MUNICIPAL BOND PORTFOLIO MANAGEMENT

MUNICIPAL BOND PORTFOLIO MANAGEMENT

Frank J. Fabozzi
T. Dessa Fabozzi
Sylvan G. Feldstein

IRWIN
Professional Publishing
Burr Ridge, Illinois
New York, New York

This publication is designed to provide accurate and authoritative
information in regard to the subject matter covered. It is sold
with the understanding that neither the author or the publisher is
engaged in rendering legal, accounting, or other professional service.
If legal advice or other expert assistance is required, the services
of a competent professional person is sought.

*From a Declaration of Principles jointly adopted by a Committee
of the American Bar Association and a Committee of Publishers.*

Senior sponsoring editor: Amy Hollands Gaber
Project editor: Stephanie M. Britt

Art coordinator: Heather Burbridge
Compositor: Alexander Graphics, Inc.
Typeface: 11/13 Times Roman
Printer: Bookpress, Inc.

Library of Congress Cataloging-in-Publication Data

Fabozzi, Frank J.
　　Municipal bond portfolio management / Frank J. Fabozzi, T. Dessa
　　Fabozzi, Sylvan G. Feldstein
　　　　p.　cm.
　　Includes index.
　　ISBN 1-55623-672-7
　　1. Municipal bonds.　2. Portfolio management.　I. Fabozzi, T.
　　Dessa, 1960–　　　　II. Feldstein, Sylvan G.　III. Title.
HG4726.F33　1995　　　　　　　　　　　　　94–15558
332.63'233—dc20

Printed in the United States of America
1 2 3 4 5 6 7 8 9 0 *BP* 1 0 9 8 7 6 5 4

Acknowledgments

The authors wish to thank the following individuals who gave freely of their time to discuss various topics covered in this book:

Jack Addams (Merrill Lynch)
Rob Barber (Merrill Lynch)
Richard B. Calhoun (Merrill Lynch)
Walter Carroll (Merrill Lynch)
Dwight Churchill (Fidelity Investments)
Ed Curland (Merrill Lynch)
Mike Demas
Geoff Domm (Merrill Lynch)
Dave Dowden (Merrill Lynch)
Michael Ferri (George Mason University)
Arnie Finklestein (Merrill Lynch)
Phil Fischer (Merrill Lynch)
Bjorn Flesaker (Merrill Lynch)
John Galante (Merrill Lynch)
Dan Hollister (Merrill Lynch)
Frank Jamison (Alex. Brown & Sons)
Frank Jones (The Guardian Life)
Andrew Kalotay (Andrew Kalotay Associates)
Kevin Klingert (BlackRock Financial Management)
David Kotok (Cumberland Advisors)
Evan Lamp (Merrill Lynch)
Tim Lenihan (Merrill Lynch)
Ted Lisec
Brent Lockwood (Alex. Brown & Sons)
Jennifer MacBlain (Merrill Lynch)
Jan Mayle (TIPS)

Edward Murphy (Merchants Mutual)
Scott Pinkus (Goldman Sachs)
Natalie Podberezsky (Merrill Lynch)
June Reed (Merrill Lynch)
Ehud Ronn (University of Texas, Austin)
Dennis Schaney (Merrill Lynch)
Yong-jai Shin (Merrill Lynch)
Sushma M. Singh (Merrill Lynch)
William Stewart (Alex. Brown & Sons)
Lisa Taylor (Merrill Lynch)
Donald Ullmann (Merrill Lynch)
George Williams (Andrew Kalotay Associates)
Bill Wood (PRAG)

We are grateful to John Hallacy, Chris Mauro, and Kurt van Kuller for their contribution to the appendix to this book. We also thank Austin Tobin of Delphis Hanover for granting us permission to reproduce the municipal yield curve data in Chapter 8 and Jeff Weiner, editor of *The Bond Buyer*, for granting us permission to reproduce the listing of the municipal bonds in the Bond Buyer Index in Chapter 16.

CONTENTS

SECTION 4
MUNICIPAL BOND PORTFOLIO MANAGEMENT   249

APPENDIX
INVESTMENT FEATURES OF NOT WIDELY UNDERSTOOD
MUNICIPAL SECURITIES   311

CHAPTER 1

INTRODUCTION

The U.S. bond market can be divided into two major sectors: the taxable bond market and the tax-exempt bond market. The former sector includes bonds issued by the U.S. government, U.S. government agencies and sponsored entities, and corporations. The tax-exempt bond market is one where bonds whose interest is exempt from federal taxation are issued and sold. Interest may or may not be taxable at the state and local level. The interest on U.S. Treasury securities is exempt from state and local taxes, but the distinction in classifying bonds as tax exempt is the tax treatment at the federal income tax level.

The majority of tax-exempt securities are issued by state and local governments and by their creations, such as "authorities" and special districts. Consequently, the terms municipal market and tax-exempt market are used interchangeably. Most, but not all, municipal bonds are tax-exempt securities.

The municipal market is a $1.2 trillion market that consists of over 1.5 million individual issues. In terms of the number of individual issues, the municipal market dwarfs U.S. taxable markets. Bonds are issued by as many as 50,000 municipal entities. Issuance since 1992 and 1993 increased significantly compared to prior years because interest rates reached low levels that encouraged the refunding of outstanding issues. In 1988, for example, new issuance was approximately $110 billion. In 1992 and 1993, issuance was more than double the 1988 level.[1]

The major motivation for investing in municipal bonds is their tax advantage. With the increases in the marginal tax rates resulting from the 1993 tax act, more investors are purchasing municipal securities. The pri-

---

[1] This information was quoted in "The Trouble with Munis," *Business Week,* September 6, 1993, pp. 44–46.

mary owners of municipal bonds are small investors (holding approximately 75% of all outstanding issues); the remainder of the investors are mutual funds, commercial banks, and property and casualty companies. Although certain institutional investors, such as pension funds, have no need for tax-advantaged investments, there have been instances when institutional investors have crossed into the municipal bond market to take advantage of higher yields.

Municipal securities come in a variety of types, with different redemption features, credit risks, and liquidity. As explained in later chapters, investors in municipal bonds are exposed to many of the same risks as investors in corporate bonds. In addition, investors in municipal bonds face the risk that changes in the tax law can adversely affect their holdings.

GOALS OF THE BOOK

The purpose of this book is fourfold. First, we describe the various types of municipal securities. New and innovative structures have been introduced into the municipal market that have unique credit risk characteristics that potential investors must carefully examine. In addition, new security types, which we call *derivative securities*, have been introduced in recent years that have more complex risk/return characteristics and better fit the investment objectives of institutional investors.

Our second goal is to set forth the state-of-the-art technology for valuing municipal bonds and measuring and controlling their interest rate risk. Until recently, the advances in valuation technology in the municipal market have lagged behind that commonly employed in the taxable market. In fact, historically, institutional investors have been simply "yield buyers"—for a given credit quality, municipal sector, and maturity sector, institutional investors have sought to maximize "yield" with little recognition given to option features embedded in an issue. As we explain in this book, the yield of a municipal bond is not a good indicator of relative value. Institutional investors' clients have an increased awareness of performance rather than portfolio yield measures; this has forced institutional investors to use the latest valuation technology in an attempt to enhance portfolio performance. Changes in the reporting of results of investment companies as set forth by the Securities and Exchange Commission and the performance reporting standards adopted by the Association of Investment and Management Research have provided further impetus to stress a portfolio's performance rather than its yield.

Our third goal is an in-depth discussion of the credit analysis of municipal bonds. In the past, investing in municipal bonds was considered second in safety only to U.S. Treasury securities; however, investors now have concerns about the credit risks of municipal bonds, regardless of whether the bonds are given investment-grade credit ratings by the commercial rating companies. There are several reasons for this.

- Several major municipal issuers have had financial crises, beginning with the City of New York's billion-dollar crisis in 1975.
- The federal bankruptcy law (effective October 1979) makes it easier for municipal bond issuers to seek protection from bondholders by filing for bankruptcy.
- The default of the Washington Public Power Supply System (WPPSS) in the early 1980's highlighted the proliferation of innovative financing techniques and legally untested security structures.
- Cutbacks in federal grant and aid programs will affect the ability of certain municipal issuers to meet their obligations.
- Fundamental changes in the American economy may cause economic hardship for municipal issuers in some regions of the country and thus make it difficult for them to meet their obligations.

These reasons are further elaborated later.

Finally, we discuss the investment management process and describe various investment strategies. We provide the framework for assessing the potential outcome of those strategies as well as give the potential uses and limitations of municipal bond index futures contracts to accomplish certain investment goals.

OVERVIEW OF THE BOOK

The book is divided into four sections. Section I provides background material. In particular, Chapter 2 describes the features and the types of municipal bonds, and Chapter 3 discusses two types of bonds in more detail: refunded and privately insured bonds. The latter in particular has become increasingly more important in the municipal market. Chapter 4 explains the creation of derivative securities. These securities are "derivative securities" because they derive their value from the municipal bonds from which they are created.

Section II covers the valuation and yield measures of municipal bonds and how to measure their potential price volatility when interest rates change. Chapters 5 and 6 describe the traditional approach to pricing municipal bonds and measuring yield. Chapter 7 explains the price volatility characteristics of municipal bonds and how volatility can be quantified. Chapter 8 describes the structure of interest rates and sets forth the principles needed to understand the latest methodology for valuing municipal bonds. Chapter 9 explains the state-of-the-art methodology for valuing municipal bonds with embedded options.

Section III sets forth the analysis needed to assess the credit quality of various types of municipal bonds. In Chapter 10 we discuss the reasons for greater concern with the creditworthiness of municipal bonds. Chapter 11 describes the companies that provide credit ratings of municipal bonds and their criteria for assessing the creditworthiness of issues. Chapter 12 outlines the elements of an unconventional perspective for assessing credit risk that may help an investor identify investment dangers associated with an issue as well as investment opportunities for enhanced return. Chapter 13 provides the elemental questions that must be asked and answered for each major type of credit and security structure before an extensive risk analysis can be completed.

In the final section, Section IV, we discuss municipal bond portfolio management, various investment strategies, and the total return framework for assessing the potential outcome of a strategy. All these topics are covered in Chapter 14. Chapter 15 explains how derivative securities are valued, their price volatility characteristics, and how they can be used in municipal bond portfolio management. In Chapter 16, we review the municipal bond index futures contract, how this contract should be priced, and how it can be used to control the interest rate risk of a municipal bond portfolio or, under certain circumstances, be used to enhance the performance of a portfolio.

The appendix describes some of the distinguishing differences between the more important local bonds and highlights those that have special strengths and weaknesses.

In the chapters that follow we provide the necessary groundwork for investors in the municipal bond market. The valuation principles discussed in this book can be used to evaluate outstanding bonds in the municipal market and can be extended to evaluate future structures of municipal bonds which are yet to be created. Given the innovations in financial engineering, new types of derivative securities will probably be created while this book is in print.

SECTION 1

MUNICIPAL BOND MARKET AND INSTRUMENTS

CHAPTER 2

FEATURES AND TYPES OF
MUNICIPALS AND THEIR RISKS

In this chapter we provide background information on various aspects of municipal securities and the market in which they trade. We begin with a review of the contractual features of municipal securities and then discuss the various types of security structures, general obligation and revenue bonds. An investor who purchases a municipal bond is exposed to the same risk as an investor in a taxable corporate bond: credit risk, interest-rate risk, reinvestment risk, call risk, volatility risk, and inflation risk. In addition, there is a risk unique to municipal bond investors: tax risk. We explain each of these risks.

When implementing trading and investment strategies, an investor must recognize tax factors unique to municipal securities that affect the outcome of a strategy, as well as the pricing of a municipal issue. These unique tax factors are explained. Finally, we review the primary and secondary municipal market.

CONTRACTUAL FEATURES OF MUNICIPAL BONDS

The promises of the issuer and the rights of the security holder are set forth in great detail in contracts called *bond indentures*. The promises are also described in the *official statement*, the equivalent of the prospectus for a municipal offering.

The essential features of a municipal issue are relatively simple. The issuer promises to pay a specified percentage of par value on designated dates and to repay a specific amount at the maturity date. Failure to pay either the principal or interest when due constitutes legal default.

FEATURES OF MUNICIPAL BONDS

In addition to the tax-exempt feature, an investor should be aware of other features of municipal bonds.

Par Value

The *par value* is the amount paid to the bondholder when the bond matures. This is also known as the maturity value, redemption value, principal, or face value.

Municipal bonds are generally issued in denominations of $5,000. The industry practice, however, is to call one $5,000 bond "five bonds," one for each $1,000 of par value. This convention was adopted because up until the 1960s most bonds were issued in $1,000 denominations, and most corporate bonds are still issued in $1,000 denominations. After issuance, the market price of a bond differs from its par value as market interest rates change. A bond selling below its par value is said to be selling at a *discount*. When a bond sells above its par value it is said to be selling at a *premium*.

When participants in the bond markets refer to the price of a bond they do not refer to its actual cash value. Instead, they refer to the price of the bond as a percentage of its par value. For example, if a bond is selling for 100, this means it is selling for 100 percent of its par value. Hence, a bond with a par value of $5,000 selling for 100 is selling for $5,000. A bond selling at a discount is selling for less than 100. For a $5,000 par value bond, a price of 80 means that the bond is selling for 80 percent of $5,000, or $4,000. When a bond is selling above 100 that means it is selling for a premium. For example, a $5,000 par value bond selling for 120¼ is selling for 120.25 percent of its par value or $6,012.50 ($5,000 × 1.2025).

Coupon Interest

The annual dollar interest that the issuer promises to pay to the bondholder is called the *coupon interest*. The *coupon rate* is the annual interest expressed as a percentage of the par value. The annual dollar interest can be determined by multiplying the coupon rate and the par value. For example, if the coupon rate is 5 percent and the par value is $5,000, the annual dollar interest is $250 (5% × $5,000).

The coupon rate can be fixed throughout the life of the issue, or it can be reset periodically. When the coupon rate is fixed throughout the issue's life, the issue is said to be a *fixed-rate* issue. When the coupon rate is reset periodically, the issue is referred to as a *floating-rate* or *variable-rate* issue. The coupon rate for such issues is based on some percent of a reference rate plus (or minus) a *spread*.

In general form, the coupon reset formula for a floating-rate issue is

Percent of reference rate ± Spread

Typically, when the reference rate is a municipal index, the coupon reset formula is

Reference rate ± Spread

Reference rates that have been used for municipal issues are J. J. Kenny Municipal Index, the Municipal Bond Buyer Index, the PSA index, a Treasury rate, and the prime rate.

The coupon rate on a floating-rate issue need not change in the same direction as the reference rate. There are derivative municipal securities whose coupon rate changes in the opposite direction to the change in the reference rate. If the reference rate increases from the previous coupon reset date, the coupon rate on the issue declines. Such issues are referred to as *inverse floating-rate issues* and are the subject of Chapter 4.

Some derivative municipal securities are a hybrid of fixed- and floating-rate bonds. In such issues, the coupon rate floats for a specified time period and then becomes fixed for the remaining life of the issue.

Some municipal issues have a fixed coupon rate and are issued at a discount from their maturity value. Issues whose original issue price is significantly less than its maturity value are referred to as *original issue discount bonds* (OIDs). The difference between the par value and the original issue price represents tax-exempt interest that the investor realizes by holding the issue to maturity. These issues are sometimes referred to as *mini-coupon issues.*

Two types of municipal issues do not distribute periodic interest to the investor. The first type is called a *zero coupon bond.* The coupon rate is zero and the original issue price is below the maturity value. Zero coupon bonds therefore are OIDs. The other type of issue that does not distribute periodic interest is one in which a coupon rate is stated but is not distributed to the investor. Instead, the interest is accrued, and all interest is paid to the investor at the maturity date along with the maturity value.

Maturity Date

The *maturity date* is the date on which the issuer is obligated to pay the par value. Corporate issuers of debt generally schedule their bonds to mature in one or two different years in the future. Municipal issuers, on the other hand, frequently schedule their bonds to mature serially over many years. Such bonds are called *serial bonds.* It is common for a municipal issue to have 10 or more different maturities.

After the last of the serial maturities, some municipal issues lump together large sums of debt into one or two years—much the way corporate bonds are issued. These bonds, called *term bonds,* have become increasingly popular in the municipal market because active secondary markets for them can develop if the term is of sufficient size.

The Legal Opinion

Municipal bonds have legal opinions. The relationship of the legal opinion to the safety of municipal bonds for both general obligation and revenue bonds is threefold. First, bond counsel should check to determine if the issuer is indeed legally able to issue the bonds. Second, bond counsel is to see that the issuer has properly prepared for the bond sale by having enacted the various required ordinances, resolutions, and trust indentures without violating any other laws and regulations. This preparation is particularly important in the highly technical areas of determining if the bond issue is qualified for tax exemption under federal law and if the issue has not been structured in such a way as to violate federal arbitrage regulations. Third, bond counsel is to certify that the security safeguards and remedies provided for the bondholders and pledged either by the bond issuer or by third parties, such as banks with letter-of-credit agreements, are actually supported by federal, state, and local government laws and regulations.

The popular notion is that much of the legal work done in a bond issue is boilerplate in nature, but from the bondholder's point of view the legal opinions and document reviews should be the ultimate security provisions. The reason is that if all else fails, the bondholder may have to go to court to enforce his or her security rights. Therefore, the integrity and competence of the lawyers who review the documents and write the legal opinions that usually are summarized and stated in the official statements are very important.

Bearer Bonds, Registered Bonds, and Book-Entry

Municipal bonds used to be issued either as bearer bonds or in registered format. As their name implies, *bearer bonds* are negotiable by anyone who holds them. Attached to bearer bonds are coupons that investors clip and submit for payment. Issuers send coupon payments to whoever submits the coupon for payment.

With *registered bonds,* the holder's name is registered with the issuer. The issuer only sends registered bondholders principal and interest payments. No coupons are attached to registered bonds—interest payments are sent directly to bondholders. Effective July 1, 1983, all new municipal bonds must be issued in registered form.

Additionally, some issuers do not issue any printed bond certificates. Instead, record of ownership is kept on computers by the representatives of the issuers. This is known as *book-entry* form, and is used to reduce the costs for the bond issuer of printing, mailing interest payments, agents, and transfer registrars.

Call and Refunding Provisions

One important question in a new bond issue is whether the issuer shall have the right to redeem the entire amount of the bonds outstanding before maturity. Issuers generally want to have this right, and investors do not want them to have it. Both sides think that at some time in the future the general level of interest rates in the market may decline to a level well below the prevailing rate at the time the bonds are issued. If so, issuers may want to redeem all of the bonds outstanding and replace them with new bond issues at lower interest rates. But this is exactly what investors do not want. If bonds are redeemed when interest rates are low, investors have to take their money back and reinvest it at a lower rate.

The verb *to call* is commonly used with the same meaning as *to redeem,* and bonds are said to be *callable* or *noncallable.* When the right to call is denied for a specified period of time after issuance, the bond is said to have *call protection,* or a *deferred call.* The earliest possible call date is referred to as the *first call.*

Call provisions, which are usually described in the bond resolution and official statement of the issue, are of such significance to the investor that the Municipal Securities Rulemaking Board requires that brokers and dealers disclose the potential impact of the call provision on the investor's potential yield.

Most call provisions permit the issuer to retire the bonds only at a price above par value, thereby providing the investor with some compensation for the risk that the issue may be called. Interest rates would have to drop by a greater amount to make it worthwhile for the issuer to refund the bond issue than if the bond could be called at par. A typical call provision allows the amount of the premium above par to decrease as the bond moves farther from the first call. For example, if the first call is 10 years from the time of issuance, the call price to the first call may be 104. In the 11th year, the bond may be callable at 103½, for example, and in the 12th year at an even lower premium over par. Some issues offer no call premium at all; that is, the call price is equal to the par value.

Issuers often call only a small part of bond issues. Those bonds are chosen at random. Usually a set percentage of bonds is called from each term maturity of a bond issue. This is called a *strip* or *partial call*. In recent years, however, some issuers have concentrated their call of bonds to a single term-maturity date from among several term maturities in the bond issue. The result is that more bonds of this maturity are likely to be called. In addition, issuers often request investors to tender their bonds. For example, an issuer may advertise that it is willing to purchase a specified amount at a specified price.

By far the most common type of call provision is the *optional call,* in which the issuer has the choice of calling the bonds. But some bonds have a *mandatory call,* in which, if certain criteria are met, the issuer must redeem the bonds whether interest rates rise or decline. This type of call provision is most often used in housing revenue bond issues. The condition used to determine if these bonds will be called is the interest rate to be paid to the bond investors versus the interest rates on the money to be loaned to homeowners. If home mortgage interest rates rapidly decline after the bonds are sold but before the money is all loaned out, the issuer may be forced to redeem some or all of the bonds with the unexpended bond proceeds. Such a condition is known as an *early redemption call.* Another condition to determine is the mortgage prepayment rate—a reflection of homeowners paying off their mortgages when they sell their homes. Once a certain amount of mortgages is prepaid, the issuer, under the bond indenture, may have to use the prepayment monies to redeem bonds.

Mandatory call features differ in another respect from optional call provisions. The length of time before bonds will be called under mandatory call provisions is generally much shorter than under optional call features. Also there is usually no call premium in the call price with mandatory redemption.

In revenue bonds, there is also a *catastrophe call* provision that requires the issuer to call the entire issue if the facility is destroyed.

Sinking Fund Provisions

With serial bonds, an issuer's repayments of debt are spread out over many years. To accomplish similar leveling out of debt repayment, term bonds may be paid off by operation of a *sinking fund*. A sinking fund means that money is applied periodically to the redemption of the bonds before maturity.

The official statement and bond indenture specifies the portion of the term issue that must be retired each year. The sinking fund provision may be designed to retire all of a bond issue by the maturity date, or it may be designed to retire only a part of the total by the maturity date. In the latter case, the balance due at maturity is called the *final maturity*.

The issuer may satisfy the sinking fund requirement generally in one of two ways. A cash payment of the face amount of the bonds to be retired may be made by the issuer to the trustee. The latter then calls the bonds by lot for redemption. Bonds have serial numbers, and numbers may be randomly selected by lot for redemption. Owners of a bond called in this manner turn them in for redemption; *interest payments stop at the redemption date*. Alternatively, the issuer can deliver to the trustee bonds with a total face value equal to the amount that must be retired. The bonds are purchased by the issuer in the secondary market at current market yields. This option is elected by the issuer when the bonds are selling below par.

From the bondholder's perspective a sinking fund requirement has two advantages. First, the risk of default is reduced due to the orderly retirement of the issue before maturity; that is, the average life is reduced. Second, if bond prices decline as a result of an increase in interest rates, price support will be provided by the issuer or its fiscal agent because it must enter the market on the buy side in order to satisfy the annual sinking fund requirements. However, the disadvantage is that the bonds may be called at the sinking fund call price at a time when interest rates are lower than rates prevailing at the time of issuance. In that case, the bonds could be selling in the market above par but may be retired by the issuer at the call price that may be equal to par value. Moreover, the issuer may have the option to call more than the scheduled amount. The issuer may exercise this option when interest rates have declined.

Other Features

We shall now describe other features that have been included in issues.

Put or Tender Option Bonds
A *put* or *tender option* bond is one in which the bondholder has the right to return the bond at a price of par to the bond trustee prior to its stated long-term maturity. The put period can be as short as one day and as long as 10 years. Usually, put bonds are backed by either commercial bank letters of credit in addition to the issuer's cash flow revenues or entirely by the cash flow revenues of the issuers.

Bonds with Warrants
Municipal bonds with warrants allow their holders to buy during a specified time period—usually two years—the bonds from the issuer at par and at predetermined coupon rates.

Super Sinkers
A *super sinker* is a specifically identified maturity for a single-family housing revenue bond issue to which all funds from early mortgage prepayments are used to retire bonds. A super sinker has a long stated maturity but a shorter, albeit unknown, actual life.

TYPES OF MUNICIPAL OBLIGATIONS

Bonds

In terms of municipal bond security structures, there are basically two different types. The first type is the general obligation bond, and the second is the revenue bond.

General obligation bonds are debt instruments issued by states, counties, special districts, cities, towns, and school districts. They are secured by the issuer's general taxing powers. Usually, a general obligation bond is secured by the issuer's unlimited taxing power. For smaller governmental jurisdictions, such as school districts and towns, the only available unlimited taxing power is on property. For larger general obligation bond issuers, such as states and big cities, the tax revenues are more diverse and may include corporate and individual income taxes, sales taxes, and property taxes. The security pledges for these larger issuers such as states are sometimes referred to as being *full faith and credit obligations.*

Additionally, certain general obligation bonds are secured not only by the issuer's general taxing powers to create monies accumulated in the general fund but also from certain identified fees, grants, and special charges that provide additional revenues from outside the general fund. Such bonds are known as being *double barreled* in security because of the dual nature of the revenue sources.

Also, not all general obligation bonds are secured by unlimited taxing powers. Some have pledged taxes that are limited as to revenue sources and maximum property-tax millage amounts. Such bonds are known as *limited-tax general obligation bonds.*

The second basic type of security structure is found in a revenue bond. Such bonds are issued for either project or enterprise financings in which the bond issuers pledge to the bondholders the revenues generated by the operating projects financed. We give examples of the specific types of revenue bonds that have been issued over the years.

Airport Revenue Bonds

The revenues securing airport revenue bonds usually come from either traffic-generated sources—such as landing fees, concession fees, and airline apron-use and fueling fees—or lease revenues from one or more airlines for the use of a specific facility such as a terminal or hangar.

College and University Revenue Bonds

The revenues securing college and university revenue bonds usually include dormitory room rental fees, tuition payments, and sometimes the general assets of the college or university as well.

Hospital Revenue Bonds

The security for hospital revenue bonds is usually dependent on federal and state reimbursement programs (Medicaid and Medicare), third-party commercial payers (such as Blue Cross and private insurance), and individual patient payments.

Single-Family Mortgage Revenue Bonds
Single-family mortgage revenue bonds are usually secured by the mortgages and mortgage loan repayments on single-family homes. Security features vary but can include Federal Housing Administration (FHA), Federal Veterans Administration (VA), or private mortgage insurance.

Multifamily Revenue Bonds
These revenue bonds are usually issued for multifamily housing projects for senior citizens and low-income families. Some housing revenue bonds are usually secured by mortgages that are federally insured; others receive federal government operating subsidies, such as under Section 8, or interest-cost subsidies, such as under Section 236; and still others receive only local property tax reductions as subsidies.

Industrial Development and Pollution Control Revenue Bonds
Bonds have been issued for a variety of industrial and commercial activities that range from manufacturing plants to shopping centers. They are usually secured by payments to be made by the corporations or businesses that use the facilities.

Public Power Revenue Bonds
Public power revenue bonds are secured by revenues to be produced from electrical operating plants. Some bonds are for a single issuer, who constructs and operates power plants and then sells the electricity. Other public power revenue bonds are issued by groups of public and private investor-owned utilities for the joint financing of the construction of one or more power plants. This last arrangement is known as a *joint power financing structure*.

Resource Recovery Revenue Bonds
A resource recovery facility converts refuse (solid waste) into commercially salable energy, recoverable products, and a residue to be landfilled. The major revenues for a resource recovery revenue bond usually are (1) the "tipping fees" per ton paid by those who deliver the garbage to the

facility for disposal; (2) revenues from steam, electricity, or refuse-derived fuel sold to either an electric power company or another energy user; and (3) revenues from the sale of recoverable materials such as aluminum and steel scrap.

Seaport Revenue Bonds
The security for seaport revenue bonds can include specific lease agreements with the benefiting companies or pledged marine terminal and cargo tonnage fees.

Sewer Revenue Bonds
Revenues for sewer revenue bonds come from hookup fees and user charges. For many older sewer bond issuers, substantial portions of their construction budgets have been financed with federal grants.

Sports Complex and Convention Center Revenue Bonds
Sports complex and convention center revenue bonds usually receive revenues from sporting or convention events held at the facilities and, in some instances, from earmarked outside revenues such as local motel and hotel room taxes.

Student Loan Revenue Bonds
Student loan repayments under student loan revenue bond programs are sometimes 100 percent guaranteed either directly by the federal government—under the Federal Direct Student Loan Program (FDSLP) or by a state guaranty agency under a more limited 1993 federal insurance program, the Federal Family Education Loans Program (FFELP).

Toll Road and Gas Tax Revenue Bonds
There are generally two types of highway revenue bonds. The bond proceeds of the first type are used to build such specific revenue-producing facilities as toll roads, bridges, and tunnels. For these pure enterprise-type revenue bonds, the pledged revenues usually are the monies collected through the tolls. The second type of highway bond is one in which the bondholders are paid by earmarked revenues outside of toll collections, such as gasoline taxes, automobile registration payments, and driver's license fees.

Water Revenue Bonds

Water revenue bonds are issued to finance the construction of water treatment plants, pumping stations, collection facilities, and distribution systems. Revenues usually come from connection fees and charges paid by the users of the water systems.

Hybrid and Special Bond Securities

Though having certain characteristics of general obligation and revenue bonds, some municipal bonds have more unique security structures as well. They include the following.

Federal Savings and Loan Insurance Corporation-Backed Bonds

In this security structure, the proceeds of a bond sale were deposited in a savings and loan association that, in turn, issued a Certificate of Deposit (CD). The CD was insured by the Federal Savings and Loan Insurance Corporation (FSLIC) up to a limit of $100,000 of combined principal and interest for each bondholder. The savings and loan association used the money to finance low- and moderate-income rental housing developments. These bonds are no longer issued, but there are billions of dollars of these bonds in the secondary market.

Insured Bonds

These are bonds that, in addition to being secured by the issuer's revenues, also are backed by insurance policies written by commercial insurance companies. The insurance, usually structured as an insurance contract, is supposed to provide prompt payment to the bondholders if a default should occur. These bonds are described in more detail in the next chapter.

Lease-Backed Bonds

Lease-backed bonds are usually structured as revenue-type bonds with annual rent payments. In some instances the rental payments may only come from earmarked tax revenues, student tuition payments, or patient fees. In other instances the underlying lessee governmental unit is to make annual appropriations from its general fund.

Letter of Credit-Backed Bonds

Some municipal bonds, in addition to being secured by the issuer's cash flow revenues, also are backed by commercial bank letters of credit. In general the letters of credit are irrevocable and, if necessary, can be used to pay the bondholders. These bonds are described in more detail in the next chapter.

Life Care Revenue Bonds

Life care bonds are issued to construct long-term residential facilities for older citizens. Revenues are usually derived from initial lump-sum payments made by the residents and some monthly rental payments.

Moral Obligation Bonds

A moral obligation bond is a security structure for state-issued bonds that indicates that if revenues are needed for paying bondholders, the state legislature involved is legally authorized, though not required, to make an appropriation out of general state-tax revenues.

Municipal Utility District Revenue Bonds

These are bonds that are usually issued to finance the construction of water and sewer systems as well as roadways in undeveloped areas. The security is usually dependent on the commercial success of the specific development project involved, which can range from the sale of new homes to the renting of space in shopping centers and office buildings.

New Housing Authority Bonds

These bonds are secured by a contractual pledge of annual contributions from HUD. Monies from Washington are paid directly to the paying agent for the bonds, and the bondholders are given specific legal rights to enforce the pledge. These bonds can no longer be issued.

Tax Allocation Bonds

These bonds are usually issued to finance the construction of office buildings and other new buildings in formerly blighted areas. They are secured by property taxes collected on the improved real estate.

"Territorial" Bonds

These are bonds issued by United States territorial possessions such as Puerto Rico, the Virgin Islands, and Guam. The bonds are tax-exempt throughout most of the country. Also, the economies of these issuers are influenced by positive special features of the United States corporate tax codes that are not available to the states.

"Troubled City" Bailout Bonds

There are certain bonds that are structured to appear as pure revenue bonds but in essence are not. Revenues come from general purpose taxes and revenues that otherwise would have gone to a state's or city's general fund. Their bond structures were created to bail out underlying general obligation bond issuers from severe budget deficits. Examples are the New York State *Municipal Assistance Corporation for the City of New York Bonds (MAC)* and the state of Illinois *Chicago School Finance Authority Bonds*.

Refunded Bonds

These are bonds that originally may have been issued as general obligation or revenue bonds but are now secured by an "escrow fund" consisting of collateral (that is, a portfolio of securities) that provides sufficient cash flow for paying the bondholders. Because the collateral is typically Treasury securities, refunded bonds are among the safest of all municipal bonds if the escrow is structured as a "pure escrow." These bonds are discussed in more detail in the next chapter.

Money Market Products

Tax-exempt money market products include notes, commercial paper, variable rate demand obligations, and a hybrid of the last two products. Generally, tax-exempt money market products have some type of credit support. This may come in the form of an irrevocable letter of credit, a line of credit, a municipal bond insurance policy, an escrow agreement, a bond purchase agreement, or a guaranteed investment contract. With a bond purchase agreement, a bank obligates itself to purchase the debt if the remarketing agent cannot resell the instrument or make a timely payment. In the case of a guaranteed investment contract, either an insurance company or a bank invests sufficient proceeds so that the cash flow generated from a portfolio of supporting assets can meet the obligation of the issue.

Notes

Municipal notes include tax anticipation notes (TANs), revenue anticipation notes (RANs), grant anticipation notes (GANs), and bond anticipation notes (BANs). These are temporary borrowings by states, local governments, and special jurisdictions. Usually, notes are issued for a period of 12 months, though it is not uncommon for notes to be issued for periods of as short as 3 months and for as long as three years. TANs and RANs (also known as TRANs) are issued in anticipation of the collection of taxes or other expected revenues. These are borrowings to even out the cash flows caused by the irregular flows of income into the treasuries of the states and local units of government. BANs are issued in anticipation of the sale of long-term bonds.

Commercial Paper

As with commercial paper issued by corporations, tax-exempt commercial paper is used by municipalities to raise funds on a short-term basis ranging from 1 day to 270 days. The dealer sets interest rates for various maturity dates, and the investor then selects the desired date. Thus, the investor has considerable choice in selecting a maturity to satisfy investment objectives. Provisions in the 1986 tax act, however, have restricted the issuance of tax-exempt commercial paper. Specifically, this act limits the new issuance of municipal obligations that are tax exempt; as a result, every maturity of a tax-exempt commercial issuance is considered a new debt issuance. Consequently, very limited issuance of tax-exempt commercial paper exists. Instead, issuers use one of the next two products to raise short-term funds.

Variable Rate Demand Obligations (VRDOs)

These instruments are floating-rate obligations that have a nominal long-term maturity but have a coupon rate that is either reset daily or every seven days. The investor has an option to put the issue back to the trustee at any time with seven days notice. The put price is par plus accrued interest.

Commercial Paper/VRDO Hybrid

This instrument is customized to meet the cash flow needs of an investor. As with taxable commercial paper, there is flexibility in structuring the maturity because the remarketing agent establishes interest rates for a range of maturities. Although the instrument may have a long nominal maturity, there is a put provision as with a VRDO. Put periods can range from 1 day to over 360 days. On the put date, the investor can put back the bonds, receiving principal and interest; or the investor can elect to extend the maturity at the new interest rate and put date posted by the remarketing agent at that time. Thus, the investor has two choices when initially purchasing this instrument: the interest rate and the put date. Interest is generally paid on the put date if the date is within 180 days. If the put date is more than 180 days forward, interest is paid semiannually. Commercial paper dealers market these products under a proprietary name. For example, the Merrill Lynch product is called Unit Priced Demand Adjustable Tax-Exempt Securities, or UPDATES. Lehman markets these simply as money market municipals. Goldman Sachs refers to these securities as flexible rate notes, and Smith Barney Shearson markets them as BITS (Bond Interest Term Series).

Derivative Securities

In recent years, a wide range of municipal products have been created from the basic fixed-rate municipal bond. This has been done by dividing the coupon interest payments and principal payments into two or more bond classes or "tranches." The term *derivative securities* has been used to describe these bond classes because they derive their value from the underlying fixed-rate municipal bond. Much of the development in this market has paralleled that of the mortgage-backed securities market.

One example of a derivative security is the inverse floating-rate security described earlier in this chapter. These, as well as other examples, are discussed in more detail in Chapter 4.

TAX PROVISIONS AFFECTING MUNICIPALS

Federal tax rates and the treatment of municipal interest at the state and local levels affect municipal bond values and strategies employed by investors. Investors in municipal securities should recognize two additional provisions in the Internal Revenue Code. These provisions deal with the alternative minimum tax and the deductibility of interest expense incurred to acquire municipal securities.

Alternative Minimum Tax

Alternative minimum taxable income (AMTI) is a taxpayer's taxable income with certain adjustments for specified tax preferences designed to cause AMTI to approximate economic income. For both individuals and corporations, a taxpayer's liability is the greater of (1) the tax computed at regular tax rates on taxable income and (2) the tax computed at a lower rate on AMTI. This parallel tax system, the alternative minimum tax (AMT), is designed to prevent taxpayers from avoiding significant tax liability as a result of taking advantage of exclusions from gross income, deductions, and tax credits otherwise allowed under the Internal Revenue Code.

There are different rules for determining AMTI for individuals and corporations. The latter are required to calculate their minimum tax liability using two methods. Moreover, there are special rules for property and casualty companies.

One of the tax preference items that must be included is certain tax-exempt municipal interest. As a result of AMT, the value of the tax-exempt feature is reduced. However, the interest of not all municipal issues is subject to the AMT. Under the current tax code, tax-exempt interest earned on all private activity bonds issued after August 7, 1986 must be included in AMTI, but there are two exceptions. First, interest from bonds that are issued by 501(c)(3) organizations (i.e., not-for-profit organizations) is not subject to AMTI. The second exception is interest from bonds issued for the purpose of refunding if the original bonds were issued before August 7, 1986. The AMT does not apply to interest on governmental or nonprivate activity municipal bonds. An implication is that those issues that are subject to the AMT trade at a higher yield than those exempt from AMT.

Deductibility of Interest Expense Incurred to Acquire Municipals

Some investment strategies involve the borrowing of funds to purchase or carry securities. Ordinarily, interest expense on borrowed funds to purchase or carry investment securities is tax deductible. One exception is relevant to investors in municipal bonds. The Internal Revenue Service specifies that interest paid or accrued on ''indebtedness incurred or continued to purchase or carry obligations, the interest on which is wholly exempt from taxes,'' is not tax deductible. It does not make any difference if any tax-exempt interest is actually received by the taxpayer in the taxable year. In other words, interest is not deductible on funds borrowed to purchase or carry tax-exempt securities.

Special rules apply to commercial banks. At one time, banks were permitted to deduct all the interest expense incurred to purchase or carry municipal securities. Tax legislation subsequently limited the deduction first to 85 percent of the interest expense and then to 80 percent. The 1986 tax law eliminated the deductibility of the interest expense for bonds acquired after August 6, 1986. The exception to this nondeductibility of interest expense rule is for *bank qualified issues*. These are tax-exempt obligations sold by small issuers after August 6, 1986 and purchased by the bank for its investment portfolio.

An issue is bank qualified if (1) it is a tax-exempt issue other than private activity bonds, but including any bonds issued by 501(c)(3) organizations; and (2) it is designated by the issuer as bank qualified, and the issuer or its subordinate entities reasonably does not intend to issue more than $10 million of such bonds. A nationally recognized and experienced bond attorney should include in the opinion letter for the specific bond issue that the bonds are bank qualified.

RISKS ASSOCIATED WITH INVESTING IN MUNICIPAL SECURITIES

The holder of a municipal bond is subject to seven risks.

1. Credit risk.
2. Interest rate risk (or market risk).
3. Reinvestment risk.
4. Call risk.
5. Volatility risk.
6. Tax risk.
7. Inflation risk.

Credit Risk or Default Risk

Credit risk or *default risk* refers to the risk that the issuer may default; that is, the issuer is unable to make timely principal and interest payments on the security. The obligations of the U.S. government are considered to be free of credit risk. For other issuers, the risk of default has been commonly measured by quality ratings assigned by commercial rating companies such as Moody's Investor Service, Standard & Poor's Corporation, and Fitch Investors Service. In Chapter 11, we describe the ratings assigned by the commercial rating companies and the factors that they consider in deriving their ratings. In addition, investment banking firms and certain institutional investors have in-house credit analysts who assess credit risk.

Section III of this book focuses on how to evaluate credit risk because the track record of the commercial rating agencies—though fairly reliable—has not been perfect.

Interest Rate or Market Risk

The price of a municipal security moves in the opposite direction of the change in interest rates. As interest rates rise (fall), the price of a fixed income security falls (rises). This property is illustrated in Chapter 5. For an investor who plans to hold a municipal security to maturity, the change in its price prior to maturity is not of concern; however, for an investor who may have to sell the security prior to the maturity date, an increase in interest rates means the realization of a capital loss. This risk is referred to as *interest-rate risk* or *market risk,* which is by far one of the major risks faced by an investor in any fixed income market.

As discussed in Chapter 7, the actual magnitude of the price response for any security depends on various characteristics of the security, such as coupon and maturity, and the options embedded in the security (e.g., call and put provisions).

Reinvestment Risk

As explained in Chapter 6, the cash flows received from any fixed income security are usually (or are assumed to be) reinvested. The additional income from such reinvestment, sometimes called *interest-on-interest,* depends upon the prevailing interest rate levels at the time of reinvestment, as well as on the reinvestment strategy. The variability in the returns from reinvestment of coupon interest from a given strategy due to changes in market rates is called *reinvestment risk.* The risk here is that the interest rate at which interim cash flows can be reinvested will fall. Reinvestment risk is greater for longer holding periods. It is also greater for securities with large, early cash flows, such as high coupon bonds. This risk is analyzed in more detail in Chapter 6.

Call Risk

As mentioned earlier in this chapter, a municipal issue may contain a provision that allows the issuer to retire or "call" all or part of the issue before the maturity date. The issuer usually retains this right to have the flexibility to refinance the bond in the future if market interest rates decline below the coupon rate.

From the investor's perspective, the call provision has three disadvantages. First, the cash flow pattern of a callable bond is not known with certainty. Second, because the issuer may call the bonds when interest rates have dropped, the investor is exposed to reinvestment rate risk. That is, the investor must reinvest the proceeds received when the bond is called at relatively lower interest rates. Finally, the capital appreciation potential of a bond is reduced because the price of a callable bond may not rise much above the price at which the issuer will call the bond.

Even though the investor is usually compensated for taking the risk of call by means of a lower price or a higher yield, it is not easy to determine if this compensation is sufficient. In any case, the returns from a bond with call risk can be dramatically different from returns obtainable from a noncallable bond. The magnitude of this risk depends upon the various parameters of the call as well as on market conditions. Call risk is so pervasive that many market participants consider it next only to interest rate risk in importance. Chapter 9 explains a framework for analyzing this risk.

Volatility Risk

As Chapter 9 explains, the price of a municipal bond with an embedded option (i.e., a call or put feature) depends on the level of interest rates and factors that influence the value of the embedded option. One of the factors is the expected volatility of interest rates. Specifically, the value of an option rises when expected interest rate volatility increases. In the case of a callable bond, the investor has granted an option to the borrower, so the price of the security falls because the investor has granted a more valuable option to the issuer. The risk that a change in volatility will adversely affect the price of a security is called *volatility risk*.

Tax Risk

A municipal bond investor faces two types of tax risk. The first type of tax risk is that the federal income tax rate will be reduced. The higher the marginal tax rate, the greater is the value of the tax-exempt nature of a municipal security. As the marginal tax rates decline, the price of a tax exempt municipal security declines. For example, in 1993 there were tax proposals to increase marginal tax rates. As a result, tax-exempt municipal bonds began trading at higher prices.

The second type of tax risk is that a municipal bond issued as tax-exempt will eventually be declared taxable by the Internal Revenue Service. This may occur because many municipal (revenue) bonds have elaborate security structures that could be subject to future adverse congressional actions and IRS interpretations. As a result of the loss of the tax exemption, the municipal bond will decline in value in order to provide a yield comparable to similar taxable bonds. As an example, in June of 1980, the Battery Park City Authority sold $97.315 million in construction loan notes. At the time of issuance, the legal counsel opined that the interest on the note would be exempt from federal income taxation. In November of 1980, however, the IRS held that interest on these notes was not exempt, resulting in a decline of the price of the notes. The issue was not resolved until September 1981 when the Authority and the IRS signed a formal agreement resolving the matter so as to make the interest on the notes tax exempt.

Inflation or Purchasing-Power Risk

Inflation risk or *purchasing-power risk* arises because of the variation in the value of cash flows from a fixed-income security, as measured in terms of purchasing power, due to inflation. For example, if investors purchase a 5-year bond in which they can realize a coupon rate of 4 percent, but the rate of inflation is 6 percent, then the purchasing power of the cash flow has declined.

PRIMARY AND SECONDARY MARKET

The municipal market can be divided into the primary market and the secondary market. The primary market is the market where all new issues of municipal bonds are sold for the first time. The secondary market is the market where previously issued municipal securities are traded.

Primary Market

A substantial number of municipal obligations are brought to market each week. A state or local government can market its new issue by offering bonds publicly to the investing community or by placing them privately with a small group of investors. When a public offering is selected, the issue usually is underwritten by investment bankers or municipal bond departments of commercial banks. Public offerings may be marketed by either competitive bidding or direct negotiations with underwriters. When an issue is marketed via competitive bidding, the issue is awarded to the bidder submitting the best bid.

Most states mandate that general obligation issues be marketed through competitive bidding, but generally this is not required for revenue bonds. Usually state and local governments require a competitive sale to be announced in a recognized financial publication, such as *The Bond Buyer,* which is a trade publication for the municipal bond industry. *The Bond Buyer* also provides information on upcoming competitive sales and most negotiated sales, as well as the results of previous week's sales.

An official statement describing the issue and the issuer is prepared for new offerings.

Secondary Market

Municipal bonds are traded in the over-the-counter market supported by hundreds of municipal bond dealers across the country. Markets are maintained on smaller issuers (referred to as "local credits") by regional brokerage firms, local banks, and by some of the larger Wall Street firms. Larger issuers (referred to as "general names") are supported by the larger brokerage firms and banks, many of whom have investment banking relationships with these issuers. There are brokers who serve as intermediaries in the sale of large blocks of municipal bonds among dealers and large institutional investors. In addition to these brokers and the daily offerings sent out over *The Bond Buyer's* "Munifacts" teletype system, many dealers advertise their municipal bond offerings for the retail market in what is known as *The Blue List.* This is a 100-plus page booklet published every weekday by the Standard & Poor's Corporation that gives municipal securities offerings and prices.

In the municipal bond markets, an odd lot of bonds is less than $100,000 in par value for retail investors. For institutions, anything below $1 million in par value is considered an odd lot. Dealer spreads depend on several factors. For the retail investor, the spread can range from as low as one-quarter of one point ($12.50 per $5,000 par value) on large blocks of actively traded bonds, to four points ($200 per $5,000 of par value) for odd lot sales of an inactive issue. For institutional investors, the dealer spread ranges from $1/4$ to $1/2$ of a point, but rarely exceeds $1/4$ of a point.

The convention for both corporate and Treasury bonds is to quote prices as a percentage of par value with 100 equal to par. Municipal bonds, however, generally are traded and quoted in terms of yield (yield to maturity or yield to call). The price of the bond in this case is called a *basis price*. The exceptions are certain long-maturity revenue bonds. A bond traded and quoted in dollar prices (actually, as a percentage of par value) is called a *dollar bond*.

CHAPTER 3

REFUNDED, INSURED, AND BANK-BACKED MUNICIPAL BONDS

In Chapter 2 we provided an overview of the various municipal bond structures and instruments. In this chapter, we focus on three types of municipal bonds whose credit risk is reduced through either an internal or external credit enhancement: refunded municipal bonds, insured municipal bonds, and bank-backed municipal bonds. We note that, of the three, refunded municipal bonds secured with irrevocable escrows of U.S. Treasury obligations are of the highest credit quality.

REFUNDED MUNICIPAL BONDS

Although originally issued as either revenue or general obligation bonds, municipals are sometimes *refunded*. A refunding usually occurs when the original bonds are escrowed or collateralized either by direct obligations guaranteed by the U.S. government, or by other types of securities. The maturity schedules of the securities in the escrow fund are such so as to pay when due bond principal, coupon, and premium payments (if any) on the refunded bonds. Once this cash flow match is in place, the refunded bonds are no longer secured as either general obligation or revenue bonds. The bonds are now supported by the securities held in the escrow fund. Such bonds, if escrowed with securities guaranteed by the U.S. government, have little if any credit risk. They are the safest municipal bond investments available.

Here we discuss refunded bonds, including (1) the general structure of an escrow fund, (2) the reasons why bond issuers refund their bonds,

(3) the major types of refunded bonds, (4) the recent controversy over "shortening" the escrow, and (5) the methods an analyst or investor can use to determine the degree of insulation from adversity of an escrow fund—and thereby, the creditworthiness of the refunded bonds.

Pure versus Mixed, or Crossover Escrow Funds

Usually, an escrow fund is an irrevocable trust established by the original bond issuer with a commercial bank or state treasurer's office. Government securities are deposited in an escrow fund that will be used to pay debt service on the refunded bonds. A *pure* escrow fund is one in which the deposited securities are solely direct or guaranteed obligations of the U.S. government; whereas a *mixed* escrow fund is one in which the permitted securities, as defined by the trust indenture, are not exclusively limited to direct or guaranteed U.S. government securities. Other securities that could be placed in mixed escrow funds include federal agency bonds, certificates of deposit from banks, other municipal bonds, and even annuity policies from commercial insurance companies. The escrow agreement should indicate what is in the escrow fund and if substitutions of lower credit quality investments are permitted.

Still another type of refunded bond is a *crossover refunding bond.* Typically, proceeds from crossover refunding bonds are used to purchase securities, which are placed in an escrow account. Usually, the crossover refunding bonds are secured by maturing principal and interest from the escrowed securities *only until the crossover date,* and the bonds to be refunded continue to be secured by the issuer's own revenues until the crossover date—usually the first call date of the bonds to be refunded. On that date, the crossover occurs, provided the issuer has not defaulted. The bonds to be refunded are redeemed from maturing securities in the escrow, which could include U.S. government securities or other investments, such as certificates of deposit. In turn, the security for the refunding bonds reverts back to the issuer's own revenues.

Here we focus primarily on the pure escrow-backed bonds, not the mixed escrow or crossover bonds.

Reasons for Refundings

Removing Restrictive Bond Covenants
Many refunded municipal bonds were originally issued as revenue bonds. Revenue bonds are usually secured by the fees and charges generated by the

completed projects, such as toll roads, water and sewer systems, hospitals, airports, and power generating plants. The specific security provisions are promised by the bond issuer in the bond trust indenture before the bonds are sold. The trust indenture describes the flow-of-funds structure, sets the rate or user-charge requirements and the additional bonds test requirements, and sets out other covenants. Many refundings occur because an issuer wants to eliminate restrictive bond covenants such as rate-increase requirements, additional bonds tests, or mandatory program expenditures. A refunding eliminates, or defeases, certain earlier covenants because the bonds are deemed to have been paid once they are refunded; therefore, they cease to exist on the books of the issuing jurisdiction.

Changing the Debt Retirement Schedule
Some bonds are refunded in order to change the issuer's debt maturity schedule—either to make the yearly debt service payments more level or to stretch out the payments.

Saving Money for the Bond Issuer
Still another reason for issuers to refund municipal bonds is to reduce their overall interest payment expenses. Typically, substantial interest cost savings can occur when interest rates decline approximately 200 to 300 basis points from the levels when the bonds were originally sold. By refunding the outstanding bonds with a new issue, the bond issuer is, in effect, refinancing the loan at a lower interest rate.

Determining the Credit Quality of the Refunded Bonds

Refunded municipal bonds are generally the safest investments because they are the most insulated from credit risk adversity, provided that the escrow funds have only direct U.S. government securities, or those backed by the U.S. government (i.e., that they are pure escrows). The following are specific questions to ask.

1. Have sufficient monies been deposited in an irrevocable escrow fund at a commercial bank or a state treasurer's office to pay the bondholder?
2. Has the bond issuer signed an escrow agreement naming the bank or state treasurer as the irrevocable trustee for the escrow fund?
3. Have certified public accountants reviewed the contents of the escrow fund to determine if it consists of either direct U.S. gov-

ernment obligations (U.S. Treasury notes, state and local government series) or obligations unconditionally guaranteed by the U.S. government?

4. Have reliable certified public accountants also certified that the cash flow from the escrow fund will provide sufficient revenue to pay the debt service as required in the refunding? It should be noted that in February of 1994 a "AAA" rated refunded bond (Northeast Randolph County Utility Board COPs in Wedowee, Alabama) defaulted because the escrow had been improperly structured. The accounting firm that did this work is no longer in business.

5. Has an experienced, nationally recognized attorney reviewed the complete transaction and given an opinion that no federal, state, or local laws have been violated?

6. What size commercial bank is involved? Preferably, a large bank that is well capitalized should be used so as to minimize the impact if an embezzlement of funds or other irregularity should ever occur.

Types of Refunded Bonds: "Pre-refunded" or ETMs

The escrow fund for a refunded municipal bond can be structured so that the refunded bonds are to be called at the first possible date or a subsequent call date established in the original bond indenture. The call price usually includes a premium of from 1 to 3 percent above par. This type of structure usually is used for those refundings that either reduce the issuer's interest payment expenses or change the debt maturity schedule. Such bonds are known in the industry as *prerefunded* municipal bonds.

Refunded bonds usually are to be retired at their first or subsequent respective callable dates, but some escrow funds for refunding bonds have been structured differently. In such refundings, the maturity schedules of the securities in the escrow funds match the regular debt-service requirements on the bonds as originally stated in the bond indentures. This type of structure usually is used when the objective is to defease any restrictive bond covenants. Such bonds are known as *escrowed-to-maturity* (*ETM*) *bonds*. In the secondary market many ETM refunded municipal bonds are outstanding.

Some Caveats For Investors

Refunded bonds can be called by the issuer before the first call date and prior to the stated maturity of the bond if there is a mandatory sinking fund provision in the original bond indenture. As an example, in 1977 the State of Massachusetts prerefunded $535 million of 9 percent general obligation bonds that had been issued in 1976 and were to mature on June 1, 2001. Under the terms of the refunding, the bonds—fully secured by U.S. government securities—were to be called on June 1, 1987, at 104 percent. However, under the original sinking fund provisions, each June 1 from 1977 to 1987 the State of Massachusetts called, at par, a predetermined portion of the outstanding 9 percent bonds as well. The par amount annually called began at 1.2 percent and gradually increased. The annual small percentage made the possibility of a call remote for large investors, but a holder of a small amount of the bonds could have had all his or her bonds called at par through the operation of the sinking fund. At various times, this could have been 20 points lower than the price at which the bonds were selling for in the secondary market.

Still another caveat for investors came to light in 1986 when two issuers in Kansas (the Kansas City, Kansas Board of Public Utilities and the State of Kansas Highway Department), and one in Pennsylvania (the Bristol Township School District) attempted to restructure their outstanding ETM bonds so as to call them prior to their stated maturity dates. The respective issuers planned to re-activate the optional call provisions under the original bond indentures. This proposed procedure became known as *escrow shortening,* and was strongly opposed by many in the industry. In Kansas, one of the escrow shortening issues failed to close, and the other was cancelled before it could be priced and sold. In Pennsylvania, a transaction did take place. Because refunded ETM bonds were believed to be legally defeased, investors thought that such bonds were no longer subject to optional calls.

There have been several responses to investors' concerns. The chief of the public finance section in the attorney general's office of the State of Texas formally opined, in 1986, that bonds issued by Texas municipalities that have been escrowed to maturity are noncallable prior to the maturity dates. In 1987, the Municipal Securities Rulemaking Board advised dealers that, in preparing refunding bond disclosure documents for issuers, such dealers should alert the issuers to the need to discuss with investors whether or not they reserved the right to exercise optional call provisions on the ETM bonds. The Public Securities Association urged issuers not to call ETM bonds unless the relevant documentation clearly disclosed that the issuer expressly reserved the right to do so. Even though the industry, in general, stepped away from encouraging issuers to do escrow shortening, uncertainty still remained as to whether optional call features are rendered inoperative upon a refunding and, therefore, as to the fair market value of outstanding ETM bonds.

It should also be noted that in early 1994 the Jefferson Memorial Hospital Association in Missouri attempted to call bonds that in 1989 it had escrowed to maturity with cash. Its argument was that since the bonds were defeased with cash, not a refunding bond issue, the 1987 industry guidelines did not apply. The issue was in litigation at the time this book was published.

Call Feature and Price Risk Protection Required for ETMs

If an ETM bond is involved, the investor should try to determine whether the call features in the refunded bond resolution have been legally defeased by the refunding issue. Sources of information could include the bond resolution for the refunding bond issue. The escrow agreement for the ETM issue, by itself, may not provide information as to whether the optional call features of the refunded ETM bonds have been legally defeased or not. If United States Treasury Obligations—State and Local Government Series (SLGs)—are used in the escrow, for economic reasons it is usually more difficult for the issuer to shorten the escrow. (Many escrows hold open-market purchased U.S. Treasuries, not SLGs.) It should be noted that it is extremely difficult to obtain the above-noted information for most outstanding ETM bonds. In the secondary market, purchasers of high coupon ETMs should ascertain what the yield would be to the first call date of the ETM, prior to the ETM refunding, and then determine if the risk-reward yield is sufficient.

INSURED MUNICIPAL BONDS

Using municipal bond insurance is one way to help reduce credit risk within a portfolio. Insurance on a municipal bond is an agreement by an insurance company to pay debt service that is not paid by the bond issuer. Municipal bond insurance contracts insure the payment of debt service on a municipal bond to the bondholder. That is, the insurance company promises to pay the issuer's obligation to the bondholder if the issuer does not do so.

The insurance usually is for the life of the issue. If trustees or investors have not had their bonds paid by the issuer on its due date, they notify the insurer and present the defaulted bond and coupon. Under the terms of the insurance contract, the insurer is generally obligated to pay sufficient monies to cover the value of the defaulted insured principal and coupon interest when they come due.

How Insured Bonds Trade and Swapping Opportunities

For calendar year 1993 a record 34 percent of total new issue volume was insured by the insurers described in this chapter.

Because of the large percentage of insured municipal bonds coming to market as well as price competition among insurers, the yield give-up for an investor who purchases insured municipals has typically been small. At the long end of the yield curve, yields on insured bonds have at times been no more than 10 basis points lower than yields on noninsured bonds. Given the enhanced credit quality the insurance provides and the cheap pricing, insured municipal bonds at this price level are attractive investments. At other times, as during the "flight to quality" by investors, the spread widens considerably. In such environments, investors who already own insured municipals may seek yield pick-up by swapping out of some of their insured bonds into noninsured though still investment grade bonds.

Do Insured Bonds Sell and Trade Like Aaa/AAA Credits?

In general, while insured municipal bonds sell at yields lower than they would without the insurance, they tend to have yields higher than other Aaa/AAA-rated bonds such as deep-discount refunded bonds. Of course, supply-and-demand forces and in-state taxation factors can distort market trading patterns from time to time. Insured bonds as a generic group may not be viewed as having the same superior degree of safety as either refunded bonds secured with escrowed U.S. Treasuries or those general obligation bonds of states that have robust and growing economies, fiscally conservative budgetary operations, and very low debt burdens.

Why Are Bonds Insured?

The overriding reason for municipal bond insurance is that it increases the marketability of some municipal bonds. This improvement in the marketability is so great in some instances that it provides a net interest cost savings to the issuer or provides access to the market that more than justifies the costs of the insurance premiums. This can be particularly important for large bond issuers of less than high quality who need to raise money in very weak market environments.

Both the bond issuer and the bond investor could be helped in the following ways.

Reduce Borrowing Costs for the Issuer

A major reason why issuers obtain municipal bond insurance is that with the insurance the commercial rating companies generally rate them in the highest categories of safety. With the high ratings, the issuer's interest costs can be significantly reduced. In fact, average gross interest savings for the bond issuer over the life of the municipal bond issue can amount to three or more times the cost of the original insurance premium.

Note, however, that since yield differentials between the credit quality rating categories are important to cost savings, and because such differentials vary with the level of interest rates, there may be periods when interest rates in general are too low for an issuer to use bond insurance. That is, the credit-rating spreads may be too narrow to provide the issuer with real dollar savings.

Still another concern that may prevent an issuer from insuring its bonds is the potential limitation that the insured bonds place on the issuer. That is, once a bond has been insured, the financial advantage to the issuer of calling the issue for early redemption or refunding is therefore reduced. This is because the present value savings needed to offset the cost of the insurance must occur over a period of years. If the insured bonds are called before the accumulation of the savings, then the issuer could experience a net interest cost loss. Therefore, the issuer must carefully weigh the reduced call or refunding option against the reduced interest rate on the insured bond issue.

Reduce Risk for the Investor

Because municipal bond insurance reduces the credit risk for the investor, the marketability of certain municipal bonds can be greatly expanded. Municipal bonds that benefit most from the insurance would include lower quality bonds, bonds issued by smaller governmental units not widely known in the financial community, bonds that have a sound though complex and difficult-to-understand security structure, and bonds issued by infrequent local-government borrowers who do not have a general market following among investors.

Of course, a major factor for an issuer to obtain bond insurance is that its creditworthiness without the insurance is substantially lower than what it would be with the insurance. That is, the interest cost savings are only of sufficient magnitude to offset the cost of the insurance premium when the underlying creditworthiness of the issuer is lower.

The Insurers

There are two major groups of municipal bond insurers. The first are the *monoline* companies that are primarily in the business of insuring municipal bonds. Almost all of the companies that are now insuring municipal bonds can be characterized as monoline in structure. The second group of municipal bond insurers are the *multiline* property and casualty companies which usually have a wide base of business, including insurance for fires, collisions, hurricanes, and health problems.

Monoline Insurers

The monoline companies are primarily in the business of insuring municipal bonds, and their respective assets, as determined in various state statutes and administrative rulings, are dedicated to paying bond principal and interest claims. The active insurers are: AMBAC Indemnity Corporation (AMBAC), Capital Guaranty Insurance Company (CGIC), Connie Lee Insurance Company, Financial Guaranty Insurance Company (FGIC), Financial Security Assurance, Inc. (FSA), and Municipal Bond Investors Assurance Corporation (MBIA Corp.) Exhibits 3–1 through 3–7 provide summary information about each of the monoline insurers.

What amounts of financial resources do these monoline insurance companies have? First, the resources found in the respective company's balance sheet are the foundation of any insurer's financial strength. These resources have also been characterized as *hard capital.*

1. *Capital and Retained Earnings (Surplus).* The amount of money identified here represents both the capital that investors have contributed to the company and any retained earnings. This category, known as an insurer's *surplus,* is available to pay the insured bondholders.

2. *Contingency Reserve.* Assets in this reserve come from transfers from the *unearned premium reserve,* and are retained by the insurance company for a period of 20 years. Under a state regulatory formula, monies in this reserve can be used to pay insured bondholders.

3. *Unearned Premium Reserve.* All insurance premiums are initially required to be placed in this reserve and then transferred to surplus and contingency reserve as the insured bonds are retired. Although monies in the unearned premium reserve generally cannot be used to pay insured bondholders, investment earnings can be.

4. *Loss Reserve.* If and when a default occurs, the insurer is required to establish such a loss reserve. The reserve is to contain an amount of monies sufficient to pay bondholders for the period that the defaulted bonds remain outstanding. Most insurers do not have such a reserve because they have not experienced such claims.

A second level of financial resources that some monoline insurers use (resources which, in our opinion, have been incorrectly characterized by some as *soft capital*) include line or letter of credit commitments from banks, future capital contributions by the monoline insurance company's investors, and special commitments from other insurance companies. This last backup is also known as a *stop-loss agreement,* and is triggered when and if catastrophic losses occur.

In addition to these two general types of capital resources, most of the monoline insurers reinsure a portion of their municipal bonds known as their *book of business* with other insurance companies when they initially insure the bonds. Usually, the monoline insurer is still legally responsible to pay the insured bondholder should the reinsurer fail to do so.

EXHIBIT 3–1
AMBAC Indemnity Corporation (AMBAC)

Credit Ratings:

Moody's: Aaa   Standard & Poor's: AAA

This company has been insuring municipal bonds since 1971. One hundred percent of AMBAC's stock is publicly traded on the New York Stock Exchange under the stock symbol of "ABK."

Insurance in Force

As of December 31, 1993, net bond interest and principal insured (i.e., bond principal as well as the coupons) was $148.92 billion. AMBAC indicated that an additional amount of $37.53 billion has been reinsured. Of AMBAC's net bond interest and principal insured, $12.58 billion (or 8.4%) is for COPs, leases, and other appropriation debt.

Since 1971 AMBAC has experienced defaults on 40 insured bonds.

Balance Sheet Resources

As of December 31, 1993, balance sheet resources amounted to $1.880 billion, of which $737.417 million represented paid-in capital and retained earnings;

Exhibit 3–1 *(continued)*

$384.230 million was in the contingency reserve; $722.817 million was in the unearned premium reserve, and $35.693 million was in the loss reserve.

As of December 31, 1993, net bond interest and principal exposure to balance sheet resources was 79.21 to 1. If the unearned premium reserve is not included. the exposure is 128.69 to 1.

Other Financial Resources

The percent value of installment premiums due on risks written in prior periods, but not yet received by AMBAC is $118.500 million. The company has a $175 million line of credit with Deutsche Bank.

Investment Portfolio (As of December 31, 1993)

Type of Investment	Market Value
Tax-Exempt Bonds	$1,482.97 million
Taxable Bonds	$ 338.80 million
Preferred Stock	-0-
Common Stock	-0-
Real Estate	-0-
Short-Term Investments	$ 109.04 million
Total:	$1,930.81 million

EXHIBIT 3–2
Bond Investors Guaranty Insurance Company (BIG)

Credit Ratings:

Moody's: Aaa   Standard & Poor's: AAA

Effective December 31, 1989, approximately two-thirds of BIG's book of business was reinsured with MBIA Corp. The reserves of BIG were also purchased and transferred to MBIA Corp.

Previously, the other one-third of BIG's book of business had been reinsured and was not included in the reinsurance with MBIA Corp.

EXHIBIT 3–3
Capital Guaranty Insurance Co. (CGIC)

Credit Ratings:

Moody's: Aaa   Standard & Poor's: AAA

CGIC is a wholly-owned subsidiary of Capital Guaranty Corporation. This insurer was established in 1986. The equity ownership of Capital Guaranty Corporation is as follows on a fully converted basis: 82.7% is publicly traded on the New York

EXHIBIT 3–3 *(continued)*

Stock Exchange under the stock symbol "CGY"; 12.2% is held by Constellation Investments, Inc. which is an affiliate of the Baltimore Gas and Electric Company; 3.4% is held by the Safeco Corporation; and 1.7% is held by The Sibag Finance Corporation, which is an affiliate of Siemens AG.

Insurance in Force

As of December 31, 1993, net bond interest and principal insured was $14.28 billion. An additional $2.73 billion has been reinsured with other insurance companies. Of CGIC's net bond interest and principal insured, $1.69 billion (or 11.83%) is for COPs, leases, and other appropriation debt.

CGIC has not experienced any bond defaults.

Balance Sheet Resources

As of December 31, 1993, balance sheet resources amounted to $284.50 million, of which $168.09 million represented paid-in capital by its owners and retained earnings; $22.90 million was in the contingency reserve; and $92.29 million was in the unearned premium reserve.

As of December 31, 1993, net bond interest and principal exposure to balance sheet resources was 50.21 to 1. If the unearned premium reserve is not included, the exposure is 74.31 to 1.

Other Financial Resources

CGIC has a $5 million line of credit with Shawmut Bank. There is also a $25 million stop-loss facility with Hannover RC.

Investment Portfolio (As of December 31, 1993)

Type of Investment	Market Value
Tax-Exempt Bonds	$105.03 million
Taxable Bonds	$140.25 million
Preferred Stock	-0-
Common Stock	-0-
Real Estate	-0-
Short-Term Investments	$ 33.11 million
Total:	$278.38 million

EXHIBIT 3–4
Connie Lee Insurance Co. (Connie Lee)

Credit Ratings

Moody's: Not Rated   Standard & Poor's: AAA

This insurer was formed in 1988. The Student Loan Marketing Association ("Sallie Mae") owns 36%; the Pennsylvania Public School Employes' Retirement System

EXHIBIT 3–4 *(continued)*

owns 20%; the U.S. Department of Education owns 14%; and the other 30% is owned by fifteen other institutional investors.

Insurance in Force

As of December 31, 1993, net bond interest and principal insured was $6.19 billion. An additional $746 million has been reinsured. Of Connie Lee's net bond interest and principal insured, $546 million (or 8.8%) is for COPs, leases and other appropriation debt.

Connie Lee has not experienced any defaults.

Balance Sheet Resources

As of December 31, 1993, balance sheet resources amounted to $177.34 million, of which $104.69 million represented paid-in capital and retained earnings; $6.96 million was in the contingency reserve; and $65.69 million was in the unearned premium reserve.

As of December 31, 1993, net bond interest and principal exposure to balance sheet resources was 34.89 to 1. If the unearned premium reserve is not included, the exposure is 55.41 to 1.

Investment Portfolio (As of December 31, 1993):

Type of Investment	Market Value
Tax-Exempt Bonds	$113.05 million
Taxable Bonds	$ 57.70 million
Preferred Stock	-0-
Common Stock	-0-
Real Estate	-0-
Short-Term Investments	$ 13.31 million
Total:	$184.06 million

EXHIBIT 3–5
Financial Guaranty Insurance Company (FGIC)

Credit Ratings

Moody's: Aaa

Standard & Poor's: AAA
Fitch: AAA

This company has been insuring municipal bonds since 1984. The General Electric Capital Corporation owns 99% of the company and The Sumitomo Marine and Fire Insurance Company, Ltd. owns 1%.

Insurance in Force

As of December 31, 1993, net bond interest and principal insured was $160.67 billion. An additional $35.25 billion has been reinsured with other insurance compa-

EXHIBIT 3–5 *(continued)*

nies. Of FGIC's net bond interest and principal insured, $3.20 billion (or 1.99%) is for COPs, leases, and other appropriation debt.

Since 1984 FGIC has experienced defaults on three insured bonds.

Balance Sheet Resources

As of December 31,1993 balance sheet resources amounted to $1.841 billion of which $777.1 million represented paid-in capital and retained earnings; $252.5 million was in the contingency reserve; $785.5 million was in the unearned premium reserve; and $25.5 million was in the loss reserve.

As of December 31, 1993, net bond interest and principal exposure to balance sheet resources was 87.27 to 1. If the unearned premium reserve is not included, the exposure is 152.22 to 1.

Other Financial Resources

The present value of installment premiums not yet received is $155.35 million. FGIC also has a standby common stock purchase agreement with General Electric Capital for $150 million.

Investment Portfolio (As of December 31, 1993)

Type of Investment	Market Value
Tax-Exempt Bonds	$1,867.83 million
Taxable Bonds	$ 65.75 million
Preferred Stock	-0-
Common Stock	-0-
Real Estate	-0-
Short-Term Investments	$ 64.19 million
Total:	$1,997.77 million

EXHIBIT 3–6
Financial Security Assurance, Inc. (FSA)

Credit Ratings

Moody's: Aaa   Standard & Poor's: AAA

This insurer was formed in 1984 to insure corporate and municipal bonds. U.S. West owns 92.5% and Tokio Marine & Fire owns 7.5% of the Company.

Insurance in Force

As of December 31, 1993, net bond interest and principal insured was $41.67 billion. An additional $19.62 billion has been reinsured. Insurance in force for COPs, leases, and other appropriation debt was $3.32 billion (or 7.96% of the total net

EXHIBIT 3–6 *(continued)*

bond interest and principal insured). Of the $61.29 billion total gross principal and interest exposure of FSA, gross municipal bond principal and interest exposure was $37.57 billion (or 61.30%).

FSA has experienced three defaults.

Balance Sheet Resources

As of December 31, 1993, balance sheet resources amounted to $680.01 million, of which $356.950 million represented paid-in capital and retained earnings; $97.10 million was in the contingency reserve; $224.78 million was in the unearned premium reserve, and $1.18 million was in the loss reserve.

As of December 31, 1993, net bond interest and principal exposure to balance sheet resources was 61.28 to 1. If the unearned premium reserve is not included, the exposure is 91.54 to 1.

Other Financial Resources

The net present value of installment premiums due on risks written in prior periods, but not yet received by FSA, is estimated to be $94.91 million. The company maintains a $325 million liquidity facility with a group of banks led by the Swiss Bank Corporation and Credit Suisse.

Investment Portfolio (As of December 31, 1993)

Type of Investment	Market Value
Tax-Exempt Bonds	$614.08 million
Taxable Bonds	$122.80 million
Preferred Stock	-0-
Common Stock	-0-
Real Estate	-0-
Short-Term Investments	$ 31.72 million
Total:	$768.59 million

EXHIBIT 3–7
Municipal Bond Investors Assurance Corporation (MBIA Corp.)

Credit Ratings

Moody's: Aaa   Standard & Poor's: AAA

In December 1986, this company became the successor to the Municipal Bond Insurance Association (MBIA), a consortium of multiline insurers. "MBIA Corp." reinsured MBIA's existing book of business, which had been insuring municipal bonds since 1974. The equity owners of "MBIA Inc.," which is the parent company of MBIA Corp., as of December 31, 1993, include the Aetna Casualty & Surety

EXHIBIT 3–7 *(continued)*

Company (9.1%); Credit Local de France (2.2%); and the other 88.7% is publicly traded on the New York Stock Exchange under the stock symbol of "MBI." Effective December 31, 1989, the company purchased the net book of insured business and reserves of the Bond Investors Guaranty Insurance Company (BIG).

Insurance in Force (For MBIA Corp. and BIG combined.)

As of December 31, 1993, net bond interest and principal insured was $266.78 billion. An additional $36.82 billion has been reinsured. Of MBIA Corp.'s net bond interest and principal insured as of December 31, 1993, $17.6 billion is for COPs, leases, and other appropriation debt. To date, there has been one bond default.

Balance Sheet Resources (For MBIA Corp. and BIG combined.)

As of December 31, 1993, balance sheet resources amounted to $3.00 billion of which $977.74 million represented paid-in capital and retained earnings; $539.10 million was in the contingency reserve; $1.47 billion was in the unearned premium reserve; and $7.47 million was in the loss reserve. As of December 31, 1993, net bond interest and principal exposure to balance sheet resources was 88.97 to 1. If the unearned premium reserve is not included, the exposure is 175.02 to 1.

Other Financial Resources

The company maintains a $575 million line of credit with Credit Suisse Bank. Additionally, the present value of installment premiums due on risks written in prior periods, but not yet received by MBIA Corp. are estimated to be approximately $186 million.

Investment Portfolio (As of December 31, 1993)

Type of Investment	Market Value
Tax-Exempt Bonds (Long-term)	$2,230.18 million
Taxable Bonds (Long-term)	$ 785.35 million
Preferred Stock	-0-
Common Stock*	$ 104.68 million
Real Estate	-0-
Short-Term Investments	$ 104.21 million
Total:	$3,224.42 million

*Equity-oriented, including an indexed mutual fund.

Multiline Companies

Several multiline property and casualty insurance companies have insured municipal bonds. We only discuss the largest insurer, the Municipal Bond

Insurance Association (MBIA), rated Aaa by Moody's and AAA by Standard & Poor's. It no longer insures municipal bonds, but it was the largest multiline insurer in the industry and for that reason is included here. Exhibit 3–8 examines MBIA.

EXHIBIT 3–8
Municipal Bond Insurance Association (MBIA)

Credit Ratings

MOODY's: Aaa   Standard & Poor's: AAA

This company represented a pool of insurers and had been insuring municipal bonds since 1974. The pool of insurers included five property and casualty insurance companies that participated in predetermined percentages. The policies of the participating insurers were "several and not joint." The individual insurance company's liability was generally limited to a previously agreed upon percentage of the debt-service risk of each bond issue. If an insurance company decided to withdraw from MBIA its existing liabilities remain in force unless assumed by a remaining participant.

Below are the five members of the MBIA pool of insurers, and their respective percentages of liability as of 1986.

Company	Percentage of Participation
The Aetna Casualty and Surety Company	33%
Fireman's Fund Insurance Company	30
The Travelers Indemnity Company	15
Aetna Insurance Company (an affiliate of Cigna)	12
The Continental Insurance Company	10
	100%

In 1987, MBIA ceased to write new insurance and reinsured most of its existing book of business with the new monoline insurer, MBIA Corp. However, its participants are still responsible for their respective shares should MBIA Corp. not pay on a defaulted bond. As of December 31, 1993 that liability represented approximately $25.1 billion in bond interest and principal.

Exhibit 3–9 shows the ownership of the monoline insurers, and Exhibit 3–10 shows their respective reinsurers. Exhibit 3–11 shows the debt service insured by each insurer; Exhibit 3–12 shows the respective balance sheet resources, and Exhibit 3–13 shows the risk-to-capital changes.

EXHIBIT 3–9
Ownership and Insured Bond Ratings* (As of December 31, 1993)

Name	Ownership (by % if available)	Ratings Moody's/S&P
AMBAC	Common Stock (100%)	Aaa/AAA
CGIC	Comon Stock (82.7%) Constellation Investors (12.2%) Safeco (3.4%) Sibag (1.7%)	Aaa/AAA
Connie Lee	Stud. Loan Marketing Assoc. (36%) Penn. Pub. School Employees' (20%) U.S. Dept. of Education (14%) Others (30%)	NR/AAA
FGIC	FGIC Holdings, Inc. (99%) The Sumitomo Marine and Fire Insurance Company, Ltd. (1%)	Aaa/AAA
FSA	U.S. West (92.5%) Tokio Marine & Fire (7.5%)	Aaa/AAA
MBIA Corp.	Aetna (9.1%) Credit Local de France (2.2%) Common Stock (88.7%)	Aaa/AAA

*For details see Exhibit 3-7.

EXHIBIT 3–10
The Major Municipal Bond Reinsurers: 1993*

Bond Insurer	Name of Reinsurer	Country	Founded	Rating (S&P)
AMBAC	AXA Reassurance	France	1937	AA
	Winterthur Swiss Insurance Co.	Switzerland	1875	AAA
	Pohjola Insurance Company	Finland	1892	AAA
CGIC	Capital Reinsurance	United States	1988	AAA
	Enhance Reinsurance	United States	1886	AAA
	Connie Lee	United States	1988	AAA
Connie Lee	Enhance Reinsurance	United States	1986	AAA
	Capital Reinsurance	United States	1988	AAA
FGIC	Capital Reinsurance	United States	1988	AAA
	Enhance Reinsurance	United States	1986	AAA
	FSA	United States	1984	AAA
FSA	Capital Reinsurance	United States	1988	AAA
	Enhance Reinsurance	United States	1986	AAA
	Tokio Marine	Japan	1879	AAA

EXHIBIT 3–10 *(continued)*

Bond Insurer	Name of Reinsurer	Country	Founded	Rating (S&P)
MBIA Corp.	Capital Reinsurance	United States	1988	AAA
	Enhance Reinsurance	United States	1986	AAA
	AXA Reassurance	France	1937	AA

*As indicated by the respective bond insurers.

EXHIBIT 3–11
Debt Service Insured (As of December 31, 1993)

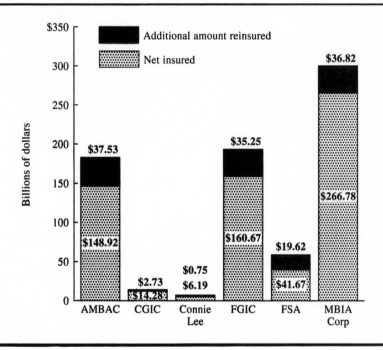

EXHIBIT 3–12
Balance Sheet Resources (As of December 31, 1993)

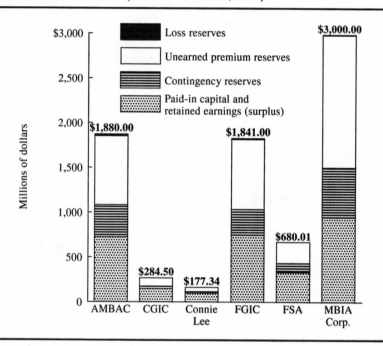

EXHIBIT 3–13
"Risk-to-Capital" Change from 1990 to 1993

Name of Insurer	6/30/90	6/30/91	9/30/92	12/31/93
AMBAC				
Net debt service to balance sheet resources	67.93	76.35	84.37	79.21
Without the unearned premium reserve	99.98	117.07	135.32	128.69
CGIC				
Net debt service to balance sheet resources	47.47	57.64	60.45	50.21
Without the unearned premium reserve	75.95	93.30	103.12	74.31
Connie Lee				
Net debt service to balance sheet resources	—	—	31.47	34.89
Without the unearned premium reserve	—	—	44.58	55.41
FGIC				
Net debt service to balance sheet resources	77.04	78.68	86.12	87.27

EXHIBIT 3–13 *(continued)*

Name of Insurer	6/30/90	6/30/91	9/30/92	12/31/93
Without the unearned premium reserve	138.51	142.04	155.25	152.22
FSA				
Net debt service to balance sheet resources	57.83	51.81	54.16	61.28
Without the unearned premium reserve	91.23	76.29	80.42	91.54
MBIA Corp.				
Net debt service to balance sheet resources	89.53	90.92	90.51	88.97
Without the unearned premium reserve	191.35	188.77	183.41	175.02

BANK-BACKED MUNICIPALS

Over the past fifteen years, municipal bonds and short-term notes have increasingly been supported by various types of credit facilities provided by commercial banks. In general, it should be noted that the first level of analysis for the investor should be the creditworthiness of the bond or note issuer. Credit facilities provided by commercial banks should not be viewed as substitutes for the credit quality of the underlying debt, but only as enhancements. For strongly secured municipals, such credit facilities can improve their marketability.

There are four basic types of bank support. Each type of credit facility is described below.

Letter of Credit

Under the traditional letter-of-credit agreement (LOC), the commercial bank is required to advance funds to the trustee even if a default has occurred under any of the documents governing the bond issue. The LOC is the strongest type of support available from a commercial bank.

LOC agreements vary from bond issue to bond issue. The strongest ones should provide the following.

1. The bank must pay the bondholders all payments when due that either are required through an acceleration of debt service caused by a default or through regular debt service.

2. Should the bond issuer be required to provide additional interest payments—if at a future date there is a determination of taxability—then the LOC should cover the additional monies required also.

3. In order to avoid "preference" payment problems caused by an issuer's bankruptcy, payments by the bank must be made at least 91 days before they are to be paid to the bondholders.

Generally, the creditworthiness of the bond issue is determined by looking at the underlying credit of the bank issuing the LOC along with the creditworthiness of the bond or note issuer. Of course, it should be noted that not all LOC-backed municipals cover debt service on defaulted municipal bonds. A careful reading of the LOC agreement, along with a legal opinion from a nationally recognized, experienced bond attorney, is required for determining the exact obligations of the bank providing the LOC.

"Irrevocable" Line of Credit

An "irrevocable" line of credit is not a guarantee of the bond issue though it does provide a level of security. It is a conditional commitment, and the investor should determine the creditworthiness of the underlying credit of the bank as well as of the bond issuer.

Revolving Line of Credit

This is a liquidity-type credit facility that provides a source of liquidity for payment of maturing debt in the event no other funds of the issuer are currently available. Because a bank can cancel a revolving line of credit without notice if the issuer fails to meet certain covenants, bond security depends entirely on the creditworthiness of the bond issuer.

Bond Purchase Agreement

This is an agreement by the bank that can be unconditional or conditional. As an example of a conditional bond purchase agreement and in regard to put bonds, often the agreement only backs the put option. If the actual underlying bonds default, the bank providing the bond purchase agreement may not be legally obligated to pay the bondholders.

CHAPTER 4

MUNICIPAL DERIVATIVE SECURITIES

In recent years, a number of municipal products have been created from basic fixed-rate municipal bonds. This has been done by splitting up cash flows of newly issued bonds or seasoned bonds with a fixed coupon rate or by combining the issuance of a fixed coupon rate bond with a financial transaction called an interest rate swap. The securities created generally have far different yield and price volatility characteristics than did the underlying fixed coupon rate municipal bond from which they were created. By expanding the risk/return profile available in the municipal marketplace, institutional investors have more flexibility in structuring municipal bond portfolios either to satisfy a specific asset/liability objective or make a more efficient interest rate or yield curve bet.

The name "derivative" has been attributed to these securities. Much of the development in this market has paralleled that of the taxable and specifically mortgage-backed securities market. The objective of this chapter is to discuss the derivative products that have been created. We explain in Chapter 15 the general principles of valuation for these securities, their investment characteristics, and their role in municipal bond portfolio management. The ability of investment bankers to create these securities has been enhanced by the development of the municipal swap market.[1] Therefore, we begin this chapter with a brief explanation of a municipal swap.

---

[1] When we use the term *investment banker* or *investment banking firm,* we refer to commercial bankers also.

SWAP MARKET

A significant innovation in the municipal market has allowed investment bankers to create derivative securities with a coupon rate that is not fixed over the term of an issue, despite issuers seeking to issue securities with a fixed coupon rate. This innovation is the municipal swap.

An *interest rate swap* is an agreement whereby two parties (called *counterparties*) agree to exchange periodic interest payments. The dollar amount of the interest payments exchanged is based on some predetermined dollar principal, which is called the *notional principal amount*. The dollar amount each counterparty pays to the other is the agreed-upon periodic interest rate times the notional principal amount. The only dollars exchanged between the parties are the interest payments, not the notional principal amount.

In the most common type of swap, one party agrees to pay the other party fixed interest payments at designated dates for the life of the contract. This party is the *fixed-rate payer*. The other party, the *floating-rate payer*, agrees to make interest rate payments that float with some index or benchmark.

Suppose, for example, that for the next five years a municipality agrees to pay an investment banking firm 6 percent per year, while the investment banking firm agrees to pay the municipality the J. J. Kenny Index. The municipality in this swap is the fixed-rate payer/floating-rate receiver; the investment banking firm is the floating-rate payer/fixed-rate receiver. Assume that the notional principal amount is $50 million, and that payments are exchanged every six months for the next five years. This means that every six months the municipality (the fixed-rate payer/floating-rate receiver) pays the investment banking firm $1.5 million (6% times $50 million divided by 2). The amount that the investment banking firm (the floating-rate payer/fixed-rate receiver) pays the municipality is the J. J. Kenny Index times $50 million divided by 2. If, for example, the index is 5 percent, the investment banking firm pays the municipality $1.25 million (5% times $50 million divided by 2).

The reference benchmarks that are commonly used for the floating rate in an interest rate swap in the taxable market are those on various money market instruments: Treasury bills, London Interbank Offered Rate (LIBOR), commercial paper, bankers acceptances, certificates of deposit, federal funds rate, and prime rate. In the municipal bond market the commonly used reference rates are the J. J. Kenny Index and the PSA Municipal Swap Index.

In our illustration, payments were assumed to be swapped based on a fixed rate and a floating rate. In another type of interest rate swap, the *basis swap*, both parties make payments based on two different floating rates. There are also swaps in which the reference rate for one party is some rate in the municipal market and for the other party it is some rate in the taxable bond market.

The swap market gives investment bankers the flexibility to create a wide range of derivative products to bet on the spread between taxable and tax-exempt rates, changes in the shape of the municipal yield curve, and changes in the quality spread between municipal issues. Generically such derivative securities created by using the municipal swap market are called *embedded swap products*.

FLOATING-RATE SECURITIES/INVERSE FLOATING-RATE BONDS

A common type of derivative security is one in which two classes of securities, a *floating-rate security* and an *inverse floating-rate bond*, are created from a fixed-rate bond. The coupon rate on the floating-rate security is reset based on the results of a Dutch auction. The auction can take place anywhere between 7 and 35 days. The coupon rate on the floating-rate security, or *floater*, changes in the same direction as market rates. The inverse floating-rate security, or *inverse floater*, receives the residual interest; that is the coupon interest paid on the inverse floater is the difference between the fixed rate on the underlying bond and the interest rate on the floater. Thus, the coupon rate on the inverse floater changes in the opposite direction of interest rates.

The sum of the interest paid on the floater and inverse floater (plus fees associated with the auction) must always equal the interest on the fixed-rate bond from which they were created. A *floor* (a minimum interest rate) is established on the inverse floater; typically the floor is zero. As a result, a *cap* (maximum interest rate) is imposed on the floater such that the combined floor of zero on the inverse floater and the cap on the floater is equal to the total interest rate on the fixed-rate bond from which they were created.

Creation of an Inverse Floater

Inverse floaters can be created two ways. First, they can be created from new issues or from bonds purchased in the secondary market. Second, they can be created via the swap market. We describe both methods in the following sections. Most inverse floaters are now created via the swap market because, as we shall explain, it allows for more flexibility and is therefore a more efficient means of creating this security.

Inverse Floaters Created from New Issues or Secondary Bonds

Inverse floaters are created by one of the following transactions.

1. A municipal dealer buys a fixed-rate municipal bond in the secondary market and places it in a trust.[2] The trust then issues a floater and an inverse floater.

2. An investment banking firm underwrites a new fixed-rate municipal issue and places it in a trust. The trust then issues a floater and an inverse floater.

Exhibit 4–1 illustrates this process.

The dealer determines the ratio of floaters to inverse floaters. For example, an investment banking firm may purchase $100 million of the underlying bond in the secondary market and issue $50 million of floaters and $50 million of inverse floaters. The dealer may opt for a 60/40 or any other split. The split of floaters/inverse floaters determines the leverage of the inverse floaters and thus affects the inverse floater's price volatility when interest rates change (as discussed in Chapter 15). To date, the most popular split of floaters and inverse floaters has been 50/50.

Suppose that interest rates are rising and an investor wishes to close out an inverse floater position. The investor in the inverse floater can pur-

---

[2]Under current regulations, if derivative securities are created by placing bonds in a trust and issuing receipts, the receipts or securities created must be sold through a private placement. There have been discussions about removing this restriction. However, one innovation has facilitated the issuance of derivative securities in the public market. At issuance, the investment banker requests multiple CUSIP numbers for a given issue. This then permits the public issuance of multiple component securities, each under a separate CUSIP number. This structure is commonly referred to as *bits and pieces*. In order to issue in the public marketplace, the issuer must request multiple CUSIPs up front. The issuer then has the option of creating derivative securities either at issuance or after issuance, utilizing the CUSIP numbers that were assigned to the deal. Often 20 or 30 CUSIP numbers are requested for a single bond issue, each representing a cash flow on the underlying fixed-rate municipal bond.

EXHIBIT 4–1
Creation of an Inverse Floater/Floater Combination

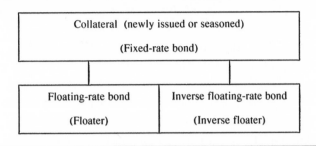

chase the corresponding floater at auction and combine the two positions to effectively own the underlying fixed-rate bond. As the market for inverse floaters is not highly liquid at this time, this represents an easy way to convert a position into a synthetic fixed-rate bond. This bond can then be hedged, if desired, by conventional methods. In the future, the investor may opt to split the issue again, retaining the inverse floater. This is a valuable option for investors. As a result, the yield on this bond is generally less than the yield on a comparable fixed-rate bond that does not have this option.

Several investment banking firms active in the municipal bond market have developed proprietary products. Merrill Lynch's institutional floaters are called FLOATS, and its inverse floaters are called RITES (Residual Interest Tax Exempt Securities). Goldman Sachs' proprietary floater products are called PARS (Periodic Auction Reset Securities), and its inverse floaters are called INFLOS, Lehman's proprietary products are called RIBS (Residual Interest Bonds) and SAVRS (Select Auction Variable Rate Securities).

Inverse Floaters Created via the Swap Market

An inverse floater can also be created when an investment banking firm underwrites a long-term fixed-rate municipal bond and simultaneously enters into an interest rate swap for a time that is generally less than the term to maturity of the bond. The investor owns an inverse floater for the term of the swap, which then converts to a fixed-rate bond (the underlying) at the end of the swap term.

To see how this can be done using an interest rate swap, let's assume the following. A municipality wants to issue $100 million on a fixed-rate basis for 20 years. An investment banking firm suggests two simultaneous transactions.

Transaction 1: Issue $100 million of a 20-year bond in which the coupon rate is determined by the following rules.

For years 1 through 5:   11% − J. J. Kenny Index
For years 6 through 10:   5%

Transaction 2: Enter into a five-year interest rate swap with the investment banker with a notional principal amount of $100 million in which semiannual payments are exchanged as follows.

Municipality pays J. J. Kenny Index
Municipality receives 6%

Notice that for the first five years the investor owns an inverse floater because as the J. J. Kenny Index increases, the coupon rate decreases. Similarly, the coupon rate increases when the J. J. Kenny Index decreases. However, though the security issued by the municipality may have an inverse floating rate, the combination of the two transactions results in a fixed rate financing for the municipality.

Rate Municipality Receives
From the investment banker for swap: 6%

Rate Municipality Pays
To investors: 11% − J. J. Kenny Index
To the investment banker for swap: J. J. Kenny Index

Net Payments
(11% − J. J. Kenny Index) + J. J. Kenny Index − 6% = 5%

The use of the swap market to create an inverse floater eliminates the need for selling the floaters through a Dutch auction.

The investor has the option of converting the indexed inverse floater to a fixed-rate bond before the end of the swap term by unwinding the swap. The cost of the conversion is satisfied either up front or is satisfied by adjusting the fixed rate the investor was to begin receiving at the end of the initial swap term. The fixed rate would be adjusted down if short-term interest rates have risen. An upward adjustment would be made if the investor converts the security when short-term interest rates have fallen. [3]

---

[3] For more information, see Lynn Stevens Hume, "Indexed Inverse Floater Deals Allow Investors to Convert to Fixed Term if Market Turns," *The Bond Buyer* (October 21, 1992).

These products are generically called *indexed inverse floaters*. Merrill Lynch sells these instruments as institutional Short RITES. Its retail inverse floating-rate product is called TEEMS (Tax Exempt Enhanced Municipal Securities). Goldman Sachs markets these as Indexed INFLOS. J. P. Morgan calls these securities Residual Adjustable Yield Securities. Lehman markets similar products as Yield Curve Enhanced Notes.[4] Lehman also markets a variation called Bulls and Bears.

Variations of the Floater/Inverse Floater Structures

Dealer firms employing twists on the structures described above have created variations of the floater/inverse floater instruments. Several are described below.

An investment bank may create *putable floating-rate securities* with inverse floaters. This is an example of a senior/subordinated class structure. The overall design is the same as with a floater and inverse floater created via the bond market. However, if the remarketing agent fails to sell out the floaters or the underlying bonds fall below a minimum collateral value and the investors in the inverse floaters do not purchase the corresponding floaters, the trustee terminates the trust and liquidates the bonds. The proceeds of the liquidation are used first to pay the par value of the floater and any accrued interest. The inverse floater investor receives the residual. Merrill Lynch markets these securities as Putable Floats/Rites.

A variation on the putable floater structure gives the owner of the floater a senior lien on only the interest portion of the issue. The investor has a parity lien with the inverse floater investor on the underlying bond principal.

Another type of security that has been created is the opposite of an inverse floater created in the swaps market. Here the investor in the first phase of the issue[5] effectively owns a floating-rate bond. After the swap term (second phase), the bond converts to the fixed-rate underlying bond. Merrill Lynch markets these bonds as Reverse Short RITES.

Synthetic floating-rate securities have been created from the cash flows of coupon paying bonds. They are called *Tender Option Bonds* (TOBs). Here the investment banker creating the securities deposits fixed-

---

[4]Chapter 15 explains the reason why an inverse floater is a play on the yield curve and hence is called Yield Curve Enhanced Notes by Lehman.

[5]The term of the first phase is the term of the underlying swap.

rate bonds in a trust. Custodial receipts for floating-rate securities (which depend on the interest on the underlying fixed-rate bond) are sold that offer the investor the ability to tender the custodial receipt for par value to the liquidity bank with seven days notice. The investor has the option to own the underlying fixed-rate bond by paying an *opt-out fee* to the investment bank. This opt-out fee is determined by the relationship between the fixed-rate bond market and the level of interest rates in the swaps market.

STRIPS AND PARTIAL STRIPS

Municipal strip obligations are created when a municipal bond's cash flows are used to back zero coupon instruments. The maturity value of each zero coupon bond represents a cash flow on the underlying security. These are similar to the strips that are created in the Treasury market. One example of this in the municipal bond market is Merrill Lynch's M-TIGRS.

Partial strips have also been created from cash bonds that are zero coupon instruments to a particular date, such as a call date, and then convert into coupon paying instruments. These are called *convertibles*, or *step-up bonds*. Merrill Lynch markets these as LIMOS, and Goldman Sachs uses the name GAINS for these instruments.

Other products can be created by allocating the interest payments and principal of a fixed coupon rate municipal bond to more than two bond classes. For example, consider a noncallable/nonputable $100 million par value issue with a coupon rate of 6 percent. From this fixed-rate issue, it would be possible to create three bond classes: (1) a 4 percent fixed-rate coupon bond with a $60 million par value, (2) a floating-rate bond with a par value of $20 million and a coupon rate that floats based on the J. J. Kenny Index plus 200 basis points, and (3) an inverse floating-rate with a par value of $20 million and that receives the residual interest from the difference of the underlying and the coupon on the floating-rate class.

Notice that the total par value of the collateral is distributed amongst the three bond classes as is the fixed coupon interest on the underlying issue. In addition to creating a floater and inverse floater, a synthetic fixed-rate municipal bond selling at a discount has also been created. This is because in this illustration the required coupon rate on the underlying municipal bond would be 6 percent for it to sell at par but the fixed-rate bond class created has the same maturity and only a 4 percent coupon rate. Thus, it sells at a discount. This synthetic bond is attractive to investors who prefer a discount security (which has higher volatility than a similar bond selling at par as explained in Chapter 7) because of an anticipated decline in interest rates but find it difficult to obtain such bonds in the marketplace.

These types of structures first were introduced by Lehman Brothers in February 1993 as part of a $95.6 million offering of the Pennsylvania Housing Agency and again a month later in a $740 million offering of the Puerto Rico Telephone Agency.[6] These are collectively called "strips and pieces."

OTHER PRODUCTS

A variety of more complex derivative securities are available. Examples are derivative securities that allow investors to bet on the spread between taxable and tax-exempt rates, changes in the shape of the municipal yield curve, and changes in the quality spread between municipal issues. We describe some of these products in this section.

Investors in *deferred interest bonds* receive a zero coupon security to a particular date (usually a call date) which then converts to pay a fixed coupon rate to the maturity of the original issue. This product is created via the swap market. The investor has the option of converting the bond to a fixed coupon rate bond before the end of the zero coupon period by unwinding the swap.

Detached calls have been sold in the municipal market. In this structure, when a municipality issues a callable bond, the investment bank issues the underlying fixed-rate callable bond separate from the call. The issuer either sells the call separately to investors or retains the call for its own use or for sale at a later date. The issuer thus gives up the right to redeem the bonds in return for the purchase price received for the call option. The bond purchaser owns a callable bond. However, the bond will not be called by the issuer, but rather may be called by the owner of the call option. The purchaser of the call option (which may be the issuer

---

[6] Aaron Pressman, "Lehman's 'Strips and Pieces' Allow Investors Multitude of Options in Structuring Portfolios," *The Bond Buyer* (March 26, 1993).

should it decide not to sell the calls to the public) has the right to call the bonds away from the callable bond holder if interest rates fall. If the holder of the detached call decides to exercise the option in this case, he or she receives a bond paying above current market interest rates. Purchasers of the call options may be investors in callable bonds wishing to protect against losing high coupon bonds if their bonds are called.

A product that Lehman Brothers calls a CMT Step Up Recovery Floater (SURF) allows municipal investors to benefit if rates in the intermediate-term taxable bond market rise faster than in the intermediate-term tax-exempt bond market.[7] An example is $11.2 million of a $43.7 million refunding issue for the Industrial Development Authority of the City of Winchester, Virginia in July 1993. Specifically, the semiannual pay issue has a maturity of 22 years and is callable after 5 years. The coupon rate for the first five years (up to the first call date) is based on the 10-year Constant Maturity Treasury (CMT), an intermediate-term taxable benchmark interest rate. The coupon rate resets at the 10-year CMT rate less a fixed spread of 145 basis points. At the first call date, the coupon rate converts into a fixed coupon rate of 5.5 percent.

At the same time of the Lehman offering, Merrill Lynch proposed as part of a $1.1 billion Puerto Rico Transportation and Highway Authority issue an embedded swap product based on a fixed rate plus the spread between the short-term taxable rate (LIBOR) and the short-term tax-exempt rate (the Public Securities Association Municipal Swap Index). This product allows investors to bet that taxable short-term rates will rise faster than tax-exempt rates. Legal complications prevented including this structure in the Puerto Rico Transportation and Highway Authority issue, but subsequent issues may include such structures.[8] Of course, it is possible to create a derivative security in which an investor can bet that the short-term taxable rate will rise slower than a short-term tax-exempt rate.

A relatively new product has been introduced that allows investors to receive future bond yields based on today's current yield ratios between taxable and tax-exempt debt. These are called *deferred fixed-rate bonds.*[9] The investor in this security receives a short-term floating-rate instrument

---

[7] Aaron Pressman, "Market Pushes More Unusual Derivatives As Standard Rate Swaps Gain Acceptance," *The Bond Buyer* (July 16, 1993).

[8] Pressman, "Market Pushes More Unusual Derivatives."

[9] For more information, see Aaron Pressman, "Merrill's New Deferred Fixed-Rate Bond Backed by Triple-A Derivatives Subsidiary," *The Bond Buyer* (October 13, 1993).

up to the first year. The investor has the option of locking in a long-term fixed rate on a monthly basis up to the first year after issuance. The fixed rate is based on a taxable index (such as the 10-year CMT rate). The fixed rate received upon conversion is set based on the ratio of tax-exempt to taxable rates when this deferred fixed-rate bond was originally sold. Thus the investor receives the latest yield based on the taxable market rates adjusted by the ratio of tax-exempt to taxable rates when the bond was issued. This was particularly attractive in the third quarter of 1993 when the ratio of tax-exempt to taxable bonds was particularly high. The interest the investor receives is exempt from taxes because the bond is a municipal obligation.

If the investor has not converted the bond after one year, the bond automatically converts to a fixed rate bond based on the same calculation. However, if the bond is called, the conversion factor is adjusted to collapse the benefits into a shorter period, such as five years (the time to the first call date on the bond), rather than over the life of the bond. Thus, the investor receives accelerated benefits, paid up to the first call date. This compensates investors for the call feature in the bond.

We have not attempted to be exhaustive in our discussion of derivative securities. Other structures have been introduced, and no doubt there are more on the drawing board. What is important to keep in mind is that these securities are created to provide an investment vehicle that can be used to satisfy some investment objective that either cannot be satisfied with existing securities or can more cost efficiently satisfy an objective. In the process of creating such a security, an issuer benefits from a lower cost of funds. The municipal swap market is the key to creating these securities.

SECTION 2

VALUATION AND PRICE VOLATILITY OF MUNICIPAL BONDS

CHAPTER 5

PRICING OF MUNICIPAL BONDS

This chapter explains how the price of a bond is determined. Our focus in this chapter is on option-free municipal bonds (bonds that are not callable or putable). Chapter 9 turns to the more complicated task of valuing municipal bonds with embedded options.

PRICING A BOND

The price of any financial instrument (municipal bond, Treasury bond, corporate bond, common stock, real estate) is equal to the present (discounted) value of its *expected* cash flow. By discounting the cash flow, allowance is made for the timing of the cash flow. Consequently, determining the price requires that an investor estimate the following: (1) the expected cash flow and (2) the appropriate discounting rate (yield).

The expected cash flow for some financial instruments is simple to determine; for others, the task may be quite complex. The appropriate yield should reflect the yield for financial instruments with *comparable* risks and features.

Assuming that the issuer does not default, it is simple to compute the cash flow for a fixed-rate, option-free municipal bond (a municipal bond that is neither callable nor putable). The cash flow is (1) the coupon interest payments to the maturity date and (2) the par (or maturity) value at maturity.

We use two bonds to illustrate how the price of a bond is calculated: a 5 percent coupon, 5-year bond; a 5 percent coupon, 20-year bond. Assuming that the next coupon payment for both bonds is six months from now, the second column of Exhibits 5–1 and 5–2 set forth the cash flow that the investor realizes every six months until the bond matures.

To calculate the price of each bond, the yield required by an investor must be determined. For the purposes of our illustrations, we shall assume that the investor wants a 6 percent yield in order to invest in either of these municipal bonds. The cash flow should be discounted at one-half the required yield, or 3 percent in our illustration. The third column of Exhibits 5–1 and 5–2 gives the present value of $1 for each period using an interest rate of 3 percent. The last column of the exhibits gives the present value of the cash flow, which is found by multiplying the cash flow in the second column by the present value of $1 at 3 percent. The sum of the present value of the cash flow is the price of the bond.

In practice, hand-held calculators and PC software are used to compute the price of a bond given the (1) coupon rate, (2) maturity date, and (3) required yield.

The required yield is determined by investigating the yields offered on comparable municipal bonds in the market. By *comparable,* we mean issues of the same credit quality, features, and term. The required yield is typically expressed as an annual interest rate. The cash flow for municipal bonds is every six months, so the market convention is to use one-half the annual interest rate as the periodic interest rate with which to discount the cash flows. This is the practice we followed in calculating the price in Exhibits 5–1 and 5–2.

The price of a zero coupon municipal bond is simply the present value of its only cash flow, the maturity value. However, in the present value computation, the number of periods used for discounting is *double* the number of years to maturity of the bond, and the discounting rate is one-half the required yield. This is done so that the return on zero coupon bonds can be compared with the return on coupon bearing instruments.

Some bonds have known, but variable, cash flows during their life. These are called *stepped coupon bonds.* Stepped coupon bonds have low or no coupon payments during the first part of their life, then pay a higher, but known, coupon in the later years. The price calculation for these bonds is the same as for fixed rate bonds. Each cash flow is discounted by the required rate of return on the bond, then summed.

For bonds with option features, the price is often calculated to the option date. For example, if a bond is callable, the price to call is calculated by summing the discounted value of the bond's cash flows to the call date, including the call price to be received on the call date. The discount rate used would be the required yield on a bond with comparable risks and a term (or maturity) equal to the time to call on the bond. For a putable bond, the bond's price to put would equal the discounted value of the cash flows (the coupon payments and put price) to the put date on the bond.

Because municipal bonds are often callable, a calculation of price to next premium call, par call (the first date that the bond becomes callable at par value), and maturity is performed.

EXHIBIT 5–1
Calculation of the Price of a Municipal Bond (5%, 5-Year)

		Issue Selling to Yield 6%	
Period	Cash Flow	Present value of $1 at 3%*	Present value
1	2.5	0.970874	2.4272
2	2.5	0.942596	2.3565
3	2.5	0.915142	2.2879
4	2.5	0.888487	2.2212
5	2.5	0.862609	2.1565
6	2.5	0.837484	2.0937
7	2.5	0.813092	2.0327
8	2.5	0.789409	1.9735
9	2.5	0.766417	1.9160
10	102.5	0.744094	76.2696
		Price =	95.7349

* Present value of $1 at 3% calculated as follows:

$$\frac{1}{(1.03)^{period}}$$

EXHIBIT 5–2
Calculation of the Price of a Municipal Bond (5%, 20-Year)

		Issue Selling to Yield 6%	
Period	Cash Flow	Present value of $1 at 3%*	Present value
1	2.5	0.970874	2.4272
2	2.5	0.942596	2.3565
3	2.5	0.915142	2.2879

EXHIBIT 5–2 (continued)

		Issue Selling to Yield 6%	
Period	Cash Flow	Present value of $1 at 3%*	Present value
4	2.5	0.888487	2.2212
5	2.5	0.862609	2.1565
6	2.5	0.837484	2.0937
7	2.5	0.813092	2.0327
8	2.5	0.789409	1.9735
9	2.5	0.766417	1.9160
10	2.5	0.744094	1.8602
11	2.5	0.722421	1.8061
12	2.5	0.701380	1.7534
13	2.5	0.680951	1.7024
14	2.5	0.661118	1.6528
15	2.5	0.641862	1.6047
16	2.5	0.623167	1.5579
17	2.5	0.605016	1.5125
18	2.5	0.587395	1.4685
19	2.5	0.570286	1.4257
20	2.5	0.553676	1.3842
21	2.5	0.537549	1.3439
22	2.5	0.521893	1.3047
23	2.5	0.506692	1.2667
24	2.5	0.491934	1.2298
25	2.5	0.477606	1.1940
26	2.5	0.463695	1.1592
27	2.5	0.450189	1.1255
28	2.5	0.437077	1.0927
29	2.5	0.424346	1.0609
30	2.5	0.411987	1.0300
31	2.5	0.399987	1.0000
32	2.5	0.388337	0.9708
33	2.5	0.377026	0.9426
34	2.5	0.366045	0.9151
35	2.5	0.355383	0.8885
36	2.5	0.345032	0.8626
37	2.5	0.334983	0.8375
38	2.5	0.325226	0.8131
39	2.5	0.315754	0.7894
40	102.5	0.306557	31.4221
		Price =	88.4426

* Present value of $1 at 3% calculated as follows:

$$\frac{1}{(1.03)^{period}}$$

Price/Yield Relationship for an Option-Free Bond

A fundamental property of a bond is that its price changes in the opposite direction of the change in the required yield. The reason for this is that the price of the bond is the present value of the cash flow. As the required yield (discounting rate) increases, the present value of the cash flow decreases—hence, the price decreases. The opposite is true when the required yield decreases: the present value of the cash flow increases, and, therefore, the price of the bond increases. This is illustrated in Exhibit 5–3 for the two 5 percent coupon bonds whose price we calculated in Exhibits 5–1 and 5–2 and for four other bonds.

EXHIBIT 5–3
Price/Yield Relationship for Six Bonds

Coupon/ Term	Price at Required Yield						
	4%	5%	6%	7%	8%	9%	10%
5%/5	104.49	100.00	95.73	91.68	87.83	84.17	80.70
5%/20	113.68	100.00	88.44	78.64	70.31	63.20	57.10
7%/5	113.47	108.75	104.27	100.00	95.94	92.09	88.42
7%/20	141.03	125.10	111.56	100.00	90.10	81.60	74.26
9%/5	122.46	117.50	112.80	108.32	104.06	100.00	96.14
9%/20	168.39	150.21	134.67	121.36	109.90	100.00	91.42

If we graphed the price/yield relationship for any option-free bond, we would find that it has the "bowed" shape shown in Exhibit 5–4. This shape is referred to as *convex*. The convexity of the price/yield relationship has important implications for the investment properties of a bond, as shown in Chapter 7.

The Relationship between Coupon Rate, Required Yield, and Price

Cash flows on a fixed-rate municipal bond are set at issuance. Because of this, as yields in the marketplace change the only variable that an investor can change in the market is the price he is willing to pay for the bond. When the coupon rate is equal to the required yield, the price of the bond is equal to its par value.

When yields in the marketplace rise above the coupon rate, the bond is not an attractive investment. Thus, the price of the bond adjusts so that

EXHIBIT 5–4

Graphical Depiction of the Price/Yield Relationship for an Option-Free Municipal Bond

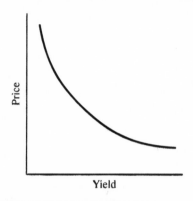

any investor who wishes to purchase the bond can realize a return above the coupon rate. To do this, the price of the bond drops below its par value. The capital appreciation and coupon received on the par value (even though the bond was purchased below par value) realized by holding the bond to maturity represents a form of return to the investor to compensate for the lower coupon rate than the yield required in the market. A bond selling below its par value is said to be selling at a *discount*. In our earlier calculation of bond price, we saw that when the required yield is greater than the coupon rate, the price of the bond is always less than the par value.

When the required yield in the market is below the coupon rate, the bond must sell above its par value. This occurs because investors who would have the opportunity to purchase the bond at par would be getting a return in excess of what the market would require. As a result, investors would bid up the price of the bond because its yield is attractive—up to a price at which it offers the required yield in the market. A bond whose price is above its par value is said to be selling at a *premium*.

We can summarize the relationship between coupon rate, required yield, and price as follows.

Coupon rate < Required yield <——> Price < Par

Coupon rate = Required yield <——> Price = Par

Coupon rate > Required yield <——> Price > Par

These relationships can be verified for the six bonds whose price we show at various required yields in Exhibit 5–3.

The Relationship between Bond Price and Time
If Interest Rates Are Unchanged

If the required yield is unchanged between the time the municipal bond is purchased and the maturity date, what happens to the price of the bond? For a municipal bond selling at par value, the coupon rate is equal to the required yield. As the municipal bond moves closer to maturity, the bond continues to sell at par value. Thus, for a municipal bond selling at par, its price remains at par **as** the bond moves toward the maturity date, if interest rates do not change.

The price of a municipal bond does *not* remain constant for a bond selling at a premium or a discount. Exhibit 5–5 shows the price movement of two hypothetical 20-year municipal bonds selling at a discount and premium, respectively, as they approach maturity. Notice that the discount bond increases in price as it approaches maturity, assuming the required yield does not change. For a premium bond, the opposite occurs. For both bonds, the price equals par value at the maturity date. This movement to par value at maturity in a stable rate environment is referred to as the *time path of the bond* and is illustrated in Exhibit 5–6.

Reasons for the Change in the Price of a Municipal Bond

The price of a municipal bond changes for one or more of the following reasons.

1. *A change in the level of general interest rates.* For example, if interest rates in the economy increase (fall), the price of a bond decreases (increases).

2. *A change in the price of a municipal bond selling at a price other than par as it moves toward maturity without any change in the required yield.* As we demonstrated, a discount bond rises in value over time if yields do not change; a premium bond declines over time if yields do not change.

3. *A change in the required yield due to a change in the ratio of the yield of municipal bonds to Treasuries.* If the Treasury rate does not change, but the ratio of municipal yields to Treasury yields changes due to actual or perceived changes in marginal federal tax rates, or changes in the

EXHIBIT 5–5
Price of Discount and Premium Municipal Bond
as the Bond Approaches Maturity

Bonds: 4% coupon, 20-year bond, selling at 76.89 to yield 6%
8% coupon, 20-year bond, selling at 111.56 to yield 6%

After	Years to maturity	Bond	
		4% coupon (discount)	7% coupon (premium)
1	19	77.51	111.25
2	18	78.17	110.92
3	17	78.87	110.57
4	16	79.61	110.19
5	15	80.40	109.80
6	14	81.24	109.38
7	13	82.12	108.94
8	12	83.06	108.47
9	11	84.06	107.97
10	10	85.12	107.44
11	9	86.25	106.88
12	8	87.44	106.28
13	7	88.70	105.65
14	6	90.05	104.98
15	5	91.47	104.27
16	4	92.98	103.51
17	3	94.58	102.71
18	2	96.28	101.86
19	1	98.09	100.96
20	0	100.00	100.00

perceived risk of the municipal market relative to the Treasury market, then the price of a municipal bond changes.

4. *A change in the perceived credit quality of the issuer.* Assuming interest rates in the economy and the ratio of municipal yields to Treasury yields do not change, the price of a municipal bond increases (decreases) if its perceived credit quality has improved (deteriorated).

Flat Price, Full Price, and Accrued Interest

When an investor purchases a municipal bond between coupon payments, and the issuer is not in default, the investor must compensate the seller of the bond for the coupon interest earned from the time of the last coupon

EXHIBIT 5–6
Time Path of a Discount and Premium Municipal Bond

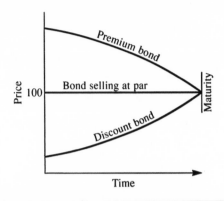

payment to the settlement date of the bond. This amount is called *accrued interest* and is computed as follows.

$$\text{Periodic coupon rate} \times \frac{\text{Number of days from last coupon to settlement date}}{\text{Number of days in coupon period}}$$

Market conventions determine the number of days in a coupon period and the number of days from the last coupon to settlement date for the accrued interest calculation. For most municipal bonds, the day count convention is 30/360, which means a year is treated as having 360 days and each month as having 30 days. Therefore, the number of days in a coupon period is 180.

As an example, consider a municipal bond whose last coupon payment was on March 1 and is purchased with a settlement date of July 17. The number of days from settlement to the next coupon payment (September 1) is determined as follows.

Remainder of July	13 days
August	30 days
September 1	1 day
	44 days

Because a coupon period has 180 days, the number of days from the last coupon to the settlement date is 136 (180 minus 44). Accrued interest for this bond is then

$$\text{Coupon rate} \times \frac{136}{180}$$

There are financial calendars available that provide the day count. Most money managers use software programs that figure this based on the information provided.

The *full price* (or *dirty price*) is the total proceeds that the buyer of the bond pays the seller. The full price is equal to the price agreed upon by the buyer and the seller plus accrued interest. The *flat price* (or *clean price*) of a bond excludes accrued interest.

CHAPTER 6

YIELD MEASURES

In Chapter 5 we explained how to compute the price of a municipal bond given the required yield. In this chapter, we show how traditional yield measures for a municipal bond are calculated given its price. We begin by discussing the sources of potential return from investing in a municipal bond. We can then see how the traditional yield measures are generally deficient in providing insight as to the potential return from holding a bond over some investment horizon. In Chapter 14 we present a better framework, total return, for assessing the potential return of a municipal bond or municipal bond portfolio.

SOURCES OF POTENTIAL RETURN

An investor who purchases a municipal bond can expect to receive a *dollar* return from one or more of the following sources

1. The coupon interest payments made by the issuer.
2. Any capital gain (or capital loss—negative dollar return) when the bond matures, is called, is put, or is sold.
3. Income from reinvestment of the coupon interest payments. This source of dollar return is referred to as *interest-on-interest*.

Market participants commonly cite four yield measures to measure the potential return from investing in a bond: current yield, yield to maturity, yield to call, and yield to put. These yield measures are expressed as a percent return rather than a dollar return. However, the yield measure should consider each of the three potential sources of return cited above. We discuss these four yield measures and assess whether they consider the three sources of potential return.

TRADITIONAL YIELD MEASURES

In this section we describe several traditional measures of yield and their limitations.

Current Yield

The current yield relates the *annual* coupon interest to the market price. The formula for the current yield is

$$\text{Current yield} = \frac{\text{Annual dollar coupon interest}}{\text{Price}}$$

For example, the current yield for a 5 percent, 20-year municipal bond whose price is $98.00 is 5.10 percent as shown below.

$$\text{Annual dollar coupon interest} = 0.05 \times \$100 = \$5$$
$$\text{Price} = \$98.00$$

$$\text{Current yield} = \frac{\$5}{\$98.00} = 0.0051 \; or \; 5.10\%$$

The current yield is greater than the coupon rate when a municipal bond sells at a discount; the reverse is true for a municipal bond selling at a premium. For a municipal bond selling at par, the current yield is equal to the coupon rate.

The drawback of the current yield is that it considers only the coupon interest, and not other sources of return that have an impact on an investor's return. No consideration is given to the capital gain that the investor realizes when a municipal bond is purchased at a discount and held to maturity; nor is any recognition given of the capital loss that the investor realizes if a municipal bond purchased at a premium is held to maturity.

Yield to Maturity

The most popular measure of yield in the bond market is the yield to maturity. The *yield to maturity* is the interest rate that makes the present value of the cash flow from a bond equal to its full price (market price plus accrued interest). Calculation of the yield to maturity of a bond is the reverse process of calculating the price of a bond described in the previous chapter. To find the price of a bond we determine the cash flow and the required yield, then we calculate the present value of the cash flow to obtain the price. To find the yield to maturity, we must first determine the cash flow. Then, we search by trial and error for the interest rate that makes the present value of the cash flow equal to the full price.

To illustrate, consider a 5 percent, 20-year municipal bond selling at 93.98. The cash flow for this bond is (1) 40 six-month payments of $2.50 and (2) $100 40 six-month periods from now. Exhibit 6–1 shows the present value of the bond at various semiannual discount (interest) rates. When a 2.75 percent interest rate is used, the present value of the cash flow is equal to 93.98, which is the price of the bond. Hence, 2.75 percent is the semiannual yield on the bond. It is the rate, when used, that makes the cash flow to equal the price of the bond.

EXHIBIT 6–1
Present Value of a 5%, 20-Year Municipal Bond for Various Semiannual Discount Rates

Interest rate	1.75%	2.00%	2.25%	2.50%	2.75%	3.00%	3.25%
Present value	121.45	113.68	106.55	100.00	93.98	88.44	83.34

The market convention adopted is to double the semiannual interest rate and call that interest rate the yield to maturity. Thus, the yield to maturity for the above bond is 5.5 percent (2 times 2.75%). The yield to maturity computed using this convention—doubling the semiannual yield—is called a *bond equivalent yield* or *coupon equivalent yield*.

The following relationship between the price of a bond, coupon rate, current yield, and yield to maturity holds.

Municipal Bond Sells At	Relationship
Par	Coupon rate = Current yield = Yield to maturity
Discount	Coupon rate < Current yield < Yield to maturity
Premium	Coupon rate > Current yield > Yield to maturity

Three Sources of Return and the Yield-to-Maturity Measure

The yield to maturity considers the coupon income and any capital gain or loss that the investor realizes by *holding a municipal bond to maturity*. The yield to maturity also considers the timing of the cash flow because the discounting rate is what causes the present value of the bond's cash flow to equal its price. It does consider interest-on-interest; *however, it assumes that the coupon payments can be reinvested at an interest rate equal to the yield to maturity.* For example, if the yield to maturity for a municipal bond is 6 percent, to earn that yield the coupon payments must be reinvested at an interest rate equal to 6 percent. The following illustration clearly demonstrates this.

- Suppose an investor has $100 and places the funds in a certificate of deposit that pays 3 percent every six months for 20 years or 6 percent per year on a bond equivalent basis. At the end of 20 years, the $100 investment will grow to $326.20.
- Suppose an investor buys a 6 percent, 20-year bond selling at par, $100. The yield to maturity for this bond is 6 percent. The investor assumes that at the end of 20 years, the total dollars from the investment will also be $326.20.

Let's look at what the latter investor actually receives. There are 40 semiannual interest payments of $3 which will total $120. When the bond matures, the investor will receive $100. Thus, the total dollars that the investor will receive on the bond is $220 if he holds the bond to maturity— less than the $326.20 necessary to produce a yield of 6 percent on a bond-equivalent basis by $106.20 ($326.20 minus $220). How is this deficiency supposed to be made up? If the investor reinvests each coupon payment until maturity at a semiannual interest rate of 3 percent (or 6 percent annual rate on a bond-equivalent basis), it can be demonstrated that the interest earned on the coupon payments will be $106.20. Consequently, of the $226.20 *total dollar return* ($326.20 less the $100 initial investment) necessary to produce a yield of 6 percent, about 47 percent ($106.20 divided by $226.20) must be generated by reinvesting the coupon payments. Thus, the inherent assumption in the yield to maturity calculation is that coupon payments are reinvested at a rate equal to the yield to maturity.

The investor only realizes the yield to maturity stated at the time of purchase if (1) the coupon payments can be reinvested at the yield to maturity, and (2) if the bond is held to maturity. With respect to the first assumption, an investor faces the risk that reinvestment rates for the future coupon payments will be less than the yield to maturity at the time the bond is purchased. This risk is referred to as *reinvestment risk.* In addition, if the bond is not held to maturity, the bond may have to be sold for less than its purchase price, resulting in a return that is less than the yield to maturity. The risk that a bond might have to be sold at a loss because interest rates rise is referred to as *interest-rate risk* or *price risk.*

Reinvestment Risk
There are two characteristics of a municipal bond that determine the degree of reinvestment risk. First, for a given yield to maturity and a coupon rate, the longer the maturity the more dependent the bond's total dollar return is on the interest-on-interest component to realize the yield to maturity quoted at the time of purchase. The reinvestment risk is greater. The implication is that the yield to maturity measure for long-term coupon municipal bonds tells little about the potential yield that an investor may realize if the bond is actually held to maturity. In high-interest rate environments, the interest-on-interest component for long-term municipal bonds may account for up to 70 percent of a municipal bond's potential total dollar return.

The second characteristic that determines the degree of reinvestment risk is the coupon rate. For a given maturity and a given yield to maturity, the higher the coupon rate, the more dependent a municipal bond's total dollar return is on the reinvestment of the coupon payments in order to produce the yield to maturity quoted at the time of purchase. This means that, holding maturity and yield to maturity constant, premium municipal bonds, having higher coupon payments to reinvest until maturity, are more dependent on interest-on-interest than are municipal bonds selling at par. In contrast, discount municipal bonds are less dependent on interest-on-interest than are municipal bonds selling at par. For zero coupon municipal bonds, none of the bond's total dollar return is dependent on interest-on-interest because no cash flow occurs until maturity. So, a zero coupon municipal bond has no reinvestment risk if held to maturity.

Interest-Rate Risk
As we explained in Chapter 5, a bond's price moves in the direction opposite to the change in interest rates. As interest rates rise (fall), the price of a bond falls (rises). For an investor who plans to hold a municipal bond to maturity, the change in the bond's price prior to maturity is of no concern (unless the investment is held in a marked-to-market account). However, for an investor who may have to sell a municipal bond prior to the maturity date, an increase in interest rates subsequent to the time the bond was purchased means the realization of a capital loss. Not all municipal bonds

have the same degree of interest-rate risk. Chapter 7 demonstrates the characteristics of a bond that determine its interest-rate risk.

Limitations of Yield to Maturity

Given the assumptions underlying yield to maturity, we now can use an illustration to drive home the key point that yield to maturity has limited value in assessing the potential performance of a municipal bond. Suppose that an investor who has a five-year investment horizon is considering the following four option-free municipal bonds.

Bond	Coupon Rate	Maturity	Yield to Maturity
W	5%	3 years	9.0%
X	6	20	8.6
Y	11	15	9.2
Z	8	5	8.0

Assuming that all four municipal bonds are of the same credit quality, which one is the most attractive to this investor?

An investor who selects municipal bond Y because it offers the highest yield to maturity fails to recognize that this municipal bond must be sold after five years. The price of the bond at that time will depend on the yield required in the market for 10 year, 11 percent coupon municipal bonds. Hence, a capital gain or capital loss could make the return higher or lower than the yield to maturity promised now. Moreover, the higher coupon rate on municipal bond Y relative to the other three bonds means that more of this bond's return is dependent on the reinvestment of coupon interest payments.

Municipal bond W offers the second highest yield to maturity. On the surface, it seems to be particularly attractive because it eliminates the problem faced by purchasing municipal bond Y, of realizing a possible capital loss when the bond must be sold prior to the maturity date. In addition, the reinvestment risk seems to be less than for the other three municipal bonds because the coupon rate is the lowest. However, the investor would not be eliminating the reinvestment risk because after three years she must reinvest the total bond proceeds received at maturity for two more years. The return that the investor realizes will depend on interest rates three years from now when the investor must reinvest the proceeds received from the maturing bond for an additional two years.

Which is the best municipal bond investment? The yield to maturity does not seem to be helping us identify the best bond. The answer depends on the expectations of the investor. Specifically, it depends on the interest rate at which the coupon interest payments can be reinvested until the end of the investor's investment horizon. Also, for bonds with a maturity longer than the investment horizon, it depends on the investor's expectations about interest rates at the end of the investment horizon. Consequently, any of these bonds can be the best investment vehicle based on some reinvestment rate and some future interest rate at the end of the investment horizon. In Chapter 14 we present an alternative and superior return measure for assessing the potential performance of bonds, total return.

Yield to Call

When a bond is callable, the practice has been to calculate a yield to call as well as a yield to maturity. The former yield calculation assumes that the issuer will call the bond at the next call date. The procedure for calculating the yield to call is the same as for any yield calculation: determine the interest rate that makes the present value of the expected cash flow equal to the full price. In the case of yield to call, the expected cash flow is the coupon payments to the next call date and the call price at that date.

To illustrate the computation, consider a 20-year, 5 percent coupon bond with a maturity value of $100 selling for $103.82. Suppose that the next call date is five years from now and the call price is $102. The cash flow for this bond if it is called in five years is (1) 10 coupon payments of $2.50 every six months and (2) $102 in 10 six-month periods from now.

The process for finding the yield to call is the same as for finding the yield to maturity. Exhibit 6–2 shows the present value for several periodic interest rates.

EXHIBIT 6–2
Present Value of a 5%, 20-Year Municipal Bond Callable in 5 Years at $102 for Various Semiannual Discount Rates

Interest rate	1.75%	2.00%	2.25%	2.50%	2.75%	3.00%	3.25%
Present value	108.51	106.13	103.82	101.56	99.36	97.22	95.14

A periodic interest rate of 2.25 percent each six months makes the present value of the cash flow equal to the price, so this is the semiannual yield to call. Therefore, the yield to call on a bond-equivalent basis is 4.5 percent.

Let's take a closer look at the yield to call as a measure of the potential return of a callable bond. The yield to call does consider all three sources of potential return from owning a bond. However, as in yield to maturity, it assumes that all cash flows can be reinvested at the computed yield—in this case the yield to call—until the assumed call date. As we noted earlier, this assumption may be inappropriate. Moreover, the yield to call assumes that (1) the investor will hold the municipal bond to the assumed call date and (2) the issuer will call the bond on that date.

These assumptions underlying the yield to call are often unrealistic. They also do not take into account how an investor reinvests the proceeds if the issue is called. For example, consider two municipal bonds, M and N. Suppose that the yield to maturity for bond M, a five-year noncallable bond, is 7 percent; for bond N the yield to call assuming the bond will be called in three years is 7.5 percent. Which bond is better for an investor with a five-year investment horizon? It is not possible to tell for the yields cited. Suppose the investor buys bond N. If the issuer calls bond N after three years, the total dollars that will be available at the end of the five-year investment horizon depends on the interest rate that can be earned from investing funds from the call date for an additional two years. In addition, if the issuer does not call the bond, a lower yield to maturity may result, or the investor may have to sell the bond at a loss if the maturity date is more than five years from today.

Yield to call can be calculated to any particular call date but suffers from the same problems as the yield to the next call date. Chapter 9 has more about the analysis of callable bonds.

Yield to Put

Yield to put is the interest rate that makes the preset value of the cash flows of the bond to the put date (i.e., coupon interest and the put price) equal to the full price of the bond. Yield to put, just like yield to maturity and yield to call, also considers all three potential sources of return. However, the inherent assumption in the calculation is that all cash flows are reinvested at the yield to put and the bond is put on the put date. Obviously, this assumption may not be realistic.

Yield to Worst

A Municipal Securities Rulemaking Board (MSRB) requirement states that municipal bonds must be quoted on a *yield to worst* basis. This is the lowest of the yield to maturity, yield to par call, and yield to next (premium) call for a callable bond. It is the lower of the yield to maturity and yield to put for putable bonds. If a bond is pre-refunded, a yield calculation to the refunding date is used instead.

Yield Measure for a Floating-Rate Note

The coupon rate for a floating-rate municipal note changes periodically based on a reference index (such as the J. J. Kenny Index or PSA Index). Because the value for the reference index in the future is not known, it is not possible to determine the note's cash flow. This means that a yield to maturity cannot be calculated.

A conventional measure used to estimate the potential return for a floating-rate security is the security's *effective margin*. This measure estimates the average spread or margin over the underlying index that the investor can expect to earn over the life of the security. The procedure for calculating the effective margin is as follows:

1. Determine the cash flow assuming that the reference rate does not change over the life of the security.
2. Select a margin.
3. Discount the cash flow found in step 1 by the current reference rate plus the margin selected in step 2.
4. Compare the present value of the cash flow as calculated in step 3 to the full price. If the present value is equal to the municipal note's full price, the effective margin is the margin assumed in step 2. If the present value is not equal to the full price, go back to step 2 and try a different margin.

For a floating-rate municipal note selling at par, the effective margin is simply the spread over the reference rate. To illustrate the calculation, suppose that a six-year floating-rate municipal note selling for 99.3830 pays a rate based on some reference rate plus 80 basis points. The coupon rate is reset every six months. Assume that the current reference rate is 4 percent. Exhibit 6–3 shows the calculation of the effective margin for this note. The second column shows the cash flow based on the current reference rate for the assumed margin. The cash flow for the first 11 periods is equal to one-half the current reference rate (2%) plus the semiannual margin of 40 basis points multiplied by 100. In the 12th six-month period, the cash flow is 2 plus the maturity value of 100. The top row of the last

EXHIBIT 6–3

Calculation of the Effective Margin for a Floating-Rate Municipal Note

Floating-rate note: Maturity 6 years
Coupon rate = Reference rate + 80 basis points
Reset every six months
Current reference rate = 4%
Price = 99.3830

Assumed Margin (in basis points)

		80	84	88	92	96	100	104
Coupon rate		4.8%	4.84%	4.88%	4.92%	4.96%	5.00%	5.04%
Semiannual rate		2.4%	2.42%	2.44%	2.46%	2.48%	2.50%	2.52%
Period	Cash Flow*	PV	PV	PV	PV	PV	PV	PV
1	2.4	2.3438	2.3433	2.3428	2.3424	2.3419	2.3415	2.3410
2	2.4	2.2888	2.2879	2.2870	2.2861	2.2852	2.2844	2.2835
3	2.4	2.2352	2.2339	2.2326	2.2312	2.2299	2.2286	2.2273
4	2.4	2.1828	2.1811	2.1794	2.1777	2.1760	2.1743	2.1726
5	2.4	2.1316	2.1295	2.1275	2.1254	2.1233	2.1213	2.1192
6	2.4	2.0817	2.0792	2.0768	2.0744	2.0719	2.0695	2.0671
7	2.4	2.0329	2.0301	2.0273	2.0246	2.0218	2.0190	2.0163
8	2.4	1.9852	1.9821	1.9790	1.9760	1.9729	1.9698	1.9667
9	2.4	1.9387	1.9353	1.9319	1.9285	1.9251	1.9217	1.9184
10	2.4	1.8933	1.8896	1.8859	1.8822	1.8785	1.8749	1.8712
11	2.4	1.8489	1.8449	1.8410	1.8370	1.8331	1.8291	1.8252
12	102	77.0372	76.8569	76.6770	76.4976	76.3186	76.1401	75.9621
PV		100.0000	99.7938	99.5882	99.3830	99.1784	98.9742	98.7706

* For periods 1–11:   Cash flow = 100 (Reference rate + Assumed margin) (0.5)
  For period 12:   Cash flow = 100 (Reference rate + Assumed margin) (0.5) + 100

seven columns shows the assumed margin. The rows below the assumed margin show the present value of each cash flow. The last row gives the total present value of the cash flow. For the seven assumed margins, the present value is equal to the price of the floating-rate note (99.3830) when the assumed margin is 96 basis points. Therefore, the effective margin is 96 basis points. (Notice that the effective margin is 80 basis points, the same as the spread over the reference rate, when the security is selling at par.)

Using the effective margin as a measure of the potential return from investing in a municipal floating-rate note has two drawbacks. First, this measure assumes that the reference rate for the benchmark will not change over the life of the security. Second, if the floating-rate note has a cap (i.e., a maximum coupon rate) or floor (i.e., a minimum coupon rate), this is not taken into consideration. The technology described in Chapter 9 allows interest rate volatility to be considered and can handle caps or floors.

PORTFOLIO YIELD

Thus far, our discussion has focused on potential yield measures for individual municipal bonds. Practitioners have adopted two conventions to calculate a portfolio yield: (1) weighted average portfolio yield and (2) internal rate of return.

Weighted Average Portfolio Yield

Probably the most common—and most flawed—method for calculating a portfolio yield is calculating the weighted average of the yields of all securities in the portfolio. The yield is weighted by the proportion of the portfolio that a security makes up. In general, if we let

w_i = the market value of security i relative to the total market value of the portfolio
y_i = the yield on security i
K = number of securities in the portfolio

then, the weighted average portfolio yield is

$$w_1 y_1 + w_2 y_2 + w_3 y_3 + \ldots + w_K y_K$$

For example, consider the following portfolio consisting of three municipal bonds

Bond	Coupon Rate	Maturity	Par Value	Market Value	Yield to Maturity
A	5.0%	5 years	$10,000,000	$ 9,208,000	6.9%
B	6.0	7 years	20,000,000	20,000,000	6.0
C	4.0	3 years	30,000,000	28,851,000	5.4

In this illustration, the total market value of the portfolio is $58,059,000, K is equal to 3, and

$$w_1 = 9,208,000/58,059,000 = 0.159 \quad y_1 = 6.9\%$$
$$w_2 = 20,000,000/58,059,000 = 0.344 \quad y_2 = 6.0\%$$
$$w_3 = 28,851,000/58,059,000 = 0.497 \quad y_3 = 5.4\%$$

The weighted average portfolio yield is then

$$0.159 \,(6.9\%) + 0.344 \,(6.0\%) + 0.497 \,(5.4\%) = 5.84\%$$

The weighted average yield measure is the most commonly used measure of portfolio yield, but it provides little insight into the potential return of a portfolio. To understand this, consider a portfolio consisting of only two bonds: a six-month bond offering a yield to maturity of 8 percent and a 30-year bond offering a yield to maturity of 5 percent. Suppose that 99 percent of the portfolio is invested in the six-month bond and 1 percent in the 30-year bond. The weighted average yield for this portfolio would be 7.97 percent. But what does this yield mean? How can it be used within an asset/liability framework? The portfolio is basically a six-month portfolio even though it has a 30-year bond. Would a financial institution feel confident offering a two-year liability contract with a yield of 5.5 percent? This would suggest a spread of 247 basis points less than the yield on the portfolio, based on the weighted average portfolio yield. This would be an imprudent policy because the yield on this portfolio over the next two years depends on interest rates six months from now.

Portfolio Internal Rate of Return

Another measure used to calculate a portfolio yield is the internal rate of the portfolio's cash flow. It is computed by first determining the cash flow for all the securities in the portfolio and then finding the interest rate that makes the present value of the cash flow equal to the market value of the portfolio.

The portfolio internal rate of return, although superior to the weighted average portfolio yield, suffers from the same general problems as the yield measures that we discussed earlier in this chapter.

CHAPTER 7

PRICE VOLATILITY CHARACTERISTICS OF MUNICIPAL BONDS

The price of a fixed-rate municipal bond changes in the opposite direction of the change in interest rates. However, not all bonds change by the same amount (in percentage terms or in dollar amount) for a given change in basis points. In order to effectively implement portfolio strategies and control the interest-rate risk of a municipal bond portfolio, it is necessary to understand the price volatility characteristics of these securities. In this chapter we review the characteristics of a bond that affect its price volatility and then describe several measures of bond price volatility. We restrict our discussion to option-free bonds. We extend the concepts reviewed in this chapter to callable bonds in Chapter 9.

PRICE/YIELD RELATIONSHIP FOR OPTION-FREE MUNICIPAL BONDS

A fundamental principle of an option-free bond (a bond without an embedded option) is that the price of a bond changes in the opposite direction of the change in the yield of the bond. This principle follows from the fact that the price of an option-free bond is equal to the present value of its expected cash flows. An increase (decrease) in the yield decreases (increases) the present value of its scheduled cash flows, and, therefore, the bond's price. Exhibit 7–1 illustrates this property for the following four bonds: (1) a 9 percent coupon bond with 5 years to maturity, (2) a 9 percent coupon bond with 20 years to maturity, (3) a 6 percent coupon bond with 5 years to maturity, and (4) a 6 percent coupon bond with 20 years to maturity.

EXHIBIT 7–1
Price/Yield Relationship for Four Hypothetical Municipal Bonds

Coupon	6.00%	6.00%	9.00%	9.00%
Maturity	5	20	5	20
Yield				
4.00%	108.9826	127.3555	122.4565	168.3887
5.00%	104,3760	112.5514	117.5041	150.2056
5.50%	102.1600	106.0195	115.1201	142.1367
5.90%	100.4276	101.1651	113.2556	136.1193
5.99%	100.0427	100.1157	112.8412	134.8159
6.00%	100.0000	100.0000	112.7953	134.6722
6.01%	99.9574	99.8845	112.7494	134.5287
6.10%	99.5746	98.8535	112.3373	133.2472
6.50%	97.8944	94.4479	110.5280	127.7605
7.00%	95.8417	89.3225	108.3166	121.3551
8.00%	91.8891	80.2072	104.0554	109.8964

If the price/yield relationship for any option-free bond is graphed, it would exhibit the shape shown in Exhibit 7–2. Notice that as the yield rises the price of the option-free bond declines. However, the relationship is not linear (it is not a straight line). The shape of the price/yield relationship for any option-free bond is referred to as *convex*, meaning that it is bowed toward the origin. As we shall see, convexity implies that prices

EXHIBIT 7–2
Price/Yield Relationship

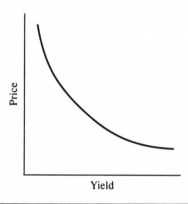

Price

Yield

rise at an increasing rate as yields fall, and that prices decline at a decreasing rate as yields rise. Obviously, with other factors equal, convexity is a positive attribute of a bond.

Keep in mind that a given price/yield relationship is appropriate only at a given point in the life of the bond. As a bond moves toward maturity, two factors influence the price of any option-free bond. First, the bond's price changes as the yield changes, as we previously discussed. Second, for discount and premium bonds, the bond's price changes even if yields remain the same. In particular, with yields held constant, the price of a discount bond increases as it moves toward maturity, reaching par value at the maturity date; for a premium bond, the bond's price decreases as it moves closer to maturity, finally declining to the par value at the maturity date.

BOND PRICE VOLATILITY

Although the prices of all option-free bonds move in the opposite direction of the change in yields, neither dollar price changes nor percentage price changes are the same for all bonds. For our four hypothetical bonds, this can be seen in Exhibit 7–3. The top panel of the exhibit shows the dollar price change, and the bottom panel shows the percentage price change for various changes in the yield assuming that the initial yield for all four bonds is 6 percent. Notice that for a given bond the absolute dollar price change and the absolute percentage price change are not the same for an equal increase and decrease in the yield, except for very small changes in the yield. Even for a small change in yield, the absolute dollar price change is less symmetric than the percentage price change. In general, the dollar price and percentage price increase when the yield declines are greater than the dollar price and percentage price decreases when the yield increases.

These two observations—the absolute and percentage price change are not equal for all bonds, and the absolute and percentage price change for equal but opposite changes in yield are asymmetrical—are explained by the characteristics of the bond that determine the shape of the price/yield relationship depicted in Exhibit 7–2. The remainder of this section explains the characteristics that account for the first observation. Later in this chapter, we provide an explanation for the second observation. Now, as the following sections show, two characteristics of an option-free bond are the primary determinants of its price volatility: coupon and term-to-maturity.[1]

Volatility in Terms of Percentage Price Chance

First, let's look at bond price volatility in terms of percentage price change for a change in yields.

For a given term to maturity and initial market yield, the percentage price volatility of a bond is greater the lower the coupon rate. This property can be seen by comparing the 9 percent and 6 percent coupon bonds with the same maturity (see the second panel of Exhibit 7–3). For example, if the initial market yield for the two 20-year bonds is 6 percent and the yield rises to 8 percent (that is, a 200 basis point increase), the 9 percent coupon bond falls in price from 134.6722 to 109.8964, a decline of 18.4 percent. However, the 6 percent 20-year bond falls by 19.8 percent, from 100.00 to 80.2072.

The second characteristic of a bond that affects its price volatility is its term-to-maturity. For a given coupon rate and initial yield, the longer the term-to-maturity, the greater the price volatility in terms of percentage price change.[2] This can be seen in the lower panel of Exhibit 7–3 by comparing the 5-year bonds to the 20-year bonds with the same coupon. For example, if the yield increases 200 basis points from 6 percent to 8 percent, the 6 percent 20-year bond's price falls by 19.8 percent (100 to 80.2072), whereas the 6 percent 5-year bond falls by only 8.11 percent (100 to 91.8891).

Volatility in Terms of Dollar Price Change

Do the same properties hold if volatility is measured in terms of dollar price change rather than percentage price change? The first panel of Exhibit 7–3 demonstrates that holding all other factors constant, the dollar price change is greater the longer the term-to-maturity. However, the first characteristic concerning the effect of the coupon rate is not true when vol-

---

[1] The time to the first coupon payment as well as the frequency of payments (monthly, semiannual, or annual) also have a small effect.

[2] There are exceptions for certain deep-discount, long-term coupon bonds.

EXHIBIT 7–3
Instantaneous Dollar and Percentage Price Change for Four Hypothetical
Municipal Bonds (Initial yield for all four bonds is 6%)

	Dollar Price Change Per $100 Par			
New Yield	*6%, 5 Year*	*6%, 20 Year*	*9%, 5 Year*	*9%, 20 Year*
4.00%	$8.9826	$27.3555	$9.6612	$33.7165
5.00	4.3760	12.5514	4.7088	15.5334
5.50	2.1600	6.0195	2.3248	7.4645
5.90	0.4276	1.1651	0.4603	1.4471
5.99	0.0427	0.1157	0.0459	0.1437
6.01	−0.0426	−0.1155	−0.0459	−0.1435
6.10	−0.4254	−1.1465	−0.4580	−1.4250
6.50	−2.1056	−5.5521	−2.2673	−6.9116
7.00	−4.1583	−10.6775	−4.4787	−13.3171
8.00	−8.1109	−19.7928	−8.7399	−24.7758

	Percent Price Change			
New Yield	*6%, 5 Year*	*6%, 20 Year*	*9%, 5 Year*	*9%, 20 Year*
4.00%	8.98%	27.36%	8.57%	25.04%
5.00	4.38	12.55	4.17	11.53
5.50	2.16	6.02	2.06	5.54
5.90	0.43	1.17	0.41	1.07
5.99	0.04	0.12	0.04	0.11
6.01	−0.04	−0.12	−0.04	−0.11
6.10	−0.43	−1.15	−0.41	−1.06
6.50	−2.11	−5.55	−2.01	−5.13
7.00	−4.16	−10.68	−3.97	−9.89
8.00	−8.11	−19.79	−7.75	−18.40

atility is measured in terms of dollar price change instead of percentage price change. In terms of dollar price change for a given maturity and initial market yield, the lower the coupon rate the smaller the dollar price change.

The Effects of Yield to Maturity

We cannot ignore that credit considerations cause different bonds to trade at different yields, even if they have the same coupon and maturity. Holding other factors constant, how does the yield-to-maturity affect a bond's price volatility? As it turns out, an increase in yield decreases the percentage price change and the absolute dollar price change. To see this, we can compare a 6 percent, 20-year bond initially selling at a yield of 6 percent, and a 6 percent, 20-year bond initially selling at a yield of 10 percent. The former is initially at a price of 100, and the latter carries a price of 65.68. If the yields on both bonds increase by 100 basis points, the first bond trades at a lower yield by 10.68 points (10.68%). After the assumed increase in yield, the second bond trades at a price of 59.88, for a price decline of only 5.80 (or 8.83%). Thus, we see that the bond that trades at a lower yield is more volatile in both percentage price changes and absolute price changes, as long as the other bond characteristics are the same.

A possibly more relevant comparison of bond price volatility would be comparing bonds that trade at different yields but starting them all on the same footing (e.g., by comparing only bonds trading at par). For par bonds trading at different yields but with the same maturity, the lower yielding bonds still exhibit both greater percentage price changes and absolute price changes for a given change in yield.

MEASURES OF BOND PRICE VOLATILITY

Money managers, arbitrageurs, and traders need to have a way to measure a bond's price volatility to implement hedging and trading strategies. Three measures that are commonly employed are (1) price value of a basis point, (2) yield value of a price change, and (3) duration.

Price Value of a Basis Point

The price value of a basis point (PVBP), also referred to as the *dollar value of an 01* (D01), is the change in the price of the bond if the yield changes by one basis point. Typically, the price value of a basis point is expressed as the absolute value of the change in price; consequently, the greater the price value of a basis point, the greater the dollar price volatility. As we saw earlier, price changes are almost symmetric for small changes in yield. Thus, it does not make a great deal of difference whether we increase or decrease yields to calculate the price value of a basis point. In practice, an average of the change resulting from both an up and a down movement in yield is used.

EXHIBIT 7-4

Calculation of the Price Value of a Basis Point for Four Hypothetical Municipal Bonds

	Bond Price			
Yield	6%, 5 Year	6%, 20 Year	9%, 5 Year	9%, 20 Year
6.00%	100.0000	100.0000	112.7953	134.6722
5.99%	100.0427	100.1157	112.8412	134.8159
6.01%	99.9574	99.8845	112.7494	134.5287

Absolute Value of Dollar Price Change for a Basis Point Change in Yield

Yield	6%, 5 Year	6%, 20 Year	9%, 5 Year	9%, 20 Year
5.99%	0.0427	0.1157	0.0459	0.1437
6.01%	0.0426	0.1155	0.0459	0.1435

Price Value of 1 Basis Point

Average	0.0427	0.1156	0.0459	0.1436

We illustrate the calculation of the price value of a basis point using the four bonds in Exhibit 7-1. For each bond, Exhibit 7-4 shows the initial price, the price after decreasing the yield by one basis point (6% to 5.99%), and the price after increasing the yield by one basis point (from 6% to 6.01%). For each bond the dollar price change is then calculated and averaged to get the price value of a basis point (PVBP).

In the municipal bond market it is common to calculate the price value of five basis points. The principle of calculating the price value of any number of basis points is the same. For example, the price value of five basis points is found by computing the difference between the initial price and the price if the yield changed by five basis points. This is shown in Exhibit 7-5 for our four hypothetical municipal bonds. The relationship is still nearly symmetric for a five basis point change in yield up or down, and the price value of five basis points is approximately equal to five times the price value of one basis point. However, for larger changes in yield, there will be a difference if the yield is increased or decreased, and the price change for a large number of basis points can no longer be approximated by the multiple times the price

EXHIBIT 7–5

Calculation of the Price Value of 5 Basis Points for Four Hypothetical Municipal Bonds

Yield	Bond Price			
	6%, 5 Year	6%, 20 Year	9%, 5 Year	9%, 20 Year
6.00%	100.0000	100.0000	112.7953	134.6722
5.95%	100.2135	100.5802	113.0252	135.3929
6.05%	99.7870	99.4245	112.5660	133.9569

Absolute Value of Dollar Price Change for a 5 Basis Point Change in Yield

Yield	6%, 5 Year	6%, 20 Year	9%, 5 Year	9%, 20 Year
5.95%	0.2135	0.5802	0.2299	0.7207
6.05%	0.2130	0.5755	0.2293	0.7153

Price Value of 5 Basis Points

	6%, 5 Year	6%, 20 Year	9%, 5 Year	9%, 20 Year
Average	0.2133	0.5779	0.2296	0.7180

change for one basis point. Most investors who derive the price values of a basis point by calculating price changes for large movements in yields (such as 100 basis points) will average the PVBPs for an up move and a down move to get the final PVBP.

Yield Value of a Price Change

Another measure of the price volatility of a bond used by some investors is the change in the yield for a specified price change. This is done by first calculating the bond's yield to maturity, and then recalculating the yield if the bond's price is increased by X dollars. The difference between the initial yield and the new yield is the yield value of an X dollar price change. The lower the yield value of an X dollar price change, the greater the dollar price volatility. The reason is that it would take a smaller change in yield to produce a price change of X dollars.

As Treasury notes and bonds are quoted in 1/32 of a percentage point of par, investors in these markets usually let X equal 1/32 of a percentage point of par. The resulting calculation gives the yield value of a 32nd. Since municipal bonds are traded in 1/8 of a percentage point of par, investors in this market are more concerned with the yield value of an 8th.

EXHIBIT 7–6
Calculation of the Yield Value of an 8th for the Two Hypothetical 6% Coupon Municipal Bonds

	Price	
Price	6%, 5 Year	6%, 20 Year
Initial	100.0000	100.0000
−1/8th	99.8750	99.8750
+1/8th	100.1250	100.1250

New Yield If Price Changes by an 8th

New Price	6%, 5 Year	6%, 20 Year
−1/8th	6.029343%	6.010820%
+1/8th	5.970701%	5.989193%

Absolute Value of Change in Yield from 6%

Price	6% 5 Year	6% 20 Year
−1/8th	0.029343%	0.010820%
+1/8th	0.029299%	0.010807%

Yield Value of an 8th

Average	0.029321%	0.010814%

The calculation of the yield value of an 8th for the two 6% coupon bonds is shown in Exhibit 7–6. In practice, the absolute changes in yield for an increase and decrease in price are calculated and then averaged to obtain the yield value of an 8th.

Duration

Another measure of the price volatility of a bond is duration. First formulated by Frederick Macaulay in 1938,[3] *duration* is a weighted average term-to-maturity of the security's cash flows. The weights are the present values of each cash flow as a percentage of the present value of all cash

---

[3] Frederick Macaulay, *Some Theoretical Problems Suggested by the Movement of Interest Rates, Bond Yields, and Stock Prices in the U.S. Since 1856* (New York: National Bureau of Economic Research, 1938).

flows (i.e., the weights are the present value of each cash flow as a percentage of the bond's full price). As we shall see, the greater the duration of a bond, the greater its percentage price volatility.

Mathematically, Macaulay duration on a coupon date for a semiannual pay municipal bond is computed as follows.

Macaulay duration (in years) =

$$\frac{1 \times PVCF_1 + 2 \times PVCF_2 + 3 \times PVCF_3 + \ldots + n \times PVCF_n}{2 \times PVTCF}$$

where

$PVCF_t$ = Present value of cash flow for period t
PVTCF = Present value of total cash flow
n = Number of six-month periods until maturity

For an option-free municipal bond on a coupon date with semiannual payments, the cash flow for periods 1 through $n - 1$ is one-half the annual coupon interest. The cash flow in period n is the semiannual coupon interest plus the maturity value. The formula can be easily extended to fractional periods when a bond is not on its coupon date.

For a bond selling on its coupon date, the total present value of the cash flows is simply the quoted price (or flat price) of the bond. For a bond not selling on a coupon date, the total present value of the cash flows is the bond's quoted price plus accrued interest (or full price).

Exhibits 7–7 and 7–8 show the details involved in calculating the Macaulay duration for the two five-year bonds selling to yield 6 percent. Here, we give the Macaulay duration for the four bonds, assuming a yield to maturity of 6 percent for each bond.

Bond	Macaulay Duration
6%, 5 year	4.39
6%, 20 year	11.90
9%, 5 year	4.19
9%, 20 year	10.98

As can be seen, the Macaulay duration of a coupon bond is less than its maturity. For a zero coupon bond, the Macaulay duration is equal to its maturity. With other factors held constant, the lower the coupon rate, the greater the duration of a bond.

EXHIBIT 7–7
Calculation of Duration and Convexity for a 6%, 5-Year Bond Selling to Yield 6%

Coupon	6.00%			
Maturity	5.00			
Yield	6.00%			
Period	Cash Flow	PV	PV × t	PV × t × (t + 1)
1	3.00	2.9126	2.9126	5.8252
2	3.00	2.8278	5.6556	16.9667
3	3.00	2.7454	8.2363	32.9451
4	3.00	2.6655	10.6618	53.3092
5	3.00	2.5878	12.9391	77.6348
6	3.00	2.5125	15.0747	105.5230
7	3.00	2.4393	17.0749	136.5994
8	3.00	2.3682	18.9458	170.5124
9	3.00	2.2993	20.6933	206.9325
10	103.00	76.6417	766.4167	8430.5841
		Price	Duration Numerator	Convexity Numerator
		100.0000	878.6109	9236.8324
		Macaulay	4.39	
		Modified	4.27	21.7665
		Dollar	4.2651	

Notice the consistency between the properties of percentage price volatility discussed earlier and the properties of duration. We showed that, with all other factors constant, the longer the maturity, the greater the percentage price volatility. A property of duration is that, with all other factors constant, the greater the maturity, the greater the duration.[4] We also showed that the lower the coupon rate, all other factors constant, the greater the percentage price volatility. As we just noted, generally the lower the coupon rate, the greater the duration. Thus, duration is telling us something about bond price volatility.

The relationship between Macaulay duration and bond price volatility is[5]

Percentage change in price =

$$-\frac{1}{(1 + \text{Yield}/2)} \times \text{Macaulay duration} \times \text{Yield change} \times 100$$

[4]This property does not necessarily hold for long-maturity, deep-discount coupon bonds.

[5]Mathematically, the relationship is obtained by taking the first derivative of the price function then dividing it by price. See Frank J. Fabozzi, *Fixed Income Mathematics* (Chicago: Probus Publishing, 1988), Appendix A.

EXHIBIT 7–8
Calculation of Duration and Convexity for a 9%, 5-Year Bond Selling to Yield 6%

Coupon	9.00%			
Maturity	5.00			
Yield	6.00%			
Period	*Cash Flow*	*PV*	*PV × t*	*PV × t × (t + 1)*
1	4.50	4.3689	4.3689	8.7379
2	4.50	4.2417	8.4834	25.4501
3	4.50	4.1181	12.3544	49.4176
4	4.50	3.9982	15.9928	79.9638
5	4.50	3.8817	19.4087	116.4522
6	4.50	3.7687	22.6121	158.2845
7	4.50	3.6589	25.6124	204.8991
8	4.50	3.5523	28.4187	255.7686
9	4.50	3.4489	31.0399	310.3988
10	104.50	77.7578	777.5781	8553.3596
		Price	*Duration Numerator*	*Convexity Numerator*
		112.7953	945.8694	9762.7321
		Macaulay	4.19	
		Modified	4.07	20.3960
		Dollar	4.5916	

The relationship is exact for infinitesimal changes in yield, but is only approximate for larger yield changes.

Generally, the first two expressions on the right-hand side in this equation are combined into one term and called *modified duration*.

$$\text{Modified duration} = \frac{\text{Macaulay duration}}{(1 + \text{Yield}/2)}$$

The relationship can then be expressed as follows.

Percentage price change = − Modified duration × Yield change × 100

To illustrate the relationship consider the 9 percent, 20-year bond selling at 134.6722 to yield 9 percent. The Macaulay duration for this bond is 10.98 years. Modified duration is 10.66, as shown here.

$$\text{Modified duration} = \frac{10.98}{(1 + 0.06/2)} = 10.66$$

If yields increase instantaneously from 6.00 percent to 6.10 percent, a yield change in decimal form of +0.0010, the formula above indicates that the percentage price change is

$$-10.66 \times (+0.0010) \times 100 = -1.07\%$$

Notice from the second panel of Exhibit 7–3 that the actual percentage price change is -1.07 percent. Similarly, if yields decrease instantaneously from 6.00 percent to 5.90 percent (a 10 basis point decrease), the formula indicates that the percentage change in price would be $+1.07$ percent. From the second panel of Exhibit 7–3, the actual percentage price change would be $+1.07$ percent. This example illustrates that for small changes in yield, duration does an excellent job of approximating the percentage price change.

Instead of a small change in yield, let's assume that yields increase by 200 basis points, from 6 percent to 8 percent (a yield change of $+0.02$). The percentage change in price estimated using duration would be

$$-10.66 \times (+0.02) \times 100 = -21.32\%$$

How good is this approximation? As can be seen from the second panel of Exhibit 7–3, the actual percentage change in price is only -18.40 percent. Moreover, if the yield decreased by 200 basis points from 6 percent to 4 percent, the approximate percentage price change based on duration would be $+21.32$, compared to an actual percentage price change of $+25.04$ percent. Thus, not only is the approximation off, but we can see that duration estimates a symmetric percentage change in price. However, as we pointed out earlier, this is not a property of the price/yield relationship for option-free municipal bonds.

Exhibit 7–9 shows the approximate percentage change in price for various changes in yield for all four municipal bonds estimated using duration.

EXHIBIT 7–9
Estimated Percentage Price Change Based on Duration (Initial yield = 6%)

New Yield	6%, 5 Year	6%, 20 Year	9%, 5 Year	9%, 20 Year
4.00%	8.54%	23.12%	8.14%	21.32%
5.00	4.27	11.56	4.07	10.66
5.50	2.14	5.78	2.04	5.33
5.90	0.43	1.16	0.41	1.07
5.99	0.04	0.12	0.04	0.11
6.01	−0.04	−0.12	−0.04	−0.11
6.10	−0.43	−1.16	−0.41	−1.07
6.50	−2.14	−5.78	−2.04	−5.33
7.00	−4.27	−11.56	−4.07	−10.66
8.00	−8.54	−23.12	−8.14	−21.32

Notice that for a 100 basis point change in yield, the formula tells us that the percentage price change will be equal to the bond's modified duration. While modified duration shows percentage price change, dollar duration shows the dollar price change of a bond and is calculated by multiplying modified duration by the bond's full price.

CONVEXITY

We are now ready to tie together the price/yield relationship and several of the properties of bond price volatility discussed in this chapter. Recall the shape of the price/yield relationship, as shown in Exhibit 7–2. We referred to that shape as convex.

In Exhibit 7–10, a tangent line is drawn to the price/yield relationship at yield y^*. The tangent shows the rate of change of price with respect to a change in interest rates at that point (yield level). The slope of the tangent line is closely related to the dollar duration. Consequently, for a given starting price, the tangent (which tells us the rate of absolute price changes) is closely related to the duration of the bond (which tells us about the rate of percentage price changes): the steeper the tangent line, the greater the duration; the flatter the tangent line, the lower the duration. Thus, for a given starting price, the tangent line and the duration can be used interchangeably and can be thought of as one and the same method of estimating the rate of price changes.

EXHIBIT 7–10
Price/Yield Relationship with Tangent Line

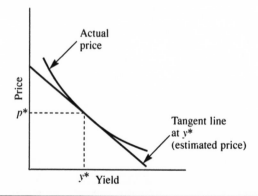

Notice what happens to duration (steepness of the tangent line) as yield changes: As yield increases (decreases), duration decreases (increases). This property holds for all option-free bonds.

If we draw a vertical line from any yield (on the horizontal axis), as in Exhibit 7–11, the distance between the horizontal axis and the tangent line represents the price approximated by using duration starting with the initial yield y^*. The approximation always understates the actual price. This agrees with what we demonstrated earlier about the relationship between duration (and the tangent line) and the approximate price change. When yields decrease, the estimated price change will be less than the actual price change, thereby underestimating the actual price change. On the other hand, when yields increase, the estimated price change will be greater than the actual price change, resulting in an overestimate for the actual price change and an underestimate of the actual price.

For small changes in yield, the tangent line and thus the duration do a good job in estimating the actual price. However, the farther away one gets from the initial yield y^*, the worse the approximation. It should be apparent that the accuracy of the approximation depends on the convexity shape (i.e., the degree of bowedness) of the price/yield relationship for the bond.

EXHIBIT 7–11
Price/Yield Showing Estimation Error

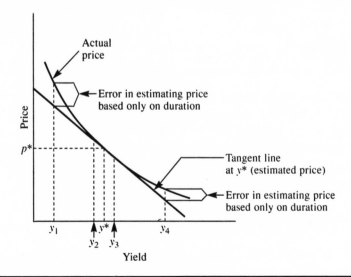

The convexity of an option-free municipal bond on a coupon date can be calculated using the following formula.

Convexity (in years) $=$

$$\frac{1\times2\times PVCF_1 + 2\times3\times PVCF_2 + 3\times4\times PVCF_3 + \ldots + n \times (n + 1)\times PVCF_n}{4 \times (1 + \text{yield}/2)^2 \times PVTCF}$$

where

$PVCF_t$ = Present value of cash flow for period t

$PVTCF$ = Present value of total cash flow

n = Number of six-month periods until maturity

Exhibits 7–7 and 7–8 show the detailed calculations for the convexity of the two 5-year bonds selling to yield 6 percent. The convexity values for the four bonds in Exhibit 7–1 are summarized in this table.

Bond	Convexity
6%/5 year	21.767
6%/20 year	186.827
9%/5 year	20.396
9%/20 year	164.106

Duration provides a first approximation to the percentage price change. Convexity provides a second approximation, based on the following relationship.[6]

Approximate percentage price change due to convexity $=$
$$0.5 \times \text{Convexity} \times (\text{Yield change})^2 \times 100$$

Here the formula gives only an approximation of that part of the price change that is due solely to the curvature of the price/yield relationship.

For example, for the 9 percent coupon bond maturing in 20 years, the approximate percentage price change due solely to convexity if the yield increases from 6 percent to 8 percent (0.02 yield change) is

$$0.5 \times 164.106 \times (0.02)^2 \times 100 = 3.28\%$$

---

[6]Mathematically this is derived from the second term of the Taylor series for the price function. See Appendix A in Fabozzi, *Fixed Income Mathematics*.

If the yield decreases from 6 percent to 4 percent (-0.02 yield change) the approximate percentage price change due solely to convexity would also be 3.22 percent.

The approximate total percentage price change based on both duration and convexity is found by simply adding the two estimates.

Estimated percentage price change =
$\qquad -$ Modified duration $\times$ Yield change $\times$ 100
$\qquad + 0.5 \times$ Convexity $\times$ (Yield change)$^2 \times$ 100

For example, if yields change from 6 percent to 8 percent, the estimated percentage price change would be

Duration	-21.32%
Convexity	$+ \ 3.28$
Total	-18.04%

Recall that the actual percentage price change was -18.40 percent. For a decrease of 200 basis points, from 6 percent to 4 percent, the approximate percentage price change would be as follows.

Duration	$+21.32\%$
Convexity	$+ \ 3.28$
Total	$+24.60\%$

The actual percentage price change was $+25.04$ percent. Consequently, for large yield movements, we obtain a better approximation for bond price movement by using both duration and convexity.

What is convexity measuring? It is measuring the rate of change of duration as yields change. For all option-free municipal bonds, duration increases as yields decline. This is a positive attribute of an option-free bond because as yields decline, price appreciation accelerates. When yield increases, the duration for all option-free bonds decreases. Once again, this is a positive attribute because as yields decline, this feature decelerates the price depreciation. This is the reason why the absolute and percentage price changes are greater when yields decline compared to when they increase by the same number of basis points. Thus, an option-free municipal bond is said to have *positive convexity*.

Although we have focused on the percentage price change due to convexity, we can also calculate a dollar price change. This is called *dollar convexity* and is found by multiplying convexity by the dollar price of the bond.

LIMITATIONS OF DURATION

Managers should recognize several limitations when using duration. We discuss each of these in this section.

Estimate Good Only for Small Yield Changes

We have not delved into the complete underlying mathematical theory behind the derivation of duration and convexity, but we can see from the above discussion one clear limitation: It is only a good approximation for a small change in yields. Thus, two bonds with the same duration may perform differently for large changes in yields.

This can be seen from Exhibit 7–12. The two bonds in the exhibit, Bonds A and B, are trading at the same price and yield. They also have the same duration. However, Bond B has greater convexity than Bond A. Thus, Bond B has better price performance regardless if yields rise or fall from the yield shown in the exhibit. Obviously, the situation depicted in the exhibit cannot last in an actual market because investors would bid up the price (or, equivalently, drive down the yield) of Bond B relative to

EXHIBIT 7–12
Comparison of Two Bonds with Different Convexities but the Same Duration

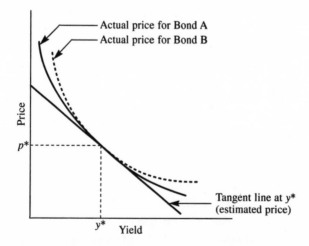

Bond B has greater convexity than Bond A

Bond A. Exhibit 7–12 is a good example of why some analysts err in using duration as the sole measure of interest rate risk when comparing yield spreads.

Portfolio Duration and Nonparallel Yield Curve Shifts

A second limitation is when we calculate the duration of a portfolio. The duration of a portfolio is calculated as the weighted average duration of the individual securities in the portfolio. But how do we interpret the portfolio duration? It is the approximate percentage change in the portfolio value when the yield changes. But what yield changes? If the portfolio consists of bonds across the maturity spectrum, which yield is assumed to change? The answer is that we assume the yield for all maturities changes by the same number of basis points. This is what is commonly referred to as the *parallel yield curve shift assumption*. The problem is that yield curves typically do not shift in a parallel fashion. When they do not, two portfolios with the same duration can perform quite differently depending on the composition of the portfolio and how the yield curve shifts. Measures have been suggested that measure the exposure of a portfolio to yield curve shifts.[7]

Yield Volatility Is Not Recognized

The third limitation of duration as a stand-alone measure of price sensitivity is that it does not recognize the volatility of yields. This is critical because the total potential price sensitivity of a portfolio depends not only on the duration but the volatility of the yield that affects that bond. For example, the duration of an investment-grade municipal bond is greater than that of a noninvestment-grade or junk municipal bond with the same maturity. There are two reasons for this. First, the coupon rate is lower on the investment grade issue, and second it trades at a lower yield level. Does this mean that a portfolio of investment-grade municipal bonds has a greater price volatility exposure? Not necessarily. It also depends on the relative volatility of yields of investment-grade municipal bonds compared to noninvestment-grade bonds. It is the combination of the duration and yield volatility that affects the portfolio's price volatility.

---

[7] See Chapter 14 in Fabozzi, *Fixed Income Mathematics* for a discussion of these measures.

Applicable Only to Option-Free Bonds

Finally, the calculation of both modified and Macaulay duration assumes that when yields change, the cash flows of a municipal bond do *not* change. This is an unrealistic assumption for callable and putable municipal bonds. In the case of a callable bond, a decline in the market yield below or near the coupon rate reduces the price appreciation. (This characteristic of a callable bond is referred to as *negative convexity*.) This is because investors are reluctant to pay the theoretical price based on the cash flows for a noncallable bond because if the bond is called the investor receives only the cash flow up to the call date and the call price at this date.

For example, consider the 9 percent, 20-year bond in Exhibit 7–1. Suppose that instead of this bond being noncallable, it is callable two years from now at 105. If yields decline from 9 percent to 6 percent, the price of this bond if it is option-free would increase from 100 to 134.6722. However, this bond is callable, so investors would not be willing to pay 134.6722 because the bond can be called in two years at 105. Using Macaulay duration or modified duration gives no recognition to any embedded option.

APPROXIMATING DURATION AND CONVEXITY FOR ANY BOND

Unfortunately, market participants often confuse the main purpose of duration by constantly referring to it as some measure of the weighted average life of a bond. This is because of the original use of duration by Macaulay. If you rely on this interpretation of duration, then it may be difficult for you to understand why a municipal bond with a maturity of 20 years can have a duration greater than 20 years. For example, in Chapter 15 we discuss derivative securities. One such derivative security that we discuss is called an inverse floating rate bond, which can be created from a fixed-rate municipal bond. Because the inverse floating rate bond's maturity is equal to that of the fixed-rate municipal bond from which it was created, how could its duration be greater than that issue's maturity?

The answer to this puzzle is that duration is the approximate percentage change in price for a small change in interest rates. In fact, a good way to remember duration is that it is the approximate percentage change in price for a 100 basis point change in interest rates. Thus, subject to the drawbacks discussed in the previous section, a bond or a portfolio with a duration of four means that the price of the bond or portfolio changes by approximately 4 percent for a 100 basis point change in yield. An inverse floating rate bond, as we see in Chapter 15, is a leveraged instrument whose price sensitivity or duration is a multiple of the fixed-rate bond from which it is created.

Once we understand that the duration is related to percentage price change, none of the formulas given above are needed to calculate the approximate duration of a municipal bond, or any of the other more complex derivative securities or options described throughout this book. All we are interested in is the percentage price change of a bond when interest rates change by a small amount. This can be found quite easily by the following procedure.

1. Increase the yield on the bond by a small number of basis points and determine the new price at this higher yield level. We denote this new price by P_+ and the new yield level as y_+.

2. Decrease the yield on the bond by the same number of basis points and calculate the new price. We denote this new price by P_- and the new yield level as y_-.

3. Let P_0 be the initial price, then approximate the duration using the following formula.

$$\text{Approximate duration} = \frac{P_- - P_+}{P_0 (y_+ - y_-)}$$

What the formula measures is the average percentage price change (relative to the initial price) for a small basis point change in yield.

To see how good this approximation is, let's apply it to the 9 percent coupon, 20-year bond trading at 6 percent. The initial price (P_0) is 134.6722. The steps are given below.

1. Increase the yield on the bond by 20 basis points from 6 percent to 6.2 percent. Thus, y_+ is 0.062. The new price (P_+) is 131.8439.

2. Decrease the yield on the bond by 20 basis points from 6 percent to 5.8 percent. Thus y_- is 0.058. The new price (P_-) is 137.5888.

3. The initial price, P_0, is 134.6722, so approximate the duration as follows.

$$\text{Approximate duration} = \frac{137.5888 - 131.8439}{134.6722 \, (0.062 - 0.058)} = 10.66$$

How good is the approximation? The modified duration as calculated by formula is 10.66. Thus, the approximation formula does an excellent job.

Similarly, the convexity of any bond can be approximated using the following formula.

$$\text{Approximate convexity} = \frac{P_+ + P_- - 2P_0}{P_0\,[0.5\,(y_+ - y_-)]^2}$$

EFFECTIVE DURATION AND EFFECTIVE CONVEXITY

The approximation formula for duration and convexity are not only useful in estimating duration and convexity for an option-free bond, but also for a bond with an embedded option. This can be done by estimating what the theoretical value of a bond with an embedded option will be after allowing for the fact that the expected cash flows can change when yields change. Thus the prices P_+ and P_- are theoretical prices. We explain in Chapter 9 how one obtains these theoretical values.

In general, we refer to "duration" as the sensitivity of the bond's price to yield changes. Modified duration measures the price responsiveness assuming that changes in yield do not change the cash flows. This measure is appropriate for option-free bonds and bonds with embedded options where the embedded option is deep out of the money (i.e., a yield

EXHIBIT 7–13
Modified Duration versus Effective Duration

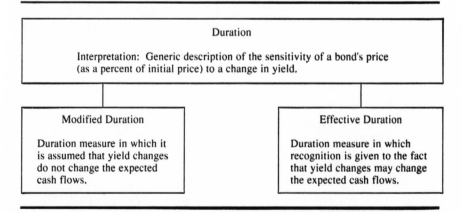

environment where the market yield is substantially higher than the coupon rate on the callable bond). In contrast, effective duration assumes that changes in yield can affect cash flows and takes this into account. This is explained in Chapter 9.

The distinction between modified duration and effective duration is shown in Exhibit 7–13.

SUMMARY

In this chapter we reviewed the price volatility characteristics of option-free bonds. Several measures, including price value of a basis point, duration, dollar duration, and convexity, were shown to summarize the important attributes of price volatility. We explained the limitations of these measures and provided a better measure for bonds with embedded options, effective duration and convexity.

CHAPTER 8

THE STRUCTURE OF INTEREST RATES IN THE MUNICIPAL BOND MARKET

The municipal bond market does not have one interest rate; rather, as in the taxable fixed-income market, it has a structure of interest rates. The interest rate that an investor will demand depends on myriad factors. In this chapter we describe these factors and how they influence interest rates.

THE BASE INTEREST RATE

The securities issued by the United States Department of the Treasury are backed by the full faith and credit of the United States government; therefore, they are viewed by market participants as having no credit risk. As such, interest rates on Treasury securities are the benchmark interest rates in the taxable fixed-income market and are the minimum interest rate or *base interest rate* that investors demand for investing in a taxable non-Treasury security.

Unlike the taxable fixed-income market, there is no risk-free interest rate benchmark. Instead, the benchmark interest rate is the yield for a generic triple-A rated general obligation bond. Thus, the yield on a benchmark triple-A rated issue or index is the base rate used in the municipal bond market.

RISK PREMIUM

Market participants talk of interest rates on particular municipal issues as trading at a *spread* to a particular benchmark triple-A rated municipal issue. For example, if the yield on a 10-year municipal security is 5 percent and the yield on a 10-year triple-A benchmark municipal is 4.3 percent, the spread is 70 basis points. This spread reflects the additional risks the investor faces by acquiring the particular municipal bond above and beyond that of the benchmark triple-A issue. Therefore this spread can be called a *risk premium* and the yield offered can be decomposed as follows.

Base interest rate + Spread

Or equivalently,

Base interest rate + Risk premium

The factors that affect the spread relative to a benchmark general obligation bond include

1. The issuer's perceived creditworthiness.
2. The term or maturity of the instrument.
3. Provisions that grant either the issuer or the investor the option to do something.
4. The taxability of interest at the state and local level.
5. Temporary supply and demand imbalances.
6. The expected liquidity of the issue.

Perceived Creditworthiness of Issuer

Default risk or *credit risk* refers to the risk that the issuer of a bond may be unable to make timely principal or interest payments. Most market participants rely primarily on commercial rating companies to assess the default risk of an issuer. We discuss these rating companies in Chapter 11.

The spread between the yield on a particular issue and a benchmark triple-A rated issue that is identical in all respects except for quality is referred to as a *quality spread* or *credit spread.*

Many municipal bonds are *insured:* a municipal bond insurer has agreed to pay interest and principal on the bonds should the issuer default on its bond payments. The rating on the bonds reflects mainly that of the insurer. The spreads on these bonds depend on the health of the insurer as well as on the credit on the underlying bonds. Prerefunded bonds are triple-A rated bonds that are backed by an escrow consisting of risk-free bonds. Thus they are perceived as having no credit risk. These are discussed further in Chapter 3.

The spreads between insured, prefunded, and noninsured bonds are affected by many factors, including the state of the economy and the relative supply in the market. As the economy deteriorates, the spread between insured or prefunded and noninsured issues generally widens. This is because investors are willing to pay up for lower credit risk issues when the economy is in an economic downturn and the expected default rate on municipal bonds rises.

Supply also has an important impact on relative bond spreads. For example, insured bonds generally trade at a lower yield than noninsured bonds. However, because of the large supply of lower credit risk (insured and prefunded) issues, in recent times these bonds have been noted as trading on top of each other. This is purely a supply effect.

Term to Maturity

As we explained in Chapter 7, the price of a municipal bond fluctuates over its life as yields in the market change. As demonstrated in that chapter, the volatility of a bond's price is dependent on its maturity. More specifically, with all other factors constant, the longer the maturity of a municipal bond, the greater the price volatility resulting from a change in market yields. Generally, bonds with a maturity of between one to five years are considered *short term*; bonds with a maturity between 6 and 20 years are viewed as *intermediate term*, and *long-term* bonds are those with a maturity greater than 20 years.

The spread between any two maturity sectors of the market is called a *maturity spread*. The relationship between the yields on comparable securities with different maturities is called the *term structure of interest rates*. This topic is of such importance that we have devoted more time to it later in this chapter.

Inclusion of Options

It is not uncommon for a municipal bond issue to include a provision that gives either the issuer or the investor an option to take some action against the other party. An option that is included in a bond issue is referred to as an *embedded option*. We discuss the various types of embedded options throughout this book.

The most common type of option in a municipal bond issue is the *call provision*. This option grants the issuer the right to retire the debt, fully or partially, before the scheduled maturity date. The inclusion of a call feature benefits municipal issuers by allowing them to replace an old bond issue with a lower interest cost issue should interest rates in the market decline. Effectively, a call provision allows the municipal issuer to alter the maturity of a bond. A call provision is detrimental to the bondholder because the bondholder must reinvest the proceeds received at a lower interest rate.

The presence of an embedded option has an effect on the spread relative to otherwise comparable municipal issues that do not have embedded options. In general, market participants require a larger spread to a triple-A benchmark municipal issue for an issue with an embedded option that is favorable to the issuer (a call option) than for a municipal issue without such an option. In contrast, market participants require a smaller spread relative to a triple-A benchmark municipal issue for an issue with an embedded option that is favorable to the investor (put option).

Tax Treatment at the State and Local Level

State and local governments may tax interest income on bond issues that are exempt from federal income taxes. Some municipalities exempt interest income from all municipal issues from taxation, others do not. Some states exempt interest income from bonds issued by municipalities within the state but tax the interest income from bonds issued by municipalities outside of the state. The implication is that two municipal securities of the same quality rating and the same maturity may trade at some spread because of the relative demand for bonds of municipalities in different states. For example, in a high income tax state such as New York, the demand for bonds of municipalities drives down their yield relative to municipalities in a low income tax state such as Florida.

Temporary Supply and Demand Imbalances

At any given time, an imbalance may exist between the supply of a particular type of issue (e.g., double-A revenue bond issued by an entity in the state of New York) and the demand for that issue. As mentioned earlier, the relatively high supply of insured versus noninsured issues has caused the yield on insured bonds to increase relative to noninsured. In addition, in years in which a flood of refundings occur, as happened in 1993, an increase in supply results in an underperformance of municipals relative to the Treasury market.

Certain states or counties because of credit or other considerations have high demand relative to supply of like bonds from other municipalities. For example, prerefunded bonds generally outperform nonprerefunded bonds. However, this is not always the case, especially in times of temporary supply/demand imbalances. For example, because the demand for Maryland bonds is high relative to other bonds, the former bonds often outperform prerefunded issues.

In addition, the municipals market is seasonal. In December and June many bonds mature or first become callable. Because of this, new bonds are issued in order to refund existing issues. This is called a *rollover*. Because the supply of municipal bonds increases during these months, the spreads between bonds of different maturities and characteristics are affected, and the spread between municipal and Treasury securities widens.

Expected Liquidity of an Issue

Municipal bonds trade with different degrees of liquidity. *Liquidity* refers to the relative marketability of a particular issue. The greater the expected liquidity of an issue, the lower the yield that investors would require on the issue relative to a benchmark issue.

THE TERM STRUCTURE OF INTEREST RATES

The term structure of interest rates plays a key role in the valuation of municipal bonds. For this reason, we discuss this topic in greater depth.

The Yield Curve

The graphical depiction of the relationship between the yield on bonds of the same credit quality but different maturities is known as the *yield curve*. In the taxable bond market, most market participants construct yield curves from observations of prices and yields in the Treasury market. Two reasons account for this tendency. First, Treasury securities are free of default risk; therefore, differences in creditworthiness do not affect yield estimates. Second, as the largest and most active bond market, the Treasury market offers the fewest problems of illiquidity or infrequent trading.

In the municipal bond market, several benchmark curves exist. In general, a benchmark yield curve is constructed for AAA-quality rated general obligation bonds. The Delphis Hanover Corporation's yield curves are popular yield curves that are often referred to in the municipals market. Delphis Hanover prices yield curves for the four investment grade credits (triple A, double A, single A, and triple B), as well as for credits in between. Exhibit 8–1 shows the yield curves in tabular form as provided by Delphis Hanover Corporation on August 26, 1993.

EXHIBIT 8–1
Delphis Hanover Yield Curves: Close of 8/26/93

Index	100 Aaa	98	96 Aa	94	92 A	90	88 Baa	86
1994	2.40	2.50	2.65	2.80	2.90	3.05	3.25	3.50
1995	3.10	3.20	3.30	3.40	3.50	3.65	3.85	4.10
1996	3.50	3.60	3.70	3.80	3.90	4.05	4.25	4.50
1997	3.75	3.85	3.95	4.05	4.15	4.30	4.50	4.75
1998	3.95	4.05	4.15	4.25	4.35	4.50	4.70	4.95
1999	4.10	4.20	4.30	4.40	4.55	4.70	4.90	5.15
2000	4.25	4.35	4.45	4.55	4.70	4.85	5.05	5.30
2001	4.35	4.45	4.55	4.65	4.80	4.95	5.15	5.40
2002	4.45	4.55	4.65	4.75	4.90	5.05	5.25	5.50
2003	4.55	4.65	4.75	4.85	5.00	5.15	5.35	5.60
2004	4.65	4.75	4.85	4.95	5.10	5.25	5.45	5.70
2005	4.75	4.85	4.95	5.05	5.20	5.35	5.55	5.80
2006	4.85	4.95	5.05	5.15	5.30	5.45	5.65	5.90
2007	4.95	5.00	5.10	5.25	5.40	5.55	5.75	5.95
2008	5.00	5.05	5.15	5.30	5.45	5.60	5.80	6.00
2009	5.05	5.10	5.20	5.35	5.50	5.65	5.85	6.05
2010	5.10	5.15	5.25	5.40	5.55	5.70	5.90	6.10
2011	5.10	5.20	5.30	5.45	5.60	5.75	5.90	6.15
2012	5.15	5.25	5.35	5.50	5.65	5.80	5.95	6.20
2013	5.15	5.25	5.35	5.50	5.65	5.80	5.95	6.20
2014	5.20	5.30	5.40	5.55	5.70	5.85	6.00	6.25
2015	5.20	5.30	5.40	5.55	5.70	5.85	6.00	6.25
2016	5.20	5.30	5.40	5.55	5.70	5.85	6.00	6.25
2017	5.20	5.30	5.40	5.55	5.70	5.85	6.00	6.25
2018	5.20	5.30	5.40	5.55	5.70	5.85	6.00	6.25
2023	5.25	5.35	5.45	5.60	5.75	5.90	6.05	6.30
2028	5.30	5.40	5.50	5.65	5.80	5.95	6.10	6.35
2033	5.30	5.40	5.50	5.65	5.80	5.95	6.10	6.35

Market participants now realize that the traditionally constructed benchmark yield curve is an unsatisfactory measure of the relation between required yield and maturity. The key reason is that securities with the same maturity may be trading at different yields. As we explain in this chapter, this phenomenon reflects the role and impact of differences in the bonds' coupon rates. Hence, developing more accurate and reliable estimates of the benchmark yield curve is necessary. As in the taxable market, current coupon bonds are used for constructing the yield curve. However, in the Treasury market current coupon bonds are issued on regular cycles. This is not the case in the municipal market. In order to derive an appropriate yield curve, the AAA curve is generally derived from market observations on yields of new issue bonds in the associated market sector.

We show the problems posed by traditional approaches to the benchmark yield curve, and we offer an increasingly popular approach to constructing a yield curve for a particular municipal issuer. The approach consists of identifying yields that apply to "zero coupon" bonds; we therefore eliminate the problem of nonuniqueness in the yield–maturity relationship.

Using the Yield Curve to Price a Bond

The price of a municipal bond is the present value of its cash flow. However, in our illustrations and our discussion of the pricing of a municipal bond in Chapter 5, we assume that one interest rate should be used to discount all the bond's cash flows. The appropriate interest rate is the yield on a benchmark municipal issue with the same maturity as the bond, plus an appropriate risk premium or spread.

There is a problem, however, with using the benchmark yield curve to determine the appropriate yield at which to discount the cash flow of a bond. To illustrate this problem, consider the following two hypothetical benchmark five-year municipal bonds, A and B. The difference between these two municipal bonds is the coupon rate, which is 9 percent for A and 3 percent for B. The cash flow for these two bonds per $100 of par value for the 10 six-month periods to maturity would be

Period	Cash flow for A	Cash flow for B
1–9	$ 4.50	$ 1.50
10	104.50	101.50

Because of the different cash flow patterns, using the same interest rate to discount all cash flows is not appropriate. Instead, each cash flow should be discounted at a unique interest rate that is appropriate for the time period in which the cash flow is received. But what should be the interest rate for each period?

The correct way to think about bonds A and B is not as bonds but as packages of cash flows. More specifically, they are packages of zero coupon instruments. Thus, the interest earned is the difference between the only cash flow—the maturity value—and the price paid. For example, bond A can be viewed as 10 zero coupon instruments: one with a maturity value of $4.50 maturing six months from now; a second with a maturity value of $4.50 maturing one year from now; a third with a maturity value of $4.50 maturing 1.5 years from now, and so on. The final zero coupon instrument matures 10 six-month periods from now and has a maturity value of $104.50. Likewise, bond B can be viewed as 10 zero coupon instruments: one with a maturity value of $1.50 maturing six months from now; one with a maturity value of $1.50 maturing one year from now; one with a maturity value of $1.50 maturing 1.5 years from now, and so on. The final zero coupon instrument matures 10 six-month periods from now and has a maturity value of $101.50. Obviously, in the case of each coupon bond, the value or price of the bond is equal to the total value of its component zero coupon instruments.

In general, any bond can be viewed as a package of zero coupon instruments. That is, each zero coupon instrument in the package has a maturity equal to the time when the coupon payment will be made or, in the case of the principal, the maturity date. The value of the bond should equal the value of all the component zero coupon instruments. If this does not hold, it is possible for a market participant to generate riskless profits by stripping the security and creating individual zero coupon securities that generate the same cash flow and can be sold separately at a profit. In the Treasury market, the stripping and reconstitution of Treasury securities has forced these securities to be priced on this basis.[1] In the municipal markets, a similar process is taking place with the creation of derivative securities. This is described in Chapter 4.

---

[1] For a further explanation, see Chapter 9 in Frank J. Fabozzi, *Bond Markets, Analysis and Strategies* (Englewood Cliffs, NJ: Prentice Hall, 1993).

To determine the value of each zero coupon instrument, it is necessary to know the yield offered on a zero coupon bond with the same maturity as the bond being valued for that issuer. This yield is called the *spot rate,* and the graphical depiction of the relationship between the spot rate and its maturity is called the *spot rate curve.* Because no municipal issuer has a zero coupon issue outstanding for each maturity on the spot rate curve, it is not possible to construct such a curve solely from observations in the market. Rather, it is necessary to derive this curve from theoretical considerations as applied to the estimated yield curve for a particular municipal issuer or a group of issuers of the same credit quality. Such a relationship—between the spot rates and maturity constructed from an issuer's yield curve—is called a *theoretical spot rate curve.*

Constructing the Theoretical Spot Rate Curve

To see how a theoretical three-year spot rate curve is constructed from a municipal issuer's yield curve, we use the following estimated par yield curve for a particular municipal issuer.

Maturity	Yield to Maturity	Market Price
1 year	3.50%	100
2 years	4.00	100
3 years	4.50	100

Each issue is trading at par value (100), so the coupon rate is equal to the yield to maturity. We simplify the illustration by assuming annual-pay bonds. The principles apply with equal force to semiannual-pay bonds.

Throughout the analysis and illustrations to come, it is important to remember the basic principle: the value of a municipal issuer's coupon securities must be equal to the value of the package of zero coupon municipal securities that duplicates the coupon bond's cash flow.

The one-year spot rate is taken as the rate on the yield to maturity on the issue with one-year to maturity, 3.5 percent. The two-year spot rate is found by using arbitrage arguments. Because the coupon rate for the two-year bond is 4 percent, its cash flow is $4 one year from now and $104 two years from now. The cash flow in the first year is $4, so its present value is found by discounting $4 by the one-year spot rate. The cash flow in the second year, $104, should be discounted at the two-year spot rate. The theoretical price of the two-year issue is then the sum of these two present values.

$$\frac{4}{(1 + z_1)^1} + \frac{104}{(1 + z_2)^2}$$

where

z_1 = The one-year spot rate
z_2 = The two-year theoretical spot rate

Because the one-year spot rate is 3.5 percent, we can compute the present value of the two-year coupon issue as follows.

$$\frac{4}{(1.035)^1} + \frac{104}{(1 + z_2)^2}$$

Because the price of the two-year coupon municipal issue is 100, the following relationship must hold.

$$100 = \frac{4}{(1.035)^1} + \frac{104}{(1 + z_2)^2}$$

Algebraically solving the above equation for the theoretical two-year spot rate gives a value of 4.01 percent. This is the rate that the market would apply to a two-year zero coupon municipal security if, in fact, such a security existed.

Given the theoretical two-year spot rate, we can obtain the theoretical three-year spot rate. The coupon rate for the three-year issue for this municipal bond issuer is 4.5 percent, so the cash flow is $4.5 one year from now, $4.5 two years from now, and $104.5 three years from now. The first two cash flows must be discounted at the one-year and two-year spot rates, respectively. The cash flow in year three should be discounted at the theoretical three-year spot rate. The sum of these present values is the theoretical price for the issue.

$$\frac{4.5}{(1.035)^1} + \frac{4.5}{(1.0401)^2} + \frac{104.5}{(1 + z_3)^3}$$

where

z_3 = The three-year theoretical spot rate

Since the price of the three-year coupon municipal security is 100 the following relationship must hold.

$$100 = \frac{4.5}{(1.035)^1} + \frac{4.5}{(1.0401)^2} + \frac{104.5}{(1 + z_3)^3}$$

Solving the above equation, we would find that the theoretical three-year spot rate is 4.531 percent.

If we had assumed issues longer than three years, we could follow the above approach sequentially to derive the theoretical four-year spot rate, then the five-year spot rate, and so on. This technique for obtaining the theoretical spot rates is called *bootstrapping*. The spot rates thus obtained represent the theoretical spot rate curve for this issuer. For our hypothetical issuer, these rates are given as follows.

1 year   3.500%
2 year   4.010
3 year   4.531

To see how this information is used to price a municipal bond of this issuer, suppose that this issuer issues an option-free bond with three years remaining to maturity and a coupon rate of 5.25 percent. The theoretical price for this bond is the present value of the cash flow where each cash flow is discounted at the corresponding theoretical spot rate. The cash flow for this bond is $5.25 for the first two years and $105.25 for the third year. The theoretical price is therefore

$$\frac{5.25}{(1.035)} + \frac{5.25}{(1.0401)^2} + \frac{100 + 5.25}{(1.04531)^3} = 102.075$$

Forward Rates

Under certain assumptions, we can extrapolate additional information from the theoretical spot rate curve. That information is the market's expectation or consensus of future interest rates. The following illustrates the process of extrapolating this information about expected future interest rates.

Consider an investor who has a two-year investment horizon and is faced with the following two alternatives involving the bonds of our hypothetical municipal issuer.

Alternative 1: Buy the two-year 4% coupon issue.

Alternative 2: Buy the one-year 3.5% coupon issue, and when it matures in one year buy another one year issue.

The investor is indifferent between the two alternatives if they produce the same return over the two-year investment horizon. The investor knows the spot rate on the one-year issue and the two-year issue. However, he does not know what yield will be available on a one-year issue that will be purchased one year from now. The yield on a one-year issue one year from now is called a *forward rate*. Given the spot rates for the one-year issue and the two-year issue, the forward rate on a one-year issue that will make the investor indifferent between the two alternatives can be determined as follows.

If an investor purchased a two-year zero coupon bond with a maturity value of $100, she would receive $100 at the end of two years. The price of the two-year zero coupon bond would be

$$\frac{100}{(1 + z_2)^2}$$

Suppose that the investor purchased a one-year zero coupon bond for X. At the end of one year, the value of this investment would be

$$X(1 + z_1)$$

Let f represent the forward rate on a one-year zero coupon bond available one year from now. If the investor were to renew her investment by purchasing that instrument at that time, then the future dollars available at the end of one year from the X investment would then be

$$X(1 + z_1)(1 + f)$$

It is easy to use the above formula to find out how many X the investor must invest in order to get $100 two years from now. This can be found as follows.

$$X(1 + z_1)(1 + f) = 100$$

Solving, we get

$$X = \frac{100}{(1 + z_1)(1 + f)}$$

Now, we are fully prepared to return to the investor's choices and analyze what that situation says about forward rates. The investor will be indifferent between the two alternatives confronting her if she makes the same dollar investment and receives $100 from both alternatives at the end of two years. That is, the investor will be indifferent if

$$\frac{100}{(1 + z_2)^2} = \frac{100}{(1 + z_1)(1 + f)}$$

Solving for f, we get

$$f = \frac{(1 + z_2)^2}{(1 + z_1)} - 1$$

We can illustrate the use of this formula with the theoretical spot rates for our hypothetical municipal issuer. We know that z_1 is 0.035 and z_2 is 0.0401. Substituting into the formula, we have

$$f = \frac{(1.0401)^2}{1.035} - 1$$
$$= .04523$$

Therefore, the forward rate on a one-year zero coupon bond one year from now is 4.523 percent.

Let's confirm our results. The price of a two-year zero coupon bond is

$$\frac{100}{(1.0401)^2} = 92.44$$

If the 92.44 amount is invested for one year at the one-year spot rate of 3.5 percent, the amount at the end of one year would be

$$92.44\,(1.03500) = 95.68$$

If this amount is reinvested for another year in a one-year zero coupon bond offering 4.523 percent, the amount at the end of one year would be

$$95.68\,(1.04523) = 100.$$

Thus, both alternatives have the same $100 payoff if the one-year zero coupon yield one year from now is 4.523 percent. This means that, if an investor is guaranteed a 4.523 percent yield on a one-year zero coupon bond of this municipal issuer one year from now, she is indifferent between the two alternatives.

We used the theoretical spot rates to compute the forward rate. The resulting calculated forward rate is called the *implied forward rate*. This is the forward rate implied by the observed market rates.

We can take this sort of analysis much farther. It is not necessary to limit ourselves to deriving implied forward rates one year from now. The yield curve can be used to calculate the implied forward rate for any time in the future for any investment horizon. As examples, the following can be calculated:

- The one-year implied forward rate two years from now.
- The two-year implied forward rate five years from now.
- The six-year implied forward rate ten years from now.
- The seven-year implied forward rate three years from now.

For our hypothetical issuer, the one-year implied forward rate two years from now can be shown to be 5.58 percent.

There is a relationship between a t-year spot rate, the current one-year spot rate, and the implied one-year forward rates. The relationship is as follows.

$$z_t = [(1 + z_1)(1 + f_1)(1 + f_2)(1 + f_3) \ldots (1 + f_{t-1})]^{1/t} - 1$$

where

f_t = The implied one-year forward rate t years from now

Earlier we showed how to calculate the theoretical price of a three-year, 5.25 percent coupon bond of our hypothetical municipal issuer using the theoretical spot rates. The same value will result by discounting the cash flows using the forward rates. Specifically, for our hypothetical municipal issuer, the current one-year forward rate, the one-year forward rate one year from now, and the one-year forward rate two years from now are respectively, 3.5 percent, 4.523 percent, and 5.58 percent; therefore, the theoretical price of a 5.25 percent coupon issue would be

$$\frac{5.25}{(1.035)} + \frac{5.25}{(1.035)(1.04523)} + \frac{100 + 5.25}{(1.035)(1.04523)(1.0558)} = 102.075$$

which is the same value as obtained earlier by discounting at the theoretical spot rates.

Why should a portfolio manager care about forward rates? There are in fact very good reasons for doing so. Foreknowledge of the forward rates implied in the current long-term rate is relevant in formulating an investment policy. To illustrate why it is important in formulating an investment policy, suppose a portfolio manager wants to invest for two years and the current one-year spot rate is 7 percent, and the two-year spot rate is 6 percent. Using the formula for the forward rate, the portfolio manager finds that by buying a two-year security she is effectively making a forward contract to lend one year from now at the rate of 5 percent for one year. If the investor believes that the one-year rate one year from now will turn out to be higher than 5 percent, it is to her advantage to invest initially in a one-year bond, then at the end of the first year to reinvest interest and principal in the one-year bond available in the second year.

The forward rates are the market's consensus of future interest rates. If portfolio managers want to bet against the market's consensus, the implied forward rates must be calculated to determine that consensus.

In addition to the role in formulating investment strategies, forward rates play a key role in the evaluation of stand-alone options and options embedded in bonds.

Determinants of the Shape of the Term Structure

If we plot the term structure—the yield to maturity, or the spot rate, at successive maturities against maturity—what is it likely to look like? Exhibit 8–2 shows four shapes that have appeared with some frequency over time in the taxable fixed-income market.

- Panel A shows an upward-sloping yield curve; that is, yield rises steadily as maturity increases. This shape is commonly referred to as a *normal* or *positive* yield curve.
- Panel B shows a *downward-sloping* or *inverted* yield curve, where yields decline as maturity increases.
- Panel C shows a *humped* yield curve.
- Panel D shows a *flat* yield curve.

In general, the municipal yield curve is positively sloped. There was a brief period when the yield curve became inverted. In fact, during the period when the Treasury yield curve was inverted, the municipal yield curve maintained its upward-sloping shape. Prior to 1986 the municipal yield curve was consistently steeper than the Treasury yield curve as measured by the spread between the 30-year and 1-year issue. Between 1986 and 1990, the steepness was comparable. In 1991, the municipal yield curve became steeper than the Treasury yield curve.

Theories that explain the yield curve are described below. Two major theories have evolved to account for these observed shapes of the yield curve: the *expectations theory* and the *market segmentation theory*.

There are several forms of the expectations theory—the *pure expectations theory*, the *liquidity theory*, and the *preferred habitat theory*. All share a hypothesis about the behavior of short-term forward rates and also assume that the forward rates in current long-term bonds are closely related to the market's expectations about future short-term rates. These three theories differ, however, on whether other factors also affect forward rates, and how. The pure expectations theory postulates that no systematic factors other than expected future short-term rates affect forward rates; the liquidity theory and the preferred habitat theory assert that there are other factors. Accordingly, the last two forms of the expectations theory are sometimes referred to as *biased expectations theories*.

The Pure Expectations Theory
According to the pure expectations theory, the forward rates exclusively represent the expected future rates. Thus, the entire term structure at a given time reflects the market's current expectations of the family of future short-term rates. Under this view, a rising term structure, as in

EXHIBIT 8–2
Four Hypothetical Yield Curves

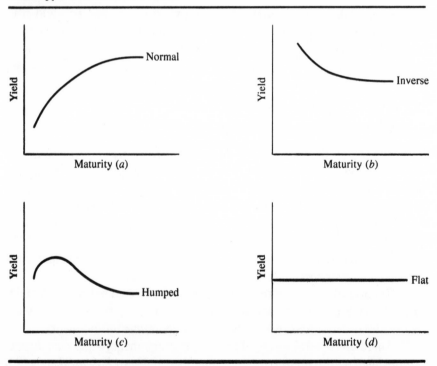

Panel A of Exhibit 8–2, must indicate that the market expects short-term rates to rise throughout the relevant future. Similarly, a flat term structure reflects an expectation that future short-term rates will be mostly constant, whereas a falling-term structure must reflect an expectation that future short rates will decline steadily.

Unfortunately, the pure expectations theory suffers from one short-coming, which, qualitatively, is quite serious. It neglects the risks inherent in investing in bonds and like instruments. If forward rates were perfect predictors of future interest rates, then the future prices of bonds would be known with certainty. The return over any investment period would be certain and independent of the maturity of the instrument initially acquired and of the time at which the investor needed to liquidate his instrument. However, with uncertainty about future interest rates—and hence about future prices of bonds—these instruments become risky investments in the sense that the return over some investment horizon is unknown.

Two risks cause uncertainty about the return over some investment horizon. The first is the uncertainty about the price of the bond at the end of the investment horizon. For example, an investor who plans to invest for five years might consider the following three investment alternatives:

1. Invest in a five-year bond and hold it for five years.
2. Invest in a 12-year bond and sell it at the end of five years.
3. Invest in a 30-year bond and sell it at the end of five years.

The return that will be realized for the second and third alternatives is unknown because the price of each long-term bond at the end of five years is unknown. In the case of the 12-year bond, the price will depend on the yield on seven-year debt securities five years from now; and the price of the 30-year bond will depend on the yield on 25-year bonds five years from now. Because forward rates implied in the current-term structure for a future 12-year bond and a future 25-year bond are not perfect predictors of the actual future rates, there is uncertainty about the price for both bonds five years from now. Thus, there is price risk—the risk that the price of the bond will be lower than currently expected at the end of the investment horizon. As explained in Chapter 7, an important feature of price risk is that it is greater the longer the maturity of the bond.

The second risk has to do with the uncertainty about the rate at which the proceeds from a bond that matures prior to the maturity date can be reinvested until the maturity date—the reinvestment risk. For example, an investor who plans to invest for five years might consider the following three alternative investments:

1. Invest in a five-year bond and hold it for five years.
2. Invest in a six-month instrument, and when it matures reinvest the proceeds in six-month instruments over the entire five-year investment horizon.
3. Invest in a two-year bond, and when it matures reinvest the proceeds in a three-year bond.

The risk in the second and third alternatives is that the return over the five-year investment horizon is unknown because rates at which the proceeds can be reinvested until maturity are unknown.

Several interpretations of the pure expectations theory have been put forth by economists. These interpretations are not exact equivalents, nor are they consistent with each other, in large part because they offer different treatments of the two risks associated with realizing a return that we have just explained.[2]

The broadest interpretation of the pure expectations theory suggests that investors expect the return for any investment horizon to be the same, regardless of the maturity strategy selected.[3] For example, consider an investor who has a five-year investment horizon. According to this theory, it makes no difference if a 5-year, 12-year, or 30-year bond is purchased and held for five years as the investor expects the return from all three bonds to be the same over five years. A major criticism of this very broad interpretation of the theory is that, because of price risk associated with investing in bonds with a maturity greater than the investment horizon, the expected returns from these three very different bond investments should differ in significant ways.[4]

A second interpretation, referred to as the *local expectations* form of the pure expectations theory, suggests that the return will be the same over a short-term investment horizon starting today. For example, if an inves-

---

[2]These formulations are summarized by John Cox, Jonathan Ingersoll, Jr., and Stephen Ross, "A Re-Examination of Traditional Hypotheses About the Term Structure of Interest Rates," *Journal of Finance* (September 1981), pp. 769–799.

[3]F. Lutz, "The Structure of Interest Rates," *Quarterly Journal of Economics* (1940–41), pp. 36–63.

[4]Cox, Ingersoll, and Ross, pp. 774–75.

tor has a six-month investment horizon, buying a 5-year, 10-year, or 20-year bond will produce the same six-month return. It has been demonstrated that the local expectations formulation, which is narrow in scope, is the only one of the interpretations of the pure expectations theory that can be sustained in equilibrium.[5]

The third and final interpretation of the pure expectations theory suggests that the return that an investor will realize by rolling over short-term bonds to some investment horizon will be the same as holding a zero coupon bond with a maturity that is the same as that investment horizon. (A zero coupon bond has no reinvestment risk, so future interest rates over the investment horizon do not affect the return.) This variant is called the *return-to-maturity expectations* interpretation. For example, once again assume that an investor has a five-year investment horizon. By buying a five-year zero coupon bond and holding it to maturity, the investor's return is the difference between the maturity value and the price of the bond, all divided by the price of the bond. According to the return-to-maturity expectations, the same return will be realized by buying a six-month instrument and rolling it over for five years. At this time, the validity of this interpretation is subject to considerable doubt.

The Liquidity Theory

We have explained that the drawback of the pure expectations theory is that it does not consider the risks associated with investing in bonds. Nonetheless, we have just shown that there is indeed risk in holding a long-term bond for one period, and that risk increases with the bond's maturity because maturity and price volatility are directly related.

Given this uncertainty, and the reasonable consideration that investors typically do not like uncertainty and wish to be compensated for accepting it, some economists and financial analysts have suggested a different theory. This theory states that investors will hold longer-term maturities if they are offered a long-term rate higher than the average of expected future rates by a risk premium that is positively related to the term to maturity.[6] Put differently, the forward rates should reflect both interest rate expectations and a "liquidity" premium (really a risk premium), and the premium should be higher for longer maturities.

---

[5]Cox, Ingersoll, and Ross, pp. 776–77.

[6]John R. Hicks, *Value and Capital*, 2d ed. (London: Oxford University Press, 1946), pp. 141–45.

According to this theory, which is called the *liquidity theory of the term structure*, the implied forward rates will not be an unbiased estimate of the market's expectations of future interest rates because they embody a liquidity premium. Thus, an upward-sloping yield curve may reflect expectations that future interest rates either (1) will rise or (2) will be flat or even fall, but with a liquidity premium increasing fast enough with maturity so as to produce an upward-sloping yield curve.

The Preferred Habitat Theory

Another theory, known as the preferred habitat theory, also adopts the view that the term structure reflects the expectation of the future path of interest rates as well as a risk premium. However, the preferred habitat theory rejects the assertion that the risk premium must rise uniformly with maturity.[7] Proponents of the preferred habitat theory say that the latter conclusion could be accepted if all investors intend to liquidate their investment at the shortest possible date while all borrowers are anxious to borrow long. This assumption can be rejected as institutions have holding periods dictated by the nature of their liabilities.

The preferred habitat theory asserts that, to the extent that the demand and supply of funds in a given maturity range do not match, some lenders and borrowers will be induced to shift to maturities showing the opposite imbalances. However, they need to be compensated by an appropriate risk premium whose magnitude reflects the extent of aversion to either price or reinvestment risk.

Thus, this theory proposes that the shape of the yield curve is determined by both expectations of future interest rates and a risk premium, positive or negative, to induce market participants to shift out of their preferred habitat. Clearly, according to this theory, yield curves sloping up, down, flat, or humped are all possible. Unquestionably strong arguments assert that the yield curve is affected by supply and demand factors within maturity and other sectors. We have noted this throughout the chapter.

Market Segmentation Theory

The market segmentation theory also recognizes that investors have preferred habitats dictated by the nature of their liabilities. This theory also

---

[7]Franco Modigliani and Richard Sutch, "Innovations in Interest Rate Policy," *American Economic Review* (May 1966), pp. 178–97.

proposes that the major reason for the shape of the yield curve lies in asset/ liability management constraints (either regulatory or self-imposed) or creditors (borrowers) restricting their lending (financing) to specific maturity sectors.[8] However, the market segmentation theory differs from the preferred habitat theory in that it assumes that neither investors nor borrowers are willing to shift from one maturity sector to another to take advantage of opportunities arising from differences between expectations and forward rates. Thus, for the segmentation theory, the shape of the yield curve is determined by supply of and demand for securities within each maturity sector.

SUMMARY

In the municipal bond market, there is not just one interest rate but a structure of interest rates. The difference between the yield on any two bonds is called the yield spread. The base interest rate in the municipal bond market is the yield on a triple-A benchmark issue or index. The yield spread between a particular municipal issue and the benchmark issue is called a risk premium. The factors that affect the spread include

1. The issuer's perceived creditworthiness.
2. The term or maturity of the instrument.
3. Provisions that grant either the issuer or the investor the option to do something.
4. The taxability of interest at the state and local level.
5. Temporary supply and demand imbalances.
6. The expected liquidity of the issue.

The relationship between yield and maturity is referred to as the *term structure of interest rates.* The graphical depiction of the relationship between the yield on bonds of the same credit quality but different maturities is known as the *yield curve.*

There is a problem with using the estimated yield curve of a particular municipal issuer or a group of issuers of the same credit quality to

---

[8]This theory was suggested in J. M. Culbertson, "The Term Structure of Interest Rates," *Quarterly Journal of Economics* (November 1957), pp. 489–504.

determine one yield at which to discount all the cash payments of any bond. Each cash flow should be discounted at a unique interest rate applicable to the time period when the cash flow is to be received. Since any bond can be viewed as a package of zero coupon instruments, its value should equal the value of all the component zero coupon instruments. The rate used to discount a zero coupon bond is called the spot rate. The theoretical spot rate curve for a municipal issuer can be estimated from the issuer's estimated yield curve using a methodology known as bootstrapping.

Under certain assumptions, the market's expectation of future interest rates can be extrapolated from the theoretical spot rate curve. The resulting rate is called the implied forward rate. The spot rate is related to the current short-term spot rate and the implied short-term forward rates.

Several theories have been proposed about the determination of the term structure: pure expectations theory, the biased expectations theory (the liquidity theory and preferred habitat theory), and the market segmentation theory. All the expectation theories hypothesize that the one-period forward rates represent the market's expectations of actual future rates. The pure expectations theory asserts that it is the only factor affecting interest rates. The biased expectations theories assert that other factors affect the structure of interest rates as well. The market segmentation theory asserts that the yield curve is influenced by supply and demand factors in each maturity sector.

CHAPTER 9

VALUATION OF MUNICIPAL BONDS WITH EMBEDDED OPTIONS

In the previous chapters we discussed pricing, yield, and bond volatility measures for option-free bonds. Applying these concepts to bonds with embedded options (e.g., callable and putable bonds) is inappropriate because the cash flows on these bonds are uncertain. Instead, the analysis for these bonds must take into account the bonds' possible cash flow outcomes.

The valuation process that we describe in this chapter allows the investor to identify if a bond is cheap, rich, or fairly priced. Rather than think in terms of price, investors prefer to look at a bond in terms of *yield spread*. If a valuation model indicates that a municipal bond is cheap by one point, investors seek to translate that amount into a basis point spread over a particular benchmark security's yield. However, as we explain in this chapter, the appropriate benchmark for measuring the yield spread is not one point on the municipal yield curve of an issuer, but instead the spread over the theoretical spot rate curve (or zero coupon curve) of the issuer. The resulting spread, which takes into account the bond's option features, is referred to as the *option-adjusted spread*.

The valuation model we present is state-of-the-art technology. It is complicated, but our hope here is to provide a general understanding of this methodology, its underlying assumptions, and its applications. In practice, few institutional investors have developed their own valuation models; instead, they rely on dealer or vendor models and input their own assumptions.

UNDERLYING PRINCIPLES

The valuation model that we discuss in this chapter requires an understanding of two fundamental principles. First, we explain the correct methodology for valuing any bullet municipal bond (i.e., one with no embedded options). Second, we provide a conceptual framework for valuing bonds with embedded options.

Overview of Bond Valuation

In previous chapters we explained that the price of a bond is the present value of the expected cash flow. All of our illustrations assumed one discount rate with which to discount all cash flows. The rate used is the yield to maturity of a corresponding on-the-run (current coupon) issue of the municipal issuer. For example, suppose that an investor seeks a value for a 10-year option-free single-A municipal bond. If the yield to maturity of the on-the-run 10-year municipal issue is 5 percent, then the value of the municipal issue would be the present value of the cash flows where all the cash flows are discounted at 5 percent. However, this is incorrect, as was explained in Chapter 8.

The problem with this valuation approach even for an option-free bond is that the rate used to discount the cash flows of a 10-year current coupon municipal issue (5 percent in our example) would be the same as that used to discount the cash flow of a 10-year zero coupon municipal issue. Such a comparison makes little sense because the cash flow characteristics of the two municipal issues are different.

As we explained in Chapter 8, any bond must be thought of as a package of cash flows; and each individual cash flow (such as a coupon payment) must be viewed as nothing more than a zero coupon instrument with a maturity date equal to the date that the cash flow will be received. As such, each cash flow or zero coupon instrument should be discounted at the rate that would be offered on a zero coupon municipal issue with a maturity equal to the date of that individual cash flow. Therefore, rather than using one discount rate for bonds with multiple cash flows, multiple discount rates should be used.

Consequently, the first step in valuing a municipal issue is to determine the appropriate zero coupon rates. Zero coupon rates are more commonly referred to as *spot rates*. Because it is unlikely that a municipal

EXHIBIT 9–1
On-the-Run Yield Curve and Theoretical Spot Rate Curve for a AAA Municipal Issuer

Year	Yield to Maturity	Price	Spot Rate	Forward Rate
1	3.5%	100	3.500%	3.500%
2	4.0	100	4.010	4.523
3	4.5	100	4.531	5.580

EXHIBIT 9–2
Theoretical Value of an Option-Free, AAA Municipal Issue with a 4.5% Coupon Bond

Year	Coupon per $100 of Par	Spot Rate	Present Value
I	4.5	3.500%	$ 4.348
2	4.5	4.010	4.160
3	104.5	4.531	91.492
		Theoretical Value: $100.00	

issuer has current zero coupon bonds with different maturities outstanding, it is necessary to estimate a theoretical spot rate curve. This curve can be estimated from the issuer's on-the-run yield curve by a methodology called bootstrapping, which we explained in Chapter 8.

Exhibit 9–1 shows the first three points on a theoretical on-the-run yield curve for a triple-A rated municipal issuer and the corresponding spot rate curve. For simplicity, we assume that all the issues are annual pay.

If this municipal issuer issued an option-free three-year 4.5 percent coupon bond, the theoretical price of this issue would be equal to the present value of each cash flow discounted at the corresponding spot rate, as is illustrated in Exhibit 9–2. The theoretical value for this bond would be $100.00.

Rather than using the theoretical spot rates, theoretical one year forward rates can be used. A *forward rate* is defined as a rate for some specified length of time beginning at some specified time in the future. Forward rates are not the investor's expectations of future interest rates; instead, they are obtained using arbitrage arguments—the same methodology used for obtaining spot rates. Exhibit 9–1 shows the on-the-run yield curve and one-year forward rates for a municipal issuer. Letting f_t denote the one-year forward rate t years from now, the present value of the cash flow for year T is as follows.

$$\frac{\text{cash flow for year } T}{(1 + f_1)\,(1 + f_2) \ldots (1 + f_T)}$$

To illustrate, consider the 4.5 percent coupon bond in Exhibit 9–2. Using the one-year forward rates in Exhibit 9–1, the theoretical value of this bond is

$$\frac{4.5}{(1.035)} + \frac{4.5}{(1.035)(1.04523)} + \frac{104.5}{(1.035)(1.04523)(1.05580)} = 100.00$$

Notice that this value agrees with that computed in Exhibit 9–2 using the spot rates.

Conceptual Approach to the Valuation of Bonds with Embedded Options

Next let's look at how a callable or putable bond should be viewed at a conceptual level. An investor in a callable bond holds a long position in the underlying noncallable (or bullet) bond and has sold an option to the issuer to call the bond (i.e., has a short position in a call option on this bond). Therefore, a callable bond of the same issuer (or on a bond with the same credit risk) is worth less to the investor than a noncallable bond with the same coupon rate. The risk is that the callable bond may be called from the investor when interest rates fall below the coupon rate, forcing the investor to reinvest the proceeds at a lower yield. An investor in a putable bond holds a long position in the underlying bullet bond and has purchased an option to put back the bond to the issuer.

Given the risk, conceptually the price of a callable and putable bond can be expressed as follows:

Callable bond price = Bullet bond price − Value of the call option

Putable bond price = Bullet bond price + Value of the put option

The general bond valuation procedure described next can be used to value the bullet bond and the bond with an embedded option. The theoretical option value can then be determined.

VALUATION MODEL

The value of any municipal bond is determined by the discounted value of the cash flows from the bond, where the discount rate is consistent with the issuer's theoretical spot rate curve or forward rate curve. However, the cash flows for a callable or a putable bond are uncertain. They depend upon both future interest rates and the volatility of those rates. All of these factors must be taken into account when valuing bonds with embedded options.

The first step in determining the value of a bond with or without embedded options is to determine the appropriate municipal yield curve.[1] This will be the yields on liquid option-free new issues that are perceived to have the same credit risk as the bond we wish to evaluate. We will call this the *benchmark curve*. We must then generate the spot and forward rates associated with this curve. The next step is to consider the possible paths that interest rates can take over the life of the bond to be analyzed.[2] As we shall illustrate, an interest rate tree of forward rates is generated, where each path represents a possible interest rate scenario over the life of the bond and each point (or node) on an interest rate path represents an interest rate at a future point in time. Next, the cash flows that would be received from the bond along each interest rate path must be determined. Finally, all cash flows must be discounted back to the present time and probability weighted to determine the bond's expected value today. We examine this process for option-free bonds and bonds with embedded options.

For an option-free bond, the process is easy. We discount the bond's cash flow in the final period (t) by the forward rate at each node for the previous period ($t - 1$) on the interest rate tree in order to determine the expected value of the bond at that period ($t - 1$). The value at each node in that period ($t - 1$) is then discounted back to the next prior period ($t - 2$). We repeat this procedure in which the cash flow (value plus coupon income) associated with each period is discounted back to the present. The resulting final price at the beginning of the tree is equal to the bond's theoretical value.

---

[1] The Treasury yield curve should not be used for the valuation of municipal bonds. Although yields of municipal and Treasury securities are generally positively correlated, they are not perfectly correlated—they can even move in opposite directions.

[2] In this model a lognormal distribution for rates is assumed. The volatility of interest rates must be estimated.

For simplicity, we first discuss the use of this model for valuing a bond with no embedded options. We then extend the model to analyze bonds with calls, puts, and other embedded options.

Generating the Interest Rate Tree

We must determine the possible interest rate scenarios. To do this we generate an interest rate tree that considers the different paths that interest rates can take over the bond's life, ensuring that this tree is consistent with the on-the-run yield curve, and with the assumed distribution and volatility of rates.

An example of an interest rate tree for a three-year bond with a 10 percent volatility of rates is shown in Exhibit 9–3. Each node (i.e., each point) shows the one-year forward rate. Also, the one-year forward rate for the next year assumes two possible values, a high rate and a low rate, each with an equal probability of occurring. The objective in the valuation process is to obtain an interest rate tree such that when any of the on-the-run issues is valued, the tree always correctly values that bond, producing the observed market price.[3]

An explanation of the methodology for deriving the interest rate tree is beyond the scope of this chapter.[4] However, it should be noted that it is based on the assumption that forward rates follow a lognormal distribution and some assumption about interest rate volatility. In our illustrations, we assume a 10 percent volatility.

Valuing a Bond Using the Interest Rate Tree

Let's look at how the interest rate tree in Exhibit 9–3 is used. Exhibit 9–4 shows the coupon interest for years prior to maturity and coupon interest plus par value at maturity for a 3-year bond. The procedure is

---

[3]In actuality, shorter maturity bonds are included in the benchmark yield curve and shorter time steps (perhaps monthly, or weekly, depending on the maturity of the bond to be analyzed) are used to evaluate the bonds. For brevity, we've chosen to show the analysis for only three time periods, though the actual number of steps often includes 100 or more. A large number of steps—and therefore interest rate paths—are required for analyzing bonds with embedded options.

[4]We refer the interested reader to Andrew Kalotay, George Williams, and Frank J. Fabozzi, "A Model for the Valuation of Bonds with Embedded Options," *Financial Analysts Journal* (May-June 1993), pp. 35–46.

EXHIBIT 9–3
Interest Rate for a Three-Year AAA Municipal Issuer
Assuming 10% Interest Rate Volatility

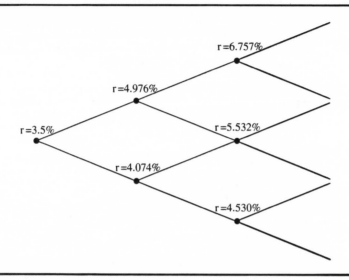

straightforward. At each node, the value of the bond is found using the following steps.

Step 1:   For a given year, determine the cash flow for the two possible interest rate paths one year from this node. The cash flow is the value of the bond one year from this point plus the coupon payment. Hold aside for now how we get these values because the process involves starting from the last year in the tree and working backwards to get the theoretical value of the bond at each node on the interest rate tree.

Step 2:   Calculate the present value of the cash flows for each of the two possible interest rate paths one year from now. The discount rate is the one-year forward rate at the node. This is illustrated in Exhibit 9–5 for any node assuming that the one-year forward rate is r_* at the node where the valuation is sought and letting

V_H = The bond's value for the higher one-year forward rate
V_L = The bond's value for the lower one-year forward rate
C = Coupon payment

EXHIBIT 9–4

Coupon and Par Value at Each Interest Rate Node for a Three-Year Municipal Bond

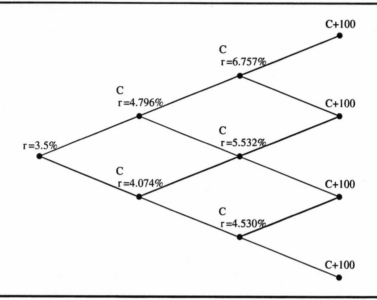

EXHIBIT 9–5
Calculating Value at a Node

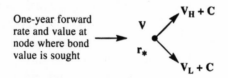

V_H = Bond's value in high-rate state one year forward.

V_L = Bond's value in low-rate state one year forward.

C = Coupon flow on the bond.

Using our notation, the cash flow at a node is either

$V_H + C$ for the higher one-year forward rate

or

$V_L + C$ for the lower one-year forward rate

The present value of these two cash flows using the one-year forward rate at the node r_* is

$$\frac{V_H + C}{(1 + r_*)} = \text{Present value for the higher one-year forward rate}$$

$$\frac{V_L + C}{(1 + r_*)} = \text{Present value for the lower one-year forward rate}$$

Step 3: Calculate the average of the two values computed in the previous step.[5] Then the value of the bond at the node is found as follows.

$$\text{Value (at a node)} = \frac{1}{2} \left[\frac{V_H + C}{(1 + r_*)} + \frac{V_L + C}{(1 + r_*)} \right]$$

The same process continues for each node on the interest rate tree. The process begins by starting in the last period and working backward.[6]

To illustrate these three steps, consider the three-year, 4.5 percent on-the-run noncallable issue shown in Exhibit 9–1.

Step 2 requires the determination of the cash flow along the interest rate tree. Exhibit 9–6 shows the interest rate tree and the cash flow at each node. The only known cash flows are the coupon payments, and, in year three, the maturity value ($100) plus the coupon interest of $4.5. To see how to use steps 2 and 3 to get the value of the bond at the top node in the second year, we use Exhibit 9–7 which has three of the nodes on the interest rate tree labeled by letter. The interest rate tree in Exhibit 9–7 is identical to that in Exhibit 9–6, but the labeling of the nodes makes it easier to follow the explanation. In addition, bond values at each node, which we determine in this section, are also displayed.

---

[5]We average the two values because it is assumed that the two possible interest rates occur with equal probability. Therefore the expected value is just the average of the discounted value of the two possible outcomes.

[6]This process is known as *backward induction*, where the value of the bond is determined by taking the final bond value and discounting it and all associated cash flows by the appropriate discount rates back to the current time period.

EXHIBIT 9–6
Cash Flows for a Three-Year, 4.5%, AAA-Rated Municipal Bond

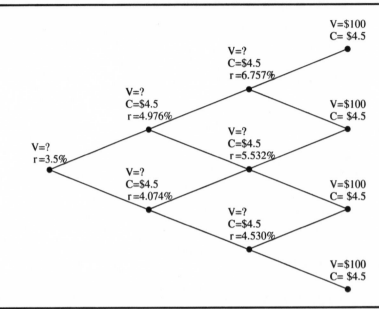

In terms of Exhibit 9–7, a value for the bond in year two is the value of the bond at the node marked with the label W. This value is the present value of the cash flows for the two nodes to the right of the node (i.e., for the two nodes in year three that are to the right of node W).

Step 2 indicates how this present value should be calculated at node W to get the bond value at this point. To get the present value, we use the forward rate at node W, 6.757 percent. For the upper node to the right of node W, the present value of the cash flow for the higher one-year forward rate is

$$\frac{100 + 4.5}{1.06757} = 97.886$$

As the cash flows at the lower node to the right of node W are identical to the upper node, the present value of the cash flow for the lower one-year forward rate is also $97.886.

Step 3 states that the present value for the two cash flows should be averaged (assuming an equal probability of each outcome) to get the value of the bond at node W. Because the two present values are the same, the

EXHIBIT 9–7
Cash Flows for a Three-Year, 4.5%, AAA-Rated Municipal Bond with Labels

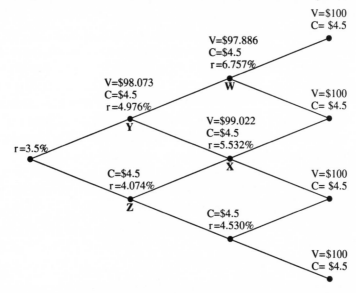

average value equals $97.886. This is the bond value shown in Exhibit 9–7 at node W.

The value of the bond at node X, and all other nodes in period two, is determined similarly. At this node, the one-year forward rate that is used to calculate the present value of the cash flows for the two nodes to the right of node X would be 5.532 percent. In step 2, since V_H and V_L to the right of node X are both $100 and the coupon is $4.50, the cash flow is identical. The present value of the cash flow at both nodes to the right of node X is then

$$\frac{100 + 4.5}{1.05532} = 99.022$$

The average of the two present values is then $99.022 and is therefore the value of the bond at node X.

As you can see, getting the bond value for the two nodes for the year just before the maturity date is simple. Now let's look at how to get the value of the bond at a node in year one. We use node Y in Exhibit 9–7. At node Y, the two nodes to the right are node W (the upper node reflecting the higher one-year forward rate) and node X (the lower node reflecting the lower one-year forward rate). Now to get the bond value at node Y, we need the cash flow at node W and node X. The cash flow is the bond's value at these two nodes plus the coupon. The cash flow at nodes W and X are then discounted at the one-year forward rate at node Y which is 4.976 percent and averaged to get the bond's value at node Y. But where do we get the bond's values at nodes W and X? We have already calculated them: They are 97.886 and 99.022, respectively. This is why this procedure is called backward induction: We work our way backward in the interest rate tree from the maturity date to the root of the tree (today). The bond values at each node were in turn used to get the bond value at an earlier period.

Thus, the value of the bond at node Y is determined from the values calculated at nodes W and X. In this case V_H is the value at node W, which is $97.886; and V_L is the value at node X, which is $99.022. Then

Present value of cash flow for the higher one-year forward rate
$$= \frac{97.886 + 4.5}{1.04976} = 97.533$$

Present value of cash flow for the lower one-year forward rate
$$= \frac{99.022 + 4.5}{1.04976} = 98.615$$

The average present value is then $98.073 [($97.533 + $98.615)/2]. This is the bond's value shown in Exhibit 9–7 at node Y.

The value of the bond at node Z is similarly determined. The value of the bond today (beginning of the tree) is determined from the values of the cash flow at nodes Y and Z.

Exhibit 9–8 shows the completed interest rate tree with the values shown at each node. Notice that the value at the root (i.e., the value today) is $100, which agrees with the observed market price. Thus, the interest rate tree is consistent with the three-year on-the-run issue. If the same procedure is followed for the other two on-the-run issues, the theoretical values would equal the observed market prices. As a result, the resulting interest rate tree is considered to be arbitrage-free. [7]

---

[7] The determination of the forward rate tree depends upon no arbitrage assumptions. A description of this is beyond the scope of this chapter. We refer the interested reader to Kalotay, Williams, and Fabozzi, "A Model for the Valuation of Bonds with Embedded Options."

EXHIBIT 9–8
Cash Flows of a Three-Year, 4.5%, AAA-Rated Municipal Bond

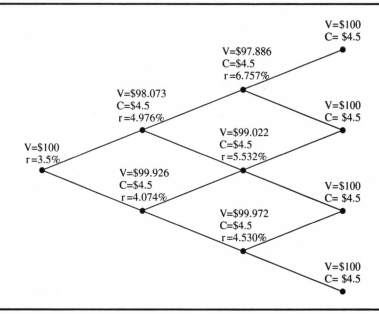

Valuing a AAA Municipal Bond

In order to value any AAA-rated municipal bond, the same interest rate tree shown in Exhibit 9–3 is used. The cash flows of the bond at each node are discounted by the benchmark forward rate at that particular node. The steps for determining the theoretical value are the same as the three steps discussed above. If the calculated bond value (theoretical value) is greater than its market price, the bond is considered to be cheap. Conversely, if the calculated value from the interest rate tree is less than the market price of the bond, the bond is considered to be rich.

To illustrate this, consider a AAA option-free, three-year, 5 percent coupon bond from the same issuer and thus subject to the same discounting rates (i.e., interest rate tree). Suppose the bond is currently trading at $101.5. Exhibit 9–9 gives the complete interest rate tree with values at each node. The theoretical value of this bond is $101.383. Because the bond's calculated (or theoretical) value is less than its current price, the bond is considered rich and should be avoided. Conversely, if the bond's

EXHIBIT 9–9
Interest Rate Tree and Values for a AAA-Rated 5% Municipal Bond

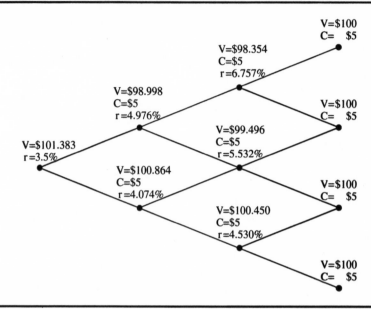

market price is $101, the bond would be considered cheap because its theoretical value is above its market price.

Also note that if the same bond's cash flows were discounted using the spot rates or the forward rates given in Exhibit 9–1, the value of the bond would be $101.383. This should not be surprising since the bond is an option-free bond. Thus, using the spot rates or forward rates gives the same value as that calculated using the interest rate tree.

Valuing an A-Rated Bond

How do we determine the value of an A-rated bond? Using the on-the-run A-rated yield curve, an interest rate tree must be generated that can be used for valuing this bond. This can be done directly by generating an interest rate tree using the benchmark A-rated yield curve. Alternatively, the zero coupon credit spreads for A-rated bonds over the AAA zero curve can be added to the yields at each node on the AAA benchmark tree. The resulting interest rate tree is then consistent with the forward rates implied by the benchmark A-rated yield curve.

For example, Exhibit 9–10 shows the interest rate tree for an A-rated issuer by adding the following zero coupon spreads to the AAA interest rate tree in Exhibit 9–3: one year, 10 basis points; two year, 10 basis points; and three year, 15 basis points.

EXHIBIT 9–10
Interest Rate Tree for an A-Rated Issuer

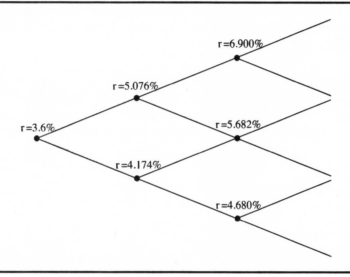

The resulting rates at each node on the interest rate tree are the A-rated benchmark one-year forward rates. To determine an A-rated bond's value, the bond's cash flows are discounted back to the present using these rates. The result is the value for the bond implied by today's benchmark yield curve for A-rated bonds. If the calculated theoretical value is greater than the market price, the bond is considered cheap; if the calculated value is less than the market price, the bond is considered rich.

The same procedure would be used for valuing bonds of other credit ratings, where the yield curve used in the analysis is the yield curve consistent with the credit of the bonds to be valued.

Valuing Callable Bonds

If a bond is callable, the valuation must take into account the possibility that the bond may be called when interest rates decline below the coupon rate.[8] To do this, we adjust the cash flow at each node to reflect a possible call at the node. Here the bond's price at each node is equal to the lower of the calculated price or the call price plus the coupon payment.

For example, assume a AAA-rated, 6 percent coupon municipal bond with two years to maturity is callable in one year and thereafter at par. The value in each year is the lower of the price assuming no call and the call price of 100. The value of the bond is then found using the three steps given earlier, using the AAA interest rate tree shown in Exhibit 9–3. This is illustrated in Exhibit 9–11.

EXHIBIT 9–11
Value of a Three-Year AAA-Rated, 6% Callable Bond
Callable at Par in One Year

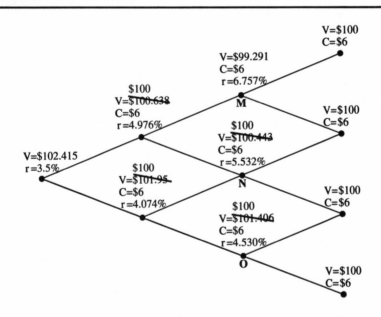

---

[8]Rational exercise of the option is assumed.

The value at node M equals $99.291, the expected value of the bond given the two possible interest rate scenarios. The value at node N, calculated from the two possible outcomes (i.e., the two nodes to the right of node N), would be $100.443. However, since interest rates have fallen below the coupon rate (6%), we assume that the issuer would call the bond at point N, resulting instead in a value of $100, not the $100.443 calculated value. [9]

The value at point O is the call price of $100 rather than the calculated price of $101.406, as the issuer would also call the bond at this point.

The value at each point of an interest rate tree for a callable bond is the minimum of (1) the calculated value or (2) the call price (plus issuance costs). The same procedure is repeated until we reach the value at the beginning of the interest rate tree, which is the value of the bond today.

Valuing Putable Bonds

Bonds with embedded put options can also be analyzed within the framework outlined above. However, for the interest rate tree, at each node we use the maximum of the put price or the calculated bond price. This is because as rates in the market rise above the coupon rate on the putable bond, investors prefer to put the bond and reinvest the proceeds in a higher coupon bond. If interest rates fall below the coupon rate of the issue, investors prefer to retain the bond. For example, assume that a AAA-rated, 5.5 percent, bond currently selling at $102 is putable one year forward and each subsequent year at $100. Using our AAA-rated benchmark yield curve and valuation, the interest rate tree and bond values are shown in Exhibit 9–12. Therefore, the calculated bond value is $102.958. As can be seen from this example, the bond will be put in the second period, when the bond sells at a discount.

Valuing Bonds with Multiple Embedded Options

This same model can be used to analyze bonds with multiple embedded options, where the bond value at each node reflects the exercise of any options at that particular node.

---

[9] We assume no issuance costs. In actuality, an issuer will call the bond if the value of the bond is greater than the call price plus issuance costs.

EXHIBIT 9–12
Value of a Three-Year AAA-Rated, 5.5% Putable Bond Putable at Par in Year One

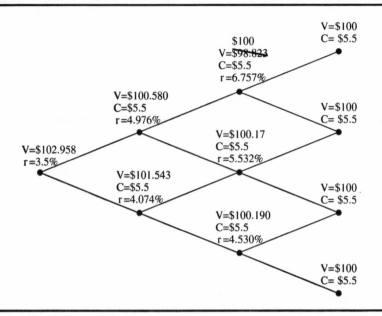

SPECIFIC ADJUSTMENTS TO THE VALUATION MODEL FOR MUNICIPAL BONDS

The analysis described up to now can also be used to value corporate bonds or callable Treasuries, where the benchmark yield curve is a corporate or Treasury yield curve. However, the model requires two adjustments to value municipal bonds because of their unique features. The first is a tax adjustment, which takes into account that capital gains on municipal bonds are taxable. The second adjustment accounts for the fact that many municipal bonds can be advance refunded. We describe both adjustments in the following sections.

Tax Adjustments to the Model

The municipal pricing model must take into account that only municipal interest is free from taxes. Capital gains on the bond are taxable and therefore affect the cash flow on the bond. The net after-tax cash flow resulting from a call should be substituted for the call price of the bond at each point in the valuation process, although the issuer's decision to call a bond is made without regard to the holder's tax status.

For example, if a bond is purchased at a discount at $99 and is callable at $100, the net cash flow on the call date for the investor would be

$$100 - t(100 - 99)$$

where t is the marginal tax rate for the investor. At a rate of 36 percent, it would be $99.64. Because bonds selling at a premium are amortized over time, the difference between the bond's price (or call price) and the adjusted tax basis (rather than the purchase price) on the bond at that particular point should be used to determine the net cash flow at each node on the interest rate tree. Exhibit 9–13 shows the adjusted values for the callable bond shown in Exhibit 9–11, assuming a purchase price of $99 and a tax rate of 36 percent.

Similarly, the adjusted tax basis for an original issue discount (OID) or zero coupon bond is the accreted value of the bond on the call date.

EXHIBIT 9–13
Value of a Three-Year AAA-Rated, 6% Callable Bond Callable at Par in One Year Adjusted for the Tax Effect

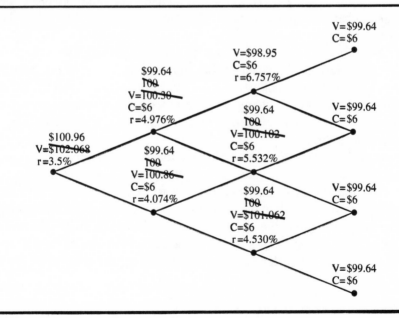

Here, when the bond is called the net cash flow should be substituted for the call price at the node where the bond is called. A similar analysis would follow for putable bonds.

Adjustments for Advance Refunding

Many municipal bonds can be advance refunded before the call date. In an advance refunding, the issuer establishes a fund of Treasury or other qualifying securities whose cash flows match the contractual cash flows of the bond until the call date, including the cost of calling the bonds. The original bonds are said to be *prerefunded,* [10] because they are effectively defeased. It can be cost-effective for issuers to do this, especially if Treasury prices are low relative to those for municipal issues. Generally, replacement bonds will be sold at lower interest rates and their proceeds are used to purchase the defeasing portfolio.

Advance refunding makes an important change in the characteristics of the outstanding bonds. Because the cash flow obligations of the original debt are now met by the proceeds from the trust, the original bonds assume the credit quality of the collateral in that trust. Because that collateral is generally the obligation of the U.S. Treasury, the prerefunded bonds assume a rating of AAA. Thus, advance refunding changes the credit risk characteristics of a bond. This must be accounted for when the bond is valued.

Consider a municipal bond that is not yet callable. The valuation procedure is just as described in this chapter, beginning at the bond's maturity and working backwards to today. In the period when the bond is callable, there are no changes to the procedure. However, once the calculation has reached the period of call protection, a new consideration must be applied.

At each point before the call date, the valuation procedure must determine the net present value savings that would result from advance refunding the bond. Just as one decides to call a bond, an advance refunding is triggered when the net present value savings from defeasance exceed the option value, which has only time value at this point. The present value of future cash flows is then replaced by the value of the defeasing portfolio, or, equivalently, the present value of the contractual cash

---

[10] These bonds are discussed in Chapter 3.

flows to the first call date, discounted on the yield curve of the trust's collateral (the Treasury curve, for example).

This procedure captures the effect seen in the marketplace: As rates fall and advance refunding is anticipated, the spreads at which a bond is valued tighten, so that the bond effectively trades at a higher credit rating.

This procedure is complicated by the fact that the Treasury yield curve and the municipal yield curve are not perfectly correlated. Also, arbitrage rules limit the allowed return on the defeasing portfolio, and they must be incorporated as well. The proper valuation procedure requires a *multifactor process,* one in which the two yield curves are simultaneously modeled, subject to both the specified correlation and the conditions of arbitrage-free pricing for each curve. This procedure is beyond the scope of this chapter.

HORIZON PRICE

In Chapter 14 we explain the total return framework for assessing the potential performance of a bond or a portfolio over some investment horizon. The calculation of the total return requires a projection of the price of the bond at a horizon date. The price at this date is called the *horizon price.*

Thus far, the model that we have described in this chapter assumes that the valuation date is the present date. However, the analysis can be extended to determine the horizon price (or value) of the bond. For example, assume a portfolio manager has a four-year investment horizon and is considering the following three AA-rated bonds.

Bond	Years to Maturity	Today's Price	Yield to Maturity
A	11 years	$ 97.5	5.25%
B	5	98.0	4.85
C	7	101.0	5.50

Since the bonds are not four years to maturity, the calculation of total return would require that this portfolio manager calculate the horizon price for each bond. In addition to determining the value of the bond at today's price and appropriate benchmark yield curve, the manager must also project the yield curve that will be in place on the horizon date. The interest rate tree then begins at the horizon date and extends to the maturity of each bond to be analyzed. The analysis is the same as for the bond being analyzed today. However, the resulting price calculated for the bond at the beginning of the tree is the expected price on the horizon date.

OTHER VALUES CALCULATED FROM THE MODEL

The valuation model we described has useful byproducts, which we discuss in the following sections.

Option Value

The difference between the calculated value of the underlying bullet (noncallable) bond and the calculated value of the callable bond is the value of the embedded call option. If the value of a callable bond is $99.5 and the value of the bullet bond is $101, the value of the embedded call option is $1.50. Although this value can be calculated, it is not by itself very useful in relative value analysis for bonds with different option features.

Effective Yield

The effective yield on a callable bond is the yield on the underlying bullet bond, given the callable bond price and spread. It is the yield that causes the discounted value of the bullet bond's cash flows to equal the bond value as calculated in the model. The difference between the nominal yield to maturity and the effective yield is the yield value of the embedded option.

Effective Duration and Convexity

As explained in Chapter 7, using modified duration for a callable bond as an interest rate sensitivity measure is incorrect because this measure does not take into consideration that the cash flow can change when yields change. In addition, it only measures the sensitivity of the bond to changes in the bond's yield to maturity, ignoring possible yield curve changes. Similarly, the traditional convexity measure also does not consider these factors. Instead of modified duration and traditional convexity, as explained in Chapter 7, effective duration and convexity should be calculated.

We present the formula for effective duration and convexity in Chapter 7. Basically, the formula requires that the yield curve be shifted by a small number of basis points and the new price be determined. The new price must reflect the fact that the change in the yield can change the cash flows.

The effective duration and convexity can also be calculated using the valuation model presented above. This is done by (1) shifting the yield curve by a small number of basis points; (2) generating a new interest rate tree; and (3) calculating the new value for the bond. The new value calculated and yield change are used in the effective duration and convexity calculation. When the valuation model described earlier is used to calculate the effective duration and effective convexity, they are also often referred to as *option-adjusted duration* and *option-adjusted convexity*.

RELATIVE VALUE ANALYSIS OF MUNICIPAL BONDS

Comparing the prices of bonds, even noncallable bonds, with different features such as maturity or coupon is difficult. How, for example, could one compare the value of a coupon paying bond with that of a zero coupon instrument on the basis of price alone? We need a better measure for comparison. The market generally uses two methods for relative valuation of bonds with embedded options: option-adjusted spread analysis and implied volatility analysis. We discuss both methods in this section.

Option-Adjusted Spread Analysis

In traditional bond analysis of option-free bonds, a spread to the appropriate benchmark yield curve is calculated for each bond. For bonds with embedded options, an option-adjusted spread (OAS) is calculated. This is the spread that, when added to the AAA benchmark interest rate tree, causes the value of the bond to equal today's market price. This spread adjusts for the option component on the bond and therefore is the spread for the hypothetical "bullet" bond with the same expected life and cash flow as the bond being analyzed. Therefore, the resulting OAS reflects the pure credit component of the bond, as it takes into account the bond's option features.

Richness or cheapness is assessed by comparing OAS's of bonds with similar credit ratings and effective durations. For example, suppose two bonds, A and B, have embedded options, are of the same credit quality, and have the same effective duration. Suppose further that the OAS of A is 15 basis points while that of B is 25 basis points. On a relative value basis, B would be preferred because it offers a higher OAS.

Although OAS can be calculated based upon a bond's benchmark credit rating curve, this value is generally calculated as a spread to a widely known or used AAA municipal benchmark curve (such as the J. J. Kenny or Delphis Hanover yield curve) so that the comparison on all bonds has one anchor. [12] Then the OAS's of bonds with the same credit ratings are compared to determine relative value. If the bond's calculated OAS is greater than that implied by the spread for a comparable bullet bond, the bond is considered cheap and would be a good value if consistent with the portfolio manager's investment objectives. If, however, the OAS is lower than the spread implied for a fairly priced bullet bond, the bond is considered rich and should be avoided.

Volatility Analysis

Implied volatility is an alternative way to measure the relative attractiveness of bonds. The implied volatility for a bond with an embedded option can be calculated given the current price and the OAS. The volatility used to generate the interest rate tree, which causes the bond's price to equal its calculated value, is the implied volatility for a bond. Given the current price, OAS, and initial volatility, we generate the interest rate tree and calculate the price of the bond. Volatility then shifts, and new trees and cash flows are generated until the discounted value of the cash flows equates to today's market price. The volatility that equates the two is the bond's *implied volatility*.

A high relative volatility (relative to estimated volatility in the marketplace) implies a high price of the embedded call option and, because

---

[12] It should be noted here that some OAS models use a credit benchmark curve in the analysis that may not represent a parallel shift over the AAA benchmark curve. Here, the OAS calculated is the yield spread to the credit benchmark curve, not to the AAA benchmark curve. Therefore, the model will calculate a different OAS to maturity or call or other specified workout date relative to the benchmark AAA curve.

the investor is short the call, a lower price for the bond. Thus the bond is cheap. For putable bonds, the opposite is true, as the investor is long the put.

APPLICATIONS OF OPTION-ADJUSTED ANALYSIS TO PORTFOLIO MANAGEMENT

Now that the valuation methodology has been explained, how is option-adjusted analysis used in portfolio management? As we have explained, OAS or implied volatility can be used to compare bonds with similar credit components. It allows bonds with different options to be compared.

Option-adjusted analysis is becoming increasingly popular in total return analysis, where it is also used to determine the horizon price for bonds. A bond's (or portfolio's) outcome can be assessed under different yield curve scenarios. For example, a manager who is attempting to hedge a portfolio with different instruments can analyze the outcome of the different hedge scenarios by calculating total return for each hedge scenario using the same interest rate assumptions. The optimal hedge scenario would be that which causes minimal fluctuations in the value of the portfolio over the specified horizon.

Option-adjusted analysis can also be used in portfolio optimization, where the focus of the analysis is option-adjusted total return (rather than nonoption-adjusted total return). In an immunization strategy, when funding a liability stream, effective duration and convexity should be used because they are a better representation of price sensitivity for bonds with embedded options than are modified duration and convexity. When constructing an indexed portfolio, the effective duration and convexity are matched to those of the index to be tracked.

SUMMARY

In this chapter we provided an overview of the latest technology for valuing municipal bonds with embedded options. This methodology is far superior to the traditional valuation and yield spread analysis for municipal bonds with embedded options because it recognizes the impact of these options on a bond's value.

Most portfolio managers do not develop their own models; instead, they use the output of models developed by dealer firms or vendors. However, portfolio managers should be familiar with the basic procedure. They should recognize the importance of the critical assumptions in the valuation model, and understand how an effective duration and convexity can be calculated and how OAS can be incorporated into the total return framework that we describe in Chapter 14. They should also know how OAS or implied volatility can be used in relative value analysis.

SECTION 3

CREDIT ANALYSIS

CHAPTER 10

REASONS FOR CREDIT CONCERNS

The purpose of Section III is to explain the basic analytical tools that an investor can use to assess the creditworthiness of a municipal issue. The analysis of municipal bonds—and particularly general obligation bonds—is more an art than a science, but we have tried to set forth the basic analytical questions and answers that should always be addressed.

WHY INVESTORS ARE NOW MORE CONCERNED ABOUT CREDIT RISK THAN EVER BEFORE

In the past investing in municipal bonds had been considered second in safety only to that of U.S. government debt obligations; however, many investors now have ongoing concerns about the credit risks of municipal bonds. This is true regardless of whether or not the bonds are given high investment-grade credit ratings by the commercial rating companies. We note, in particular, that by 1994 mutual funds had become dominant municipal bond purchasers and sellers. A fund manager is very concerned about a bond's up-to-date credit quality since the deterioration of a bond in his or her fund, when recognized by the fund's outside evaluators, immediately results in the decline of the fund's price. This price, or net asset value (NAV), is printed daily in the newspapers and is a critical factor in the successful marketing of the fund to the public.

Defaults and the Federal Bankruptcy Law

The first reason for this concern results primarily from the New York City billion-dollar financial crisis in 1975. The financial crisis sent a loud and clear warning to municipal bond investors in general that, regardless of the supposedly ironclad protections for the bondholder, when issuers such as large cities have severe budget-balancing difficulties, the political hue and cry and the financial stakes of public-employee unions, vendors, and community groups may be dominant forces in the budgetary process.

This reality was further reinforced by the Bankruptcy Reform Act of 1978, which took effect on October 1, 1979. This act makes it easier for municipal bond issuers to seek protection from bondholders by filing for bankruptcy. Of course, the investor should always avoid bonds of issuers who may go into bankruptcy. The judicial process usually involves years of court hearings and litigation that no bond investor should want to be a party to regardless of whether or not he or she may eventually win.

Key provisions of the amendments to the 1978 act were passed in 1988; we discuss these later in this chapter.

Innovative Financing Techniques and Legally Untested Security Structures

The second reason for increased interest in credit risk analysis results from the proliferation in the municipal bond market of innovative financing techniques to secure new bond issues. In addition to the more traditional general obligation bonds and toll road, bridge, and tunnel revenue bonds, there are now more nonvoter-approved, innovative, and legally untested security mechanisms. These innovative financing mechanisms include "moral obligation" housing bonds, "take or pay" electric utility bonds with "step-up" provisions requiring the participants to increase payments to make up for those that may default, "lease rental" bonds, medicare- and medicaid-dependent hospital bonds, commercial bank-backed letter of credit bonds, "put" bonds, and tax-exempt commercial paper. What distinguishes these newer bonds from the more traditional general obligation and revenue bonds is that no history of court decisions and other case law firmly establishes the rights of the bondholders and the obligations of the issuers. For the newer financing mechanisms, it is not possible to determine the probable legal outcome if the bond securities were challenged in court. Therefore, credit analysis has become important in order to identify those bonds that—because of strong finances and other characteristics—are not likely to result in serious litigation.

Of course, the need for the independent review of the creditworthiness of bonds secured by legally untested structures is perhaps most recently shown in the troubled bonds of the Washington Public Power Supply System (WPPSS). Both of the major commercial rating companies gave their highest ratings to these bonds in the early 1980s. One of them, Moody's, had given the WPPSS Projects 1, 2, and 3 bonds its very highest credit rating of Aaa and the Projects 4 and 5 bonds its rating of A-1. This latter investment-grade rating is defined as having the strongest investment attributes within the upper-medium grade of creditworthiness. The other major commercial company, Standard & Poor's, also had given the WPPSS Projects 1, 2, and 3 bonds its highest rating of AAA and the Projects 4 and 5 bonds its rating of A +, which is comparable to Moody's A-1 rating. While these high-quality ratings were in effect, WPPSS sold over $8 billion in long-term bonds. By 1994 Moody's as well as Standard & Poor's rated the Projects 1, 2, and 3 bonds double A. Moody's had no rating for the defaulted Projects 4 and 5 bonds and Standard & Poor's only rated them D.

Cutbacks in Programs

The third reason for the credit risk concern—began with the scaling down of federal grants and aid programs in the 1980s. Over the previous 20 years, many state and local governments had grown dependent on federal grant programs as direct subsidies to their own capital construction and operating budgets. Federal grants had provided indirect subsidies to their local economies as well.

Fiscally conservative federalism can be expected to continue. With the continued support from a broad-based, fiscally conservative national political constituency, we can expect the scaling-down process of federal aid to state and local governments to continue. The increased population growth in the more conservative Sun Belt regions of the country would indicate a further strengthening of this electoral base for fiscal conservatism. What this means for credit analysis is that many general obligation and revenue bond issuers may undergo serious financial stresses as the federal grant and aid reductions are implemented over the coming years.

Secular Declines within the American Economy

The fourth reason for investor concern is that the American economy is undergoing a fundamental change, which is resulting in a decline of various sectors of the economy. This decline has widespread implications for whole regions of the country. Many general obligation and revenue bond issuers can be expected to undergo significant economic deterioration that could negatively impact their tax collections and wealth indicators such as personal income, bank deposits, retail sales, and real property valuations.

An example of this would be in the Midwest, where the basic structure of employment is shifting away from higher-paying manufacturing jobs to lower-paying trade and service jobs. Another example of change is in the energy states, some of whom have experienced significant economic deteriorations.

The Strong Public Demand for Municipal Bonds

The fifth reason for the increased interest in municipal bond credit risk analysis is derived from the changing nature of the municipal bond market. The municipal bond market is characterized by strong buying patterns among both private investors and institutions. This trend was caused by high federal, state, and local income tax rates. Tax-exempt bonds increasingly have become an important and convenient way for sheltering income. One corollary of the strong buyer's demand for tax exemption was an erosion of the traditional security provisions and bondholder safeguards that had grown out of the default experiences of the 1930s. General obligation bond issuers with high tax and debt burdens, declining local economies, and chronic budget-balancing problems had little difficulty finding willing buyers. Also, revenue bonds increasingly were brought to market with legally untested security provisions, modest rate covenants, reduced debt reserves, and weak additional bonds tests.

In regard to the rate covenant, although the rates charged preferably should provide cover to the extent necessary to pay for debt service, operations, and prudent reserves, more and more rate covenants began to be structured to provide cover only to the extent necessary to pay debt service, operations, and *required* improvements. Excess monies were credited against the succeeding year's revenue requirements. Such an arrangement is known as *Chinese coverage*. This form of coverage had been an exception in the past but has now become more of a norm in the industry. The widespread weakening of security provisions means that it is more important than ever before that the prudent investor carefully evaluate the creditworthiness of a municipal bond before making a purchase.

Trading Strategies

The last reason for the increased interest in credit risk analysis results from a fundamental philosophical change that is developing among institutional investors. More and more municipal bond buyers no longer buy and hold their municipal bonds to maturity—which had been the traditional investment approach. Some investors see the opportunity for substantial capital gains through active trading. This could occur if they buy in a sector of the municipal bond market that has become underpriced or "cheap" and sell when the sector becomes overpriced or "rich." Of course, knowing which bonds are likely credit-rating downgrades or upgrades can be very valuable to such an investor.

WHY IT IS IMPORTANT TO KNOW THE CREDIT RISK BEFORE BUYING A MUNICIPAL BOND

The purpose of a common stock analysis is for the analyst to predict the future earnings and profitability of individual corporations and product sectors. The role of municipal bond credit analysis is less dramatic but is nevertheless very important. Furthermore, several different approaches to municipal bond credit analysis exist. There are no universally accepted theories of municipal credit analysis, as there are in the fields of common stock and corporate bond analysis.

As an example of the diversity of municipal bond analysis, one can look at the relationship of intergovernmental aid programs to general obligation bond security. One viewpoint held in the investment community is that the bonds of any local government—such as a city, town, county, or school district—that is heavily dependent on outside revenue sources are less attractive as an investment than bonds for a community that has a strong taxable economic base. However, the financial and budgetary operations of the bond issuer may be significantly strengthened by the outside support. For instance, the school district of Hoboken, New Jersey issued its own general obligation bonds and maintained its own budgetary accounts. In the late 1970s the school district received approximately 75 percent of its revenues from the state, and an annually declining amount from local property taxpayers. In this instance, a New Jersey state constitutional provision and a resulting statute provide that if a community's property tax base declines, the state correspondingly makes up the difference with increased payments of state aid to education. Did this feature make the general obligation school bonds of Hoboken stronger or weaker credit risks?

While the field of municipal bond credit analysis is not characterized by standardized and universally accepted analytical techniques, there is general acceptance of the three basic purposes of a bond analysis. Additionally, although the municipal bond investor will not make a "killing" on the basis of a competent creditworthiness analysis, he or she should be aware of three risk factors, nevertheless. By knowing the degree of creditworthiness, an investor can better protect and utilize investment funds.

The Potential for Default

First, the municipal bond credit risk analysis should determine whether the bond issuer is likely, under a reasonable economic and financial scenario, to default either permanently or temporarily in making bond and interest payments when due. That is, the first purpose of a municipal bond credit analysis is to determine if the bond is going to have serious problems in which the investor could lose capital.

Over the past 25 years some municipal bonds and notes have indeed defaulted. Some have had to go to the federal bankruptcy courts. The Advisory Commission on Intergovernmental Relations reported in a 1985 study that, between 1972 and 1983 alone, there were recorded defaults by at least 113 issuers. Of these, ten were general obligation debts, six were for water supply systems and sewers, five each were for housing and hospitals, three were for utilities other than water and sewers, and 82 were for bonds issued to finance private-purpose commercial and industrial facilities. Clearly, such bonds and notes were ones that the prudent investor should have avoided.

Degrees of Safety

Second, besides identifying the likely default candidates, a related purpose of the risk analysis is to identify among the nondefault candidates those that are financially and legally stronger than others, as well as those that are the most strongly secured bonds. Terms such as *gilt-edged* are usually reserved for describing municipal bonds with very little credit risk and very remote default possibilities, whereas bonds identified as either "being not for widows and orphans" or as being "businessmen's risks" would be at the lower end of the investment-risk spectrum.

Furthermore, although the rating companies give ratings that show degrees of safety, a shortcoming of relying on their ratings exclusively is that they tend to review a credit only when it comes to the new-issue market. With credit deterioration possible over a very short period of time, the investor must look beyond the assigned credit rating.

Short-Term versus Long-Term Opportunities

The third and final purpose of the credit risk analysis is to provide the investor with an indication of what direction the creditworthiness of a particular municipal bond is headed. Is the bond becoming stronger, deteriorating in quality, or remaining the same? Knowing the direction in which the bond is headed can provide tremendous short-term trading opportunities for the sophisticated investor who buys or sells on the basis of potential credit upgrades or downgrades. Additionally, the credit-risk analysis of a bond may uncover certain attractive features of the bond security that are not generally recognized in the marketplace and are not adequately reflected in the credit ratings, but eventually may be. Such bonds provide short-term investment opportunities as well.

As an example, certain bonds issued by the New York City Housing Authority were originally secured only by authority revenues and the guarantee of the City of New York. In the late 1970s they were converted to a federal program whereby the debt service began to be paid directly by the federal government to the paying agent for the bonds. For some years, however, the bonds continued to be rated only B by Moody's. Some investors, aware of this new security feature, bought the bonds when they were priced as B-rated credits. After the Authority applied for the credit upgrade, Moody's assigned Aaa ratings to the bonds. Once this became known in the marketplace, the value of the bonds increased by 200–250 basis points.

A final point in determining the credit direction of a bond is for the investor to be aware that because demographic, economic, and financial changes can take place very rapidly, the time horizon of this credit-risk analysis should not be expected to cover a longer period than a few years.

THE MUNCIPAL BANKRUPTCY LAW

In 1988, President Reagan signed into law a bill amending Chapter 9 of the Bankruptcy Reform Act of 1978 (the "Amendment"). Chapter 9 provides the legal and procedural mechanism for public entities, such as states, municipalities, and other political units of local government to seek the protection of the United States bankruptcy courts. In effect, the Amendment strengthens the legal argument in a federal bankruptcy court that general creditors of a municipality cannot reach the "special revenues'' that have been pledged to secure the municipality's revenue bond issues. The Amendment, in effect, appears to insulate and segregate so-called ''special revenues'' that secure local government municipal revenue bonds in the event that the issuing municipality should file for bankruptcy.

When Chapter 9 appeared in 1978, it was unclear as to what would happen to holders of revenue bonds in a bankruptcy filing, and noted legal authorities held that a Chapter 9 proceeding would automatically terminate the pledge of revenues securing the issuer's revenue bonds. The primary and practical effect of the new changes is to make stronger the credit quality of those local government revenue bonds secured by ''special revenues'' [as defined in section 902(3) of the Bankruptcy Code], which had been issued by weaker municipalities. Conversely, the new law also appears to insulate general obligation bondholders from the claims of those special revenue bondholders. In this regard it makes the general obligation bonds stronger of local issuers who also may have outstanding revenue bonds that are poorly secured by special revenues. The effective date of the changes is for those bankruptcies that have been filed on or after November 3, 1988.

EXHIBIT 10–1
Federal Bankruptcy Filings Under Chapter 9 (1980–March, 1994)

No.	Year	Code	Debtor	Court District
1	1992	(B)	Town of North Courtland	N. Alabama
2	1991	(B)	City of Lipscomb	N. Alabama
3	1986	(D)	Cooper River School District	Alaska
4	1983	(B)	South Tucson, Arizona	Arizona
5	1990	(C)	Corning Hospital District	E. California
6	1986	(D)	Lassen Community College District	California
7	1985	(C)	Monterey County Special Health Care Authority	N. California
8	1983	(D)	San Jose School District	N. California
9	1991	(D)	Richmond Unified School District	N. California
10	1981	(E)	The Management Institute of San Leandro	N. California
11	1992	(D)	Ellicott School Building Authority	Colorado
12	1992	(E)	Powderhorn Metropolitan District No. II	Colorado
13	1991	(A)	Cottonwood Water and Sanitation District	Colorado
14	1991	(E)	Northern Metropolitan District, Adams County, Colorado	Colorado
15	1991	(E)	Castle Pines North Metropolitan District	Colorado

EXHIBIT 10–1 *(continued)*

No.	Year	Code	Debtor	Court District
16	1991	(E)	Colorado Springs Cottonwood General Improvement District	Colorado
17	1991	(E)	Paint Brush Hills Metropolitan District	Colorado
18	1990	(E)	Wolf Creek Valley Metropolitan District No. II, Mineral County, Colorado	Colorado
19	1990	(E)	Wolf Creek Valley Metropolitan District No. IV, Mineral County, Colorado	Colorado
20	1990	(E)	Dawson Ridge Metropolitan District No. 1	Colorado
21	1990	(E)	Villages at Castle Rock Metropolitan District No. 7	Colorado
22	1990	(E)	Will-O-Wisp	Colorado
23	1989	(E)	Colorado Centre Metropolitan District	Colorado
24	1989	(E)	Villages at Castle Rock Metropolitan District No. 4	Colorado
25	1989	(E)	Hamilton Creek Metropolitan District, Summit County, Colorado	Colorado
26	1987	(A)	Eagles Nest Metropolitan District	Colorado
27	1992	(F)	Westport Transit District	Connecticut
28	1991	(B)	City of Bridgeport	Connecticut
29	1989	(F)	Lake Grady Road and Bridge District, Extension #1, Hillsborough County, Florida	Florida
30	1987	(F)	Lake Grady Road and Bridge District, Hillsborough County, Florida	Florida
31	1987	(A)	Water & Sewer District "A" Pasco County, Florida	Florida
32	1985	(A)	Bell County Garbage and Refuse Disposal District	Kentucky
33	1984	(A)	Whitley County Water District	E. Kentucky
34	1992	(C)	Addison Hospital	Michigan
35	1987	(B)	Village of Merrill, Michigan	Michigan
36	1987	(B)	City of Mound Bayou, Mississippi	Mississippi
37	1984	(C)	Pulaski Memorial Hospital	Missouri
38	1984	(B)	Wellston City, Missouri	Missouri
39	1992	(D)	Chilhowee R-IV School District	W. Missouri
40	1991	(E)	City of Columbia Falls, Montana Special Improvement Districts Nos. 25, 26, and 28	Montana
41	1992	(A)	Sanitary and Improvement District No. 113	Nebraska
42	1992	(A)	Sanitary and Improvement District No. 284	Nebraska
43	1991	(A)	Sanitary and Improvement District No. 289	Nebraska

EXHIBIT 10–1 *(continued)*

No.	Year	Code	Debtor	Court District
44	1991	(A)	Sanitary and Improvement District No. 89	Nebraska
45	1991	(A)	Sanitary and Improvement District No. 151	Nebraska
46	1990	(A)	Sanitary and Improvement District No. 235	Nebraska
47	1990	(A)	Sanitary and Improvement District No. 330	Nebraska
48	1989	(A)	Sanitary and Improvement District No. 257	Nebraska
49	1989	(A)	Sanitary and Improvement District No. 264	Nebraska
50	1988	(A)	Sanitary and Improvement District No. 252 of Douglas County, Nebraska	Nebraska
51	1988	(A)	Sanitary and Improvement District No. 52 of Sarpy County, Nebraska	Nebraska
52	1987	(A)	Sanitary and Improvement District No. 117 of Sarpy County, Nebraska	Nebraska
53	1987	(A)	Sanitary and Improvement District No. 93 of Sarpy County, Nebraska	Nebraska
54	1987	(A)	Sanitary and Improvement District No. 122 of Sarpy County, Nebraska	Nebraska
55	1987	(A)	Sanitary and Improvement District No. 103 of Sarpy County, Nebraska	Nebraska
56	1987	(A)	Sanitary and Improvement District No. 92 of Sarpy County, Nebraska	Nebraska
57	1987	(A)	Sanitary and Improvement District No. 75 of Sarpy County, Nebraska	Nebraska
58	1987	(A)	Sanitary and Improvement District No. 69 of Sarpy County, Nebraska	Nebraska
59	1987	(A)	Sanitary and Improvement District No. 267 of Douglas County, Nebraska	Nebraska
60	1987	(A)	Sanitary and Improvement District No. 253 of Douglas County, Nebraska	Nebraska
61	1987	(A)	Sanitary and Improvement District No. 301 of Douglas County, Nebraska	Nebraska
62	1987	(A)	Sanitary and Improvement District No. 251 of Douglas County, Nebraska	Nebraska
63	1987	(A)	Sanitary and Improvement District No. 3 of Saunders City, Nebraska	Nebraska
64	1987	(A)	Sanitary and Improvement District No. 6 of Platte County, Nebraska	Nebraska
65	1986	(A)	Sanitary and Improvement District No. 67 of Sarpy County, Nebraska	Nebraska
66	1986	(A)	Sanitary and Improvement District No. 187 of Douglas County, Nebraska	Nebraska

EXHIBIT 10–1 *(continued)*

No.	Year	Code	Debtor	Court District
67	1986	(A)	Sanitary and Improvement District No. 97 of Sarpy County, Nebraska	Nebraska
68	1986	(A)	Sanitary and Improvement District No. 229 of Douglas County, Nebraska	Nebraska
69	1986	(A)	Sanitary and Improvement District No. 87 of Douglas County, Nebraska	Nebraska
70	1986	(A)	Sanitary and Improvement District No. 250 of Douglas County, Nebraska	Nebraska
71	1986	(A)	Sanitary and Improvement District No. 4 of Saunders City, Nebraska	Nebraska
72	1985	(A)	Sanitary and Improvement District No. 265 of Douglas County, Nebraska	Nebraska
73	1985	(A)	Sanitary and Improvement District No. 7 of Lancaster County, Nebraska	Nebraska
74	1985	(A)	Sanitary and Improvement District No. 65 of Sarpy County, Nebraska	Nebraska
75	1984	(A)	Sanitary and Improvement District No. 63 of Sarpy County, Nebraska	Nebraska
76	1983	(A)	Sanitary and Improvement District No. 4 of Lancaster County, Nebraska	Nebraska
77	1983	(A)	Sanitary and Improvement District No. 42 of Sarpy County, Nebraska	Nebraska
78	1982	(A)	Sanitary and Improvement District No. 5 of Cass County, Nebraska	Nebraska
79	1983	(C)	Jersey City Medical Center	N. Jersey
80	1989	(A)	Valliant Public Works Authority	E. Oklahoma
81	1982	(B)	Wapanucka, Oklahoma	E. Oklahoma
82	1988	(B)	Borough of Shenandoah	Pennsylvania
83	1981	(E)	North & South Shenango Joint Municipal Authority	W. Pennsylvania
84	1988	(F)	Low Country Regional Transportation Authority	South Carolina
85	1991	(A)	Sale Creek Utility District	E. Tennessee
86	1988	(B)	City of Copperhill	Tennessee
87	1986	(F)	Chattanooga Area Regional Transportation Authority	Tennessee
88	1982	(A)	Pleasant View Utility District of Cheatham County, Tenn.	Mdle. Tenn.
89	1993	(A)	Big Oaks Municipal Utility District	S. Texas
90	1993	(B)	Denton County Reclamation and Road District	E. Texas
91	1993	(A)	Harris County Municipal Utility	S. Texas
92	1992	(A)	Northwest Dallas County Flood Control District	N. Texas
93	1992	(B)	Southeast Williamson County Road	W. Texas

EXHIBIT 10–1 *(concluded)*

No.	Year	Code	Debtor	Court District
94	1992	(B)	Southwest Williamson County Road District No. 1	W. Texas
95	1988	(C)	South Eastland County Hospital District d/b/a Blackwell Hospital	Texas
96	1987	(A)	Northwest Harris County Municipal Utility District No. 19	S. Texas
97	1980	(A)	Grimes County Municipal Utility District No. 1	S. Texas
98	1992	(A)	West Harris County Municipal Utility District No. 7	S. Texas
99	1990	(C)	Timpangos Community Mental Health	Utah
100	1992	(A)	Jefferson County Solid Waste Authority	W. Virginia
101	1988	(A)	Arbuckle, WV Public Service District	W. Virginia
102	1985	(A)	Badger Mountain Irrigation District	E. Washington
103	1991	(A)	Whatcom County Water District	W. Washington
104	1991	(B)	City of North Bonneville	W. Washington
105	1994	(E)	Aurora Centretech Metropolitan District	Colorado

Code: A = Municipal Utilities; B = City, Village or County; C = Hospital/Health Care;
D = School/Education; E = Special Municipal District; F = Transportation

The authors would like to thank James E. Spiotto of Chapman and Cutler, 1994, for providing the data for this table.

The Primary Changes

Section 927, added to Chapter 9, states that "The holder of a claim payable solely from *special revenues* of the debtor under applicable nonbankruptcy law shall not be treated as having recourse against the debtor on account of such claim . . ." (emphasis added). This is known as the limitation on recourse section. Section 928, also added, states that "*special revenues* acquired by the debtor after the commencement of the case shall remain subject to any lien resulting from any security agreement entered into by the debtor before the commencement of the case . . ." (emphasis added). This latter provision appears to protect that security interest of the revenue bondholder during a bankruptcy of the issuing municipality.

How "Special Revenues" Are Defined

Section 902 of Title II of the United States Code was amended to specify what types of pledged revenues, identified as "special revenues," will remain subject to a lien in favor of revenue bondholders in the event of the bankruptcy of the issuer. It should be noted that, in general, real estate and income taxes are not defined as being special revenues under Section 902. It does identify five categories of special revenues. They are

1. "Receipts derived from the ownership, operation, or disposition of projects, or systems of the debtor that are primarily used or intended to be used primarily to provide transportation, utility, or other services, including the proceeds of borrowings to finance the projects or systems." Such qualifying revenues would appear to include monies derived from the operation of local government electric, water, and transportation systems.

2. "Special excise taxes imposed on particular activities or transactions." Such qualifying revenues would appear to include excise taxes on hotel and motel rooms as well as on the sale of alcoholic beverages. *It would not appear, however, that a general state sales tax would qualify as a special excise tax under this provision.*

3. "Incremental tax receipts from the benefited area in the case of tax-increment financing." This provision seems to cover tax receipts securing tax allocation and special assessment bonds, even though they are part of a general tax levy, because they result from increased property valuations in the improved area above and beyond the pre-improvement tax base.

4. "Other revenues or receipts derived from particular functions of the debtor whether or not the debtor has other functions . . ." This provision could apply to municipal bonds secured by regulatory fees and stamp taxes imposed for the recording of deeds or any identified function, as well as to other revenues such as tolls or fees identified as related to a particular service or benefit.

5. "Taxes specifically levied to finance one or more projects or systems, excluding receipts from general property, sales, or income taxes (other than tax-increment financing) levied to finance the general purposes of the debtor." The Amendment appears to validate the rights of revenue bondholders when the revenues securing their bonds are derived from incremental sales or property taxes that were specifically levied to pay bondholders for financing capital improvement projects. *Such taxes* *levied to pay for a local government's operating expenses would appear not to be covered by this provision.*

A federal bankruptcy court could retain the power to enjoin the special revenues upon a specific showing of need—for example, when a secured creditor was about to apply proceeds of a gross revenue pledge in a matter inconsistent with the new Amendment. Nonetheless, the rights of holders of revenue bonds to payments secured by special revenues should likely be strengthened in being exempt from the automatic stay provisions of the Bankruptcy Code as amended.

CHAPTER 11

COMPANIES THAT RATE MUNICIPAL BONDS

In this chapter we explain the ratings systems and differences between the two major commercial rating companies, Moody's and Standard & Poor's. The rating system of a third and smaller company, Fitch, is given at the end of the chapter. The major rating companies are part of large, growth-oriented conglomerates and typically charge fees to issuers, bond insurers, and underwriters for their ratings. Moody's is an operating unit of Dun & Bradstreet Companies; Standard & Poor's is part of McGraw-Hill Inc. As of 1994 Moody's charged fees as high as $125,000 per bond sale; Standard & Poor's generally charged up to $50,000.

MOODY'S

The municipal bond rating system used by Moody's grades the investment quality of municipal bonds in a nine-symbol system that ranges from Aaa, the highest investment quality, to the lowest credit rating, C. The respective nine alphabetical ratings and their definitions are shown in Exhibit 11–1.

Municipal bonds in the top four categories (Aaa, Aa, A, and Baa) are considered to be of investment-grade quality. Additionally, bonds in the Aa through B categories that Moody's concludes have the strongest investment features within the respective categories are designated by the symbols Aa1, A1, Baa1, Ba1, and B1, respectively. Moody's also may use the prefix *Con.* before a credit rating to indicate that the bond security is dependent on (1) the completion of a construction project, (2) earnings of a project with little operating experience, (3) rentals being paid once the facility is constructed, or (4) some other limiting condition. It should

EXHIBIT 11–1
Moody's Municipal Bond Ratings

Rating	Definition
Aaa	Best quality; carry the smallest degree of investment risk.
Aa	High quality; margins of protection not quite as large as the Aaa bonds.
A	Upper medium grade; security adequate but could be susceptible to impairment.
Baa	Medium grade; neither highly protected nor poorly secured—lack outstanding investment characteristics and sensitive to changes in economic circumstances.
Ba	Speculative; protection is very moderate.
B	Not desirable investment; sensitive to day-to-day economic circumstances.
Caa	Poor standing; may be in default but with a workout plan.
Ca	Highly speculative; may be in default with nominal workout plan.
C	Hopelessly in default.

also be noted that as of 1994 Moody's applied numerical modifiers 1, 2, and 3 in each generic rating classification from Aa through B to municipal bonds that are issued for industrial development and pollution control and secured by company revenues. The modifier 1 indicates that the security ranks in the higher end of its generic rating category; the modifier 2 indicates a midrange ranking, and the modifier 3 indicates that the bond ranks in the lower end of its generic rating category.

The municipal note rating system used by Moody's is designated by the four investment-grade categories of Moody's Investment Grade (MIG) shown in Exhibit 11–2.

EXHIBIT 11–2
Moody's Municipal Note Ratings

Rating	Definition
MIG 1	Best quality
MIG 2	High quality
MIG 3	Favorable quality
MIG 4	Adequate quality

A short-term issue having a "demand" feature (i.e., payment relying on external liquidity and usually payable upon demand rather than fixed maturity dates) is differentiated by Moody's with the use of the symbols VMIG1 through VMIG4.

EXHIBIT 11–3
Moody's Tax-Exempt Commercial Paper Ratings

Rating	Definition
Prime 1 (P–1)	Superior capacity for repayment
Prime 2 (P–2)	Strong capacity for repayment
Prime 3 (P–3)	Acceptable capacity for repayment

Moody's also provides credit ratings for tax-exempt commercial paper. These are promissory obligations (1) not having an original maturity in excess of nine months and (2) backed by commercial banks. Moody's uses three designations, as shown in Exhibit 11–3, all considered to be of investment grade, for indicating the relative repayment capacity of the rated issues.

STANDARD & POOR'S

The municipal bond rating system used by Standard & Poor's grades the investment quality of municipal bonds in a 10-symbol system that ranges from AAA, the highest investment quality, to D, the lowest credit rating. Bonds within the top four categories (AAA, AA, A, and BBB) are considered by Standard & Poor's to be of investment-grade quality. The respective 10 alphabetical ratings and definitions are given in Exhibit 11–4.

Standard & Poor's also uses a plus (+) or minus (−) sign to show relative standing within the rating categories ranging from AA to BB. Additionally, Standard & Poor's uses the letter *p* to indicate a provisional rating that is intended to be removed upon the successful and timely completion of the construction project. A double dagger (‡) on a mortgage-backed revenue bond rating indicates that the rating is contingent upon receipt by Standard & Poor's of closing documentation confirming investments and cash flows. An asterisk (*) following a credit rating indicates that the continuation of the rating is contingent upon receipt of an executed copy of the escrow agreement.

The municipal note rating system used by Standard & Poor's grades the investment quality of municipal notes in a four-symbol system that ranges from SP–1 +, highest investment quality, to the lowest credit rating, SP–3. Notes within the top three categories (i.e., SP–1 +, SP–1, and

EXHIBIT 11–4
Standard & Poor's Municipal Bond Ratings

Rating	Definition
AAA	Highest rating; extremely strong security.
AA	Very strong security; differs from AAA in only a small degree.
A	Strong capacity but more susceptible to adverse economic effects than above two categories.
BBB	Adequate capacity but adverse economic conditions more likely to weaken capacity.
BB	Lowest degree of speculation; risk exposure.
B	Speculative; risk exposure.
CCC	Speculative; major risk exposure.
CC	Highest degree of speculation; major risk exposure.
C	No interest is being paid.
D	Bonds in default with interest and/or repayment of principal in arrears.

SP–2) are considered by Standard & Poor's as being of investment-grade quality. The respective ratings and summarized definitions are shown in Exhibit 11–5.

Standard & Poor's also rates tax-exempt commercial paper in the same four categories as taxable commercial paper. Exhibit 11–6 gives the four tax-exempt commercial paper rating categories.

HOW THE RATING COMPANIES DIFFER

Although there are many similarities in how Moody's and Standard & Poor's approach credit ratings, there are certain differences in their respective approaches as well. As examples we shall present below some of the differences in approach between Moody's and Standard & Poor's when they assign credit ratings to general obligation bonds.

The credit analysis of general obligation bonds issued by states, counties, school districts, and municipalities initially requires the collection and assessment of information in four basic categories.

1. *Information on the issuer's debt structure so that the overall debt burden can be determined.* The debt burden usually is composed of (1) the respective direct and overlapping debts per capita as well as (2) the respective direct and overlapping debts as percentages of real estate valuations and personal incomes.

EXHIBIT 11–5
Standard & Poor's Municipal Note Ratings

Rating	Definition
SP–1	Very strong or strong capacity to pay principal and interest. Those issues determined to possess overwhelming safety characteristics will be given a plus (+) designation.
SP–2	Satisfactory capacity to pay principal and interest.
SP–3	Speculative capacity to pay principal and interest.

EXHIBIT 11–6
Standard & Poor's Tax-Exempt Commercial Paper Ratings

Rating	Definition
A–1 +	Highest degree of safety.
A–1	Very strong degree of safety.
A–2	Strong degree of safety.
A–3	Satisfactory degree of safety.

2. *Information on the issuer's ability and political discipline for maintaining sound budgetary operations.* The focus of attention here is usually on the issuer's general operating funds and whether or not it has maintained at least balanced budgets over the previous three to five years.

3. *Determination of the specific local taxes and intergovernmental revenues available to the issuer.* Also important are obtaining historical information on tax-collection rates, which are important when looking at property tax levies, and on the dependency of local budgets on specific revenue sources, which is important when looking at the impact of federal monies.

4. *An assessment of the issuer's overall socioeconomic environment.* Questions that have to be answered here include determining the local employment distribution and composition, population growth, and real estate property valuation and personal income trends, among other economic indexes.

Although Moody's and Standard & Poor's rely on these same four informational categories in arriving at their respective credit ratings of general obligation bonds, what they emphasize among the categories can result at times in dramatically different credit ratings for the same issuer's bonds.

Moody's and Standard & Poor's have major differences in their respective approaches toward these four categories. The two rating companies also bring other differences in conceptual factors to bear before assigning their respective general obligation credit ratings. The differences between the rating companies are very important; and although there are some zigs and zags in their respective rating policies, clear patterns of analysis exist and have resulted in split credit ratings for a given issuer. The objective here is to outline what these differences between Moody's and Standard & Poor's actually are. The rating companies have stated in their publications what criteria guide their respective credit-rating approaches, but the conclusions here about how they go about rating general obligation bonds are derived not only from these sources, but also from reviewing their credit reports and rating decisions on individual bond issues.

Evaluating the Four Basic Informational Categories

Simply stated, Moody's tends to focus on the debt burden and budgetary operations of the issuer; Standard & Poor's considers the issuer's economic environment as the most important element in its analysis. Although in most instances these differences of emphasis do not result in dramatically split credit ratings for a given issuer, in at least one instance a major difference in ratings on general obligation bonds has occurred.

The general obligation bonds of the Chicago School Finance Authority in early 1994 were rated only Baa-1 by Moody's, but Standard & Poor's rated the same bonds AA–. In assigning the credit rating of Baa-1, Moody's based its rating on the following debt- and budget-related factors: (1) The deficit funding bonds are to be retired over a 15-year period, an unusually long time for such an obligation; (2) the overall debt burden is high; and (3) the school board faces long-term difficulties in balancing its operating budget because of reduced operating taxes, and uncertain public employee union relations.

Standard & Poor's credit rating of AA – appears to be based primarily upon the following two factors: (1) Chicago is well diversified and fundamentally sound; and (2) the unique security provisions for the bonds in the opinion of the bond counsel insulate the pledged property taxes from the school board's creditors in the event of a school-system bankruptcy.

Comparing State and Local Government General Obligation Bonds

The commercial rating companies differ in how they apply their analytical tools to the rating of state general obligation bonds and local government general obligation bonds. Moody's basically believes that the state and local bonds are not fundamentally different. Moody's applies the same debt- and budget-related concerns to state general obligation bonds as they do to general obligation bonds issued by counties, school districts, towns, and cities.

Moody's has even assigned ratings below A to state general obligation bonds. When the state of Delaware was having serious budgetary problems in the period beginning in 1975 and extending through 1978, Moody's gradually downgraded its general obligation bonds from Aa to Baa1. It should be noted that when Moody's downgraded Delaware general obligation bonds to Baa1 and highlighted its budgetary problems, the state government promptly began to address its budgetary problems. By 1986 the bond rating was up to Aa. In May of 1982 Moody's downgraded the state of Michigan's general obligation bonds from A to Baa1 on the basis of the weak local economy and the state's budgetary problems. By 1986 the rating was back up to A-1. Another example of Moody's maintaining a state credit rating below A was Alaska, where until 1974 the state general obligation bonds were rated Baa1. Here, Moody's cited the heavy debt load as a major reason for the rating.

Unlike Moody's, Standard & Poor's seems to make more of a distinction between state and local government general obligation bonds. Because states have broader legal powers in the areas of taxation and policy-making that do not require home-rule approvals, broader revenue bases, and more diversified economies, Standard & Poor's seems to view state general obligation bonds as being significantly stronger than those of their respective underlying jurisdictions. Standard & Poor's by 1994 has only given one rating below A to a state (the State of Louisiana bonds). It should also be noted that Moody's rates the general obligation bonds of the Commonwealth of Puerto Rico "Baa-1," whereas S & P's rating is "A." Additionally, of the 40 state general obligation bonds that both Moody's and Standard & Poor's rated, the latter had given ratings in the AA range or better to 35 states. On the other hand, Moody's had given ratings of Aa or better to only 33 states.

On the whole, for reasons just outlined, Standard & Poor's seems to tend to have a higher credit assessment of state general obligation bonds than does Moody's. Furthermore, Moody's views these broader revenue resources as making states more vulnerable in difficult economic times to demands by local governments for increased financial aid.

Assessing the Moral Obligation Bonds

In more than 20 states, state agencies have issued housing revenue bonds that carry a potential state liability for making up deficiencies in their one-year debt service reserve funds (backup funds), should any occur. In most cases if a drawdown of the debt reserve occurs, the state agency must report the amount used to its governor and the state budget director. The state legislature, in turn, may appropriate the requested amount, though it has no legally enforceable obligation to do so. Bonds with this makeup provision are the so-called moral obligation bonds.

Below is an example of the legal language in the bond indenture that explains this procedure.

> In order to further assure the maintenance of each such debt service reserve fund, there shall be annually apportioned and paid to the agency for deposit in each debt service reserve fund such sum, if any, as shall be certified by the chairman of the agency to the governor and director of the budget as necessary to restore such fund to an amount equal to the fund requirement. The chairman of the agency shall annually, on or before December first, make and deliver to the governor and director of the budget his certificate stating the sum or sums, if any, required to restore each such debt service reserve fund to the amount aforesaid, and the sum so certified, if any, shall be apportioned and paid to the agency during the then current state fiscal year.

Moody's views the moral obligation feature as being more literary than legal when applied to legislatively permissive debt service reserve makeup provisions. Therefore, it does not consider this procedure a credit strength. Standard & Poor's, to the contrary, does. It views moral obligation bonds as being no lower than one rating category below a state's own general obligation bonds. Its rationale is based upon the implied state support for the bonds and the market implications for that state's own general obligation bonds should it ever fail to honor its moral obligation.

As for the result of these two different opinions of the moral obligation, several municipal bonds have had split ratings. As an example, in

1994 the Nonprofit Housing Project Bonds of the New York State Housing Finance Agency, received the Moody's credit rating of Ba, which is a speculative investment category. Standard & Poor's, because of the moral obligation pledge of the state of New York, gives the same bonds a credit rating of BBB −, which is an investment-grade category.

Assessing the Importance of Withholding State Aid to Pay Debt Service

Still another difference between Moody's and Standard & Poor's involves their respective attitudes toward state aid security-related mechanisms. Since 1974 it has been the policy of Standard & Poor's to view as a very positive credit feature the automatic withholding and use of state aid to pay defaulted debt service on local government general obligation bonds. Usually the mechanism requires the respective state treasurer to pay debt service directly to the bondholder from monies due the local issuer from the state. By 1994, several states have enacted security mechanisms that in one way or another allow certain local government general obligation bondholders to be paid debt service from the state aid appropriations, if necessary. In most instances the state aid withholding provisions apply to general obligation bonds issued by school districts. (The states involved are Colorado, Georgia, Virginia, South Dakota, Indiana, Kentucky, New Jersey, New York, Pennsylvania, South Carolina, and West Virginia.)

Although Standard & Poor's does review the budgetary operations of the local government issuer to be sure there are no serious budgetary problems, the assigned rating reflects the general obligation credit rating of the state involved, the legal base of the withholding mechanism, the historical background and long-term state legislative support for the pledged state aid program, and the specified coverage of the state aid monies available to maximum debt-service requirements on the local general obligation bonds. Normally, Standard & Poor's applies a blanket rating to all local general obligation bonds covered by the specific state aid withholding mechanism. The rating is one or two notches below the rating of that particular state's general obligation bonds. Whether the rating is either one notch below or two notches below depends on the coverage figures, the legal security, and the legislative history and political durability of the pledged state aid monies involved. It should also be noted that Standard & Poor's stated policy is to give blanket ratings; a specified rating is only granted when an issuer or bondholder applies for it.

Although Moody's recognizes the state aid withholding mechanisms in its credit reviews, it believes that its assigned rating must in the first instance reflect the underlying ability of the issuer to make timely debt-service payments. Standard & Poor's, to the contrary, considers a state aid withholding mechanism that provides for the payment of debt service equally as important a credit factor as the underlying budget, economic, and debt-related characteristics of the bond issuer.

Assessing the Importance of Accounting Records

Another area of difference between Moody's and Standard & Poor's concerns their respective attitudes toward the accounting records kept by general obligation bond issuers. In 1980 Standard & Poor's stated that if the bond issuer's financial reports are not prepared in accordance with generally accepted accounting principles (GAAP) it will consider this a "negative factor" in its rating process. Standard & Poor's has not indicated how negative a factor it is in terms of credit rating changes but has indicated that issuers will not be rated at all if either the financial report is not timely (i.e., available no later than six months after the fiscal year end) or is substantially deficient in terms of reporting. Moody's policy here is quite different. Because Moody's reviews the historical performance of an issuer over a three- to five-year period, requiring GAAP reporting is not necessary from Moody's point of view, although the timeliness of financial reports is of importance.

EXHIBIT 11–7
Fitch Municipal Bond Ratings

Rating	Definition
AAA	Highest credit quality.
AA	Very high credit quality.
A	High credit quality.
BBB	Satisfactory credit quality.
BB	Speculative.
B	Highly speculative.
CCC	May lead to default.
CC	Default seems probable.
C	In imminent default.
DDD, DD and D	In default

FITCH

A third, and smaller, rating company is Fitch. The alphabetical ratings and definitions used by Fitch are given in Exhibit 11–7. Plus ($+$) and minus ($-$) signs are used with a rating to indicate the relative position of a credit within the rating category. Plus and minus signs are not used for the AAA category.

CHAPTER 12

FRAMEWORK FOR ASSESSING CREDIT RISK

The economic deterioration of some regions of the country, the proliferation in the marketplace of innovative bond security structures, and the federal government's pullback of grant monies for local governments force the municipal bond investor today to apply an eclectic research methodology for determining creditworthiness. Because the research procedures of the past do not always provide the structure for analyzing many of the risks that now face investors, the investor must tailor the methodology to match each particular type of bond security. Certain basic features of the analysis remain more important now than ever before.

This chapter outlines the elements of an unconventional, or *left-handed,* perspective for assessing credit risk that may help to identify a few investment dangers as well as opportunities. This approach is applicable to revenue bonds and the innovative financial-deficiency-makeup structures, but it may be relevant to general obligation bonds as well. At the end of this chapter we address how an investor should also judge a bond by the character of the issuer.

WHAT ARE THE AGREEMENTS?

One mistake the investor can make is not fully investigating with whom the issuer is temporarily investing its money. The insolvency of ESM Government Securities Inc. of Ft. Lauderdale, Florida in 1985 again heightened awareness concerning the potential problems associated with repurchase agreements, or *repos* as they are known in the capital markets and municipal finance industry. In the case of ESM, several municipalities invested cash from operating, capital, and debt service funds and failed to take possession of the collateralized securities or have them held by a third party in an account in their name. When business operations ceased, the municipalities were unable to prove that they had a "perfected lien" in the securities.

These problems related to repos, however, are not new. In 1982 a New York City based firm, Lombard-Wall, Inc., filed for reorganization relief under Chapter 11 of the Federal Bankruptcy Code. At the time of the bankruptcy Lombard-Wall had repos outstanding with over 50 municipal bond and note issuers or their designated bank trustees across the country. While the issuers faced significant potential losses, an upsurge in the bond market ultimately saved Lombard-Wall. In 1984, two more small securities dealers, Lion Capital Group and RTD Securities, declared voluntary bankruptcy. Many municipalities and school districts, mainly in New York State, held repos with these firms which they believed to have been fully collateralized. However, the collateral was not held in an account of the municipal corporation and was subsequently claimed by more than one party as collateral for loans that had been made.

The investor should distinguish between investment agreements made with established investment banking firms, government bond dealers, and banking institutions on the one hand, and those entered into with under-capitalized government securities arbitrage and trading firms. Large financial institutions have certain public image sensitivities that, particularly in stable economic times, can be viewed by the investor as a credit strength.

WHO IS THE TRUSTEE?

With the development of innovative and highly complicated cash-flow structured municipal financings, bond and note trustees need to become more involved with and knowledgeable about the specific construction project's overall status. Historically, however, trustees have seen their primary responsibilities as acting as paying agents on the debt, receiving the due monies, and receiving interest income on the various investments made under the indentures. The trustee is not a participant in the project transaction, but does represent the bond and noteholder, and many believe, should vigorously monitor the construction project, particularly one that has a more complicated financing structure. For example, this is particularly important in the case of construction loan notes that require the timely completion and certification of the project for FHA insurance. Most trustees have not attempted to anticipate problems and thus avoid them. In general, bond security structures that appear to require vigorous monitoring by the trustee should not be assumed to be a credit strength.

IS WHAT YOU SEE, WHAT YOU GET?

Another mistake an investor can make is to treat unaudited financial statements as if they were audited. A case in point was the bonds issued by Tampa General Hospital in 1982. At the time of the original bond sale, the hospital issued unaudited financial information that showed only a modest loss from operations of $436,000 on revenues of $73,053,000.[1] Later, the audited report for this Florida hospital showed an actual operating loss of $3,592,000 as well as deepening financial problems. It turned out that the hospital faced stiff competition from neighboring hospitals and health-care facilities, and had an uncertain financial future resulting in part from federal medicare cutbacks. These bonds are in the speculative category of creditworthiness.

Another pitfall for the investor is that construction schedules and revenue collections may not be met as projected. Of course, the commercial rating companies sometimes use "interim" ratings on new 20- to 30-year bonds secured by the revenues to be generated by the completed projects and additions. Examples include electric generating plants and hospitals. For such projects the ratings assigned by the rating companies assume that the construction schedules and revenues projected in the feasibility studies are accurate. Yet there always is a risk when project financing is involved, no matter how well reasoned the feasibility study may appear to be. Remember, feasibility studies are commissioned by the issuer and not by the investor or the analyst. As an example of this risk, in 1981 the Sebring Utilities Commission in Florida sold $92,750,000 in 30-year revenue bonds to construct a power plant. The feasibility study had concluded that surplus power could be sold to others on the spot market. The sale of this power was a necessary ingredient for the economic success of the project.

---

[1] When issued these bonds were rated conditional Baa–1 by Moody's, and provisional A– by Standard & Poor's.

However, after the plant was completed and had become operational, it could not sell the generated power. As a result the bonds had become very speculative. When they were issued they had been given a conditional A by Moody's. Later, they were rated Caa.

Still another example is the $5,070,000 in bonds issued by Northwest General Hospital in 1980 to finance the construction of additions and renovations to a hospital in Detroit. Of course, some events could not have been anticipated in a feasibility study; however, the issue came to market based on utilization trends contained in a feasibility study, and the bond issue correspondingly was considered by some to be of above-average investment quality. Within a few years the hospital was experiencing severe financial problems. Anticipated rental income did not materialize; the hospital's only surgeon resigned and was not replaced; project construction was significantly delayed; and the occupancy rate was 10 to 15 percent below the original feasibility study projections. Additionally, the hospital's administrator died and all the members of the Board of Trustees resigned. Clearly, investors who believed in the infallibility of the feasibility study for these bonds did not have their hopes materialize.[2]

DO INNOVATIVE SECURITY STRUCTURES ALWAYS POSE EQUAL CREDIT RISKS FOR THE INVESTOR?

In light of the Washington State Supreme Court decision on June 15, 1983, concerning the Washington Public Power Supply System (WPPSS) Projects 4 and 5 bonds, the investor must now question whether the security structure of an issue is innovative and to what extent the legal structure is untested. In recent years, more and more municipal bonds have come to market with legal structures that are conceptually innovative, believed by very responsible attorneys to be legal, but that are also unproven as to their validity in relevant courts of law. Specifically, these structures are financial-deficiency-makeup concepts that in worst-case scenarios require communitywide financial support. Because of possibly strong sur-

---

[2]These bonds originally had been rated conditional Baa–1 by Moody's. As of 1994, they were rated C.

rounding economies and approving legal opinions, many investors have felt comfortable in purchasing these bonds even when the yields reflected an assumed high level of safety. However, in difficult economic scenarios one can assume that the structures more than likely will be legally tested if local governmental revenue-raising powers are pledged and have to be used. While such bonds may still have a place in an investor's portfolio, the yields should be high enough to compensate for the real risks involved. Many times they are not.

The ultimate assessment of risk for any financial-deficiency-makeup structure such as take-or-pay bonds (and even for lease rentals) now has to be derived from three factors in addition to the fact that there is an approving legal opinion. The factors are

1. Does the project to be financed by the bond proceeds have wide community support and serve a generally accepted, noncontroversial public purpose? Sports stadiums, large construction projects with complicated construction procedures, and private-purpose endeavors may fall outside this category.

2. Is the project well reasoned, tightly managed by proven construction managers, and designed to be self-supporting within reasonable economic parameters? In other words, the smaller the degree of construction risk and the greater the financial viability of the completed project, the stronger the credit should be. The analysis, of course, is improved by periodic visits to the construction site and by an ongoing assessment of the quality of management. Historically the chances appear to be better that the courts will force debt-service payments, if a project has been completed.

3. Is there a strong history of political and financial support by the relevant state and local governments for bond structures that have similar financial-deficiency-makeup provisions?

As implied above, legally untested take-or-pay and lease-rental bonds may well have some features that might be legally questionable and that are not nailed down by the courts. Yet some may be perfectly good investments with nominal risk if they include other basic security features such as the above three elements. Even within the state of Washington, examples include the bonds of the Grant County P.U.D. #2 (for Wanapum hydro and Priest Rapids hydro), the Douglas County P.U.D. #1 (Wells hydro), and the Chelan County P.U.D. #1 (Columbia River–Rock Island hydro, Lake Chelan hydro, and Rocky Reach hydro).

Because of the legal cloud over the enforceability of the take-or-pays resulting from the WPPSS court decision, these bonds may now be viewed by some as being of weaker credit quality. Yet all of these projects meet the above criteria and are still very sound credits from a fundamental standpoint. They are bond issues that were sold years ago to finance hydroelectric generating facilities that are now on-line. Additionally, they provide power at very low cost to investor-owned utilities that are financially weak but that clearly support the projects. While the current purchasers of the power may or may not legally have to take the power, it is available and its cost is so low that it is in their economic self-interest to do so for a very long time.

THE LEGAL OPINION

The popular notion is that much of the legal work done in a bond issue is boiler plate in nature, but from the bondholder's point of view the legal opinions and document reviews should be the ultimate security provisions. This is because if all else fails, the bondholder may have to go to court to enforce his or her security rights. Therefore, the integrity and competency of the lawyers who review the documents and write the legal opinions that usually are summarized and stated in the official statements are very important.

The relationship of the legal opinion to the safety of municipal bonds for both general obligation and revenue bonds is threefold. First, the lawyer should check to determine if the issuer is indeed legally able to issue the bonds. Second, the lawyer is to see that the issuer has properly prepared for the bond sale by having enacted the various required ordinances, resolutions, and trust indentures without violating any other laws and regulations. This preparation is particularly important in the highly technical areas of determining whether the bond issue is qualified for tax exemption under federal law and whether the issue has not been structured in such a way as to violate federal arbitrage regulations. Third, the lawyer is to certify that the security safeguards and remedies provided for the bondholders and pledged either by the bond issuer or by third parties, such as banks with letter-of-credit agreements, are actually supported by federal, state, and local government laws and regulations.

General Obligation Bonds

General obligation bonds are debt instruments issued by states, counties, towns, cities, and school districts. They are secured by the issuers' general taxing powers. The investor should review the legal documents and opinion as summarized in the official statement to determine what specific *unlimited* taxing powers, such as those on real estate and personal property, corporate and individual income taxes, and sales taxes, are legally available to the issuer, if necessary, to pay the bondholders. Usually for smaller governmental jurisdictions, such as school districts and towns, the only available unlimited taxing power is on property. If there are statutory or constitutional taxing-power limitations, the legal documents and opinion should clearly describe what impact they have on the security for the bonds.

For larger general obligation bond issuers, such as states and big cities that have diverse revenue and tax sources, the legal opinion should indicate the claim of the general obligation bondholder on the issuer's general fund. Does the bondholder have a legal claim, if necessary, to the first revenues coming into the general fund? This is the case with bondholders of State of New York general obligation bonds. Does the bondholder stand second in line? This is the case with bondholders of State of California general obligation bonds. Or are the laws silent on the question altogether? This is the case for most other state and local governments.

Additionally, certain general obligation bonds, such as those for water and sewer purposes, are secured in the first instance by user charges and then by the general obligation pledge. (Such bonds are popularly known as being *double barreled.*) If so, the legal documents and opinion should state how the bonds are secured by revenues and funds outside the issuer's general taxing powers and general fund.

Revenue Bonds

Revenue bonds are issued for enterprise financings that are secured by the revenues generated by the completed projects themselves, or for general public-purpose financings in which the issuers pledge to the bondholders the tax and revenue resources that were previously part of the general fund. This latter type of revenue bond is usually created to allow issuers to raise debt outside general obligation debt limits and without voter approvals. The trust indenture and legal opinion for both types of revenue bonds should provide the investor with legal comfort in six bond-security areas:

1. The limits of the basic security.
2. The flow-of-funds structure.
3. The rate, or user-charge, covenant.
4. The priority-of-revenue claims.
5. The additional-bonds test.
6. Other relevant covenants.

Limits of the Basic Security

The trust indenture and legal opinion should explain what are the revenues for the bonds and how they realistically may be limited by federal, state, and local laws and procedures. The importance of this is that although most revenue bonds are structured and appear to be supported by identifiable revenue streams, those revenues sometimes can be negatively affected directly by other levels of government. As an example, the Mineral Royalties Revenue Bonds that the State of Wyoming sold in 1981 had most of the attributes of revenue bonds. The bonds had a first lien on the pledged revenues, and additional bonds could only be issued if a coverage test of 125 percent was met. Yet the basic revenues themselves were monies received by the state from the federal government as royalty payments for mineral production on federal lands. The U.S. Congress was under no legal obligation to continue this aid program. Therefore the legal opinion as summarized in the official statement must clearly delineate this shortcoming of the bond security.

Flow-of-Funds Structure

The trust indenture and legal opinion should explain what the bond issuer has promised to do concerning the revenues received. What is the order of the revenue flows through the various accounting funds of the issuer to pay for the operating expenses of the facility, to provide for payments to the bondholders, to provide for maintenance and special capital improvements, and to provide for debt-service reserves? Additionally, the trust indenture and legal opinion should indicate what happens to excess revenues if they exceed the various annual-fund requirements.

The flow of funds of most revenue bonds is structured as *net revenue* (i.e., debt service is paid to the bondholders immediately after revenues are paid to the basic operating and maintenance funds, but before paying all other expenses). A *gross revenue* flow-of-funds structure is one in which the bondholders are to be paid even before the operating expenses of the facility are paid. Examples of gross revenue bonds are those issued by the New York Metropolitan Transportation Authority. However, although it is true that these bonds legally have a claim to the fare-box revenues before all other claimants, it is doubtful that the system could function if the operational expenses, such as wages and electricity bills, were not paid first.

Rate, or User-Charge, Covenants

The trust indenture and legal opinion should indicate what the issuer has legally committed itself to do to safeguard the bondholders. Do the rates charged only have to be sufficient to meet expenses, including debt service, or do they have to be set and maintained at higher levels so as to provide for reserves? In regard to the rate covenant, the investor should determine if the rates charged are to provide cover only to the extent necessary to pay for debt service, operations, and required improvements with excess monies being credited against the succeeding year's revenue requirements. Such an arrangement is known as *Chinese* or *revolving coverage,* and it is not a strong credit feature. The legal opinion should also indicate whether or not the issuer has the legal power to increase rates or charges on users without having to obtain prior approvals by other governmental units.

Priority-of-Revenue Claims

The legal opinion as summarized in the official statement should clearly indicate whether or not others can legally tap the revenues of the issuer even before they start passing through the issuer's flow-of-funds structure. An example would be the Highway Revenue Bonds issued by the Puerto Rico Highway Authority. These bonds are secured by the revenues from the Commonwealth of Puerto Rico gasoline tax. However, under the Commonwealth's constitution, the revenues are first subject to being applied to the commonwealth government's own general obligation bonds if no other funds are available for them.

Additional-Bonds Test

The trust indenture and legal opinion should indicate under what circumstances the issuer can issue additional bonds that share equal claims to the issuer's revenues. Usually, the legal requirement is that the maximum annual debt service on the new bonds as well as on the old bonds be covered by the projected net revenues by a specified minimum amount. This can be as low as one time coverage. Some revenue bonds have stronger additional-bonds tests to protect the bondholders. As an example, the State of Florida Orlando-Orange County Expressway Bonds have an additional-bonds test that is twofold. First, under the Florida constitution the previous year's *pledged historical revenues* must equal at least 1.33 times maximum annual debt service on the outstanding and to-be-issued bonds. Second, under the original trust indenture *projected revenues* must provide at least 1.50 times estimated maximum annual debt service on the outstanding and to-be-issued bonds.

Other Relevant Covenants
Lastly, the trust indenture and legal opinion should indicate whether there are other relevant covenants for the bondholder's protection. These usually include pledges by the issuer of the bonds to have insurance on the project (if it is a project-financing revenue bond), to have the accounting records of the issuer annually audited by an outside certified public accountant, to have outside engineers annually review the condition of the capital plant, and to keep the facility operating for the life of the bonds.

In addition to the above aspects of the specific revenue structures of general obligation and revenue bonds, two other developments over the recent past make it more important than ever that the legal documents and opinions summarized in the official statements be carefully reviewed by the investor. The first development involves the mushrooming of new financing techniques that rest on legally untested security structures. The second development is the increased use of legal opinions provided by local attorneys who may have little prior municipal bond experience. (Legal opinions had traditionally been written by recognized municipal bond attorneys.)

Legally Untested Security Structures and New Financing Techniques

In addition to the more traditional general obligation bonds and toll road, bridge, and tunnel revenue bonds, as noted earlier there are now more nonvoter-approved, innovative, and legally untested security mechanisms. These innovative financing mechanisms include lease-rental bonds, moral obligation bonds, take-or-pay power bonds with step-up provisions requiring the participants to increase payments to make up for those that may default, and commercial bank-backed letter of credit "put" bonds. What distinguishes these newer bonds from the more traditional general obligation and revenue bonds is that they have a limited history of court decisions and other case law to firmly protect the rights of the bondholders. For the newer financing mechanisms, the legal opinion should include an assessment of the probable outcome if the bond security were challenged in court. Note, however, that most official statements do not provide this to investors because they have not demanded it.

The Need for Reliable Legal Opinions

For many years, concern over the reliability of the legal opinion was not as important as it is now. As the result of the numerous bond defaults and related shoddy legal opinions in the 19th century, the investment community demanded that legal documents and opinions be written by recognized municipal bond attorneys. As a consequence, over the years a small group of primarily Wall Street-based law firms and certain recognized firms in other financial centers dominated the industry and developed high standards of professionalism.

Now, however, more and more issues have their legal work done by local law firms, some of whom had little experience in municipal bond work. This development, along with the introduction of more innovative and legally untested financing mechanisms, has created a greater need for reliable legal opinions. An example of a specific concern involves the documents that the issuers' lawyers must complete so as to avoid arbitrage problems with the Internal Revenue Service. Legal opinions written entirely by unknown law firms and local lawyers raise serious credibility questions for the investor. On negotiated bond issues, one remedy has been for the underwriters to have their own counsels review the documents and to provide separate legal opinions. If the bond has come to market through a competitive sale and there is a question about a local attorney performing the functions traditionally performed by recognized bond attorneys, then the prudent investor may wish to avoid the bond altogether.

Also, more recently some public issuers have provided legal opinions written solely by public officials—usually the state attorney general. Since many institutional buyers of municipal bonds are also subject to state regulatory procedures, there has been a reluctance by some investors to purchase such bonds. Their reasoning is that the ability to seek legal redress for improper work on a bond issue could be compromised by the regulatory relationship.

WHAT IS THE ISSUER'S CHARACTER?

Still another question to ask before purchasing a municipal bond is just what kind of people are the issuers? Are they conscientious public servants with clearly defined public goals? Do they have histories of successful management of public institutions? Have they demonstrated commitments to professional and fiscally stringent operations? Additionally, issuers in highly charged and partisan environments in which conflicts chronically occur between political parties or among factions or personalities within the governing bodies are clearly the bond issuers to scrutinize closely and possibly to avoid. In fact, such issuers should be scrutinized regardless of the strength of the surrounding economic environment.

For General Obligation Bonds

For general obligation bond issuers the focus is on the political relationships that exist on the one hand among chief executives, such as mayors, county executives, and governors, and on the other hand among their legislative counterparts. Issuers with unstable political elites are of particular concern. Of course, rivalry among political actors is not necessarily bad. What is undesirable is competition so bitter and personal that real cooperation among the warring public officials in addressing future budgetary problems may be precluded. An example of an issuer that was avoided in the past because of such dissension is the City of Cleveland. The political problems of the city in 1978 and the bitter conflicts between Mayor Kucinich and the city council resulted in a general obligation note default in December of that year.

For Revenue Bonds

When investigating revenue bond issuers, it is important to determine not only the degree of political conflict, if any, that exists among the members of the bond-issuing body, but also the relationships and conflicts among those who make the appointments to the body. Additionally, the investor should determine whether the issuer of the revenue bond has to seek prior approval from another governmental jurisdiction before the user-fees or other charges can be levied. If this is the case, then the stability of the political relationships between the two units of government must be determined.

An example of the importance of this information can be seen when reviewing the creditworthiness of the water and electric utility revenue bonds and notes issued by Kansas City, Kansas. Although the revenue bonds and notes were issued by city hall, it was the six-member board of public utilities, a separately elected body, that had the power to set the water and electricity utility rates. In the spring of 1981, because of political dissension among the board members caused by a political struggle between a faction on the board of public utilities and the city commissioners (including the city's finance commissioner), the board refused to raise utility rates as required by the covenant. The situation only came under control when a new election changed the makeup of the board in favor of those supported by city hall.

In addition to the above institutional and political concerns, for revenue bond issuers in particular an assessment of the technical and managerial abilities of the staff should be made. The professional competency of the staff is a more critical factor in revenue bond analysis than it is in the analysis of general obligation bonds, which are secured in the final instance by the full faith and credit and unlimited taxing powers of the issuers. Many revenue bonds are secured by the ability of the revenue projects to be operational and financially self-supporting.

The professional staffs of authorities that issue revenue bonds for the construction of public power-generating facilities, apartment complexes, resource recovery systems, hospitals, water and sewer systems, and other large public works projects should be carefully reviewed. Issuers who have histories of high-management turnovers, project cost overruns, or little experience should be avoided by the conservative investor, or at least considered higher risks than their assigned credit ratings may indicate. Additionally, it is helpful for revenue bond issuers to have their accounting records annually audited by outside certified public accountants, so as to ensure the investor of a more accurate picture of the issuer's financial health.

ON THE FINANCIAL ADVISER AND UNDERWRITER

Shorthand indications of the quality of the investment are (1) who the issuer selected as its financial adviser, if any, (2) its principal underwriter if the bond sale was negotiated, and (3) its financial adviser if the bond issue came to market competitively. Additionally, many prudent underwriters will not bid on competitive bond issues if there are significant credit-quality concerns. Therefore, it is also useful to learn who was the underwriter for the competitive bond sales as well.

Identifying the financial advisers and underwriters is important for two reasons.

The Need for Complete, Not Just Adequate, Investment and Call Feature Risk Disclosures

The first reason relates to the quality and thoroughness of information provided to the investor by the issuer. The official statement, or private placement papers if the issue is placed privately, is usually prepared with the assistance of lawyers and a financial adviser or by the principal underwriter. There are industrywide disclosure guidelines that are generally adhered to, but not all official statements provide the investor with complete discussions of the risk potentials that may result from either the specific economics of the project or the community settings and the operational details of the security provisions. Usually the author of this document is the one who decides what either to emphasize or downplay in the official statement. The more professional and established the experience of the author to provide the investor with unbiased and complete information about the issuer and call features of the bond issue, the more comfortable the investor can be with information provided by the issuer and in arriving at an investment decision.

The Importance of Firm Reputation for Thoroughness and Integrity

By itself, the reputation of the issuer's financial adviser or underwriter should not be the determinant credit-quality factor, but it is a factor the investor should consider. This is particularly the case for marginally feasible bond issues that have complex flow-of-funds and security structures. The securities industry is different from other industries, such as real estate, in that trading and investment commitments are usually made verbally over the phone with a paper trail following days later. Many institutional investors, such as banks, bond funds, and casualty insurance companies, have learned to judge issuers by the "company" they keep. Institutions tend to be conservative, and they are more comfortable with financial information provided by established financial advisers and underwriters who have recognized reputations for honesty. Individual investors would do well to adopt this approach as well.

SUMMARY

In this chapter we have attempted to identify certain features of bond and note security structures that the investor should consider while looking for credit strengths and weaknesses. We hope that they might provide some insights into the subtleties of the world of municipal credit risk analysis and give some ideas for future thought as well.

CHAPTER 13

GUIDELINES FOR ASSESSING CREDIT RISK

The credit analysis of many types of municipal bonds and notes is more of an art than a science. Nonetheless, most municipal bond analysts would agree that for each particular type of security structure elemental questions must be asked and answered before an extensive credit risk analysis can be completed.

When Arthur Buck and Luther Gulick wrote their classic book on municipal research in 1926, no types of municipal securities existed other than the general obligation and public utility-secured bonds and notes.[1] In this chapter we identify many more security structures. Many of these structures are innovative and reflect the increased broadening of the use of municipal securities for various public and private purposes that has occurred since the Buck and Gulick book was written. Some of these innovative structures, such as zero coupon bonds, also have been used by issuers to enhance the marketing of their bonds in a municipal bond market that has become increasingly more volatile. In any event, this chapter discusses the basic questions that should be asked to determine the relative creditworthiness of these bonds and notes.

AIRPORT REVENUE BONDS

For airport revenue bonds, the questions vary according to the type of bond security involved. There are two basic security structures.

---

[1] A. E. Buck, ed., in collaboration with other staff members of the National Institute of Public Administration and the New York Bureau of Municipal Research *Municipal Finance* (New York: Macmillan, 1926).

The first type of airport revenue bond is one based on traffic-generated revenues that result from competitiveness and passenger demand for the airport. The financial data on the operations of the airport should come from independently audited financial statements going back at least three years. If a new facility is planned, a feasibility study prepared by a recognized consultant should be reviewed. The feasibility study should have two components: (1) a market and demand analysis to define the service area and examine demographic and airport utilization trends and (2) a financial analysis to examine project operating costs and revenues.

Revenues at an airport may come from landing fees paid by the airlines for their flights, concession fees paid by restaurants, shops, newsstands, and parking facilities, and from airline apron and fueling fees.

Also, in determining the long-term economic viability of an airport, the investor should determine whether the wealth trends of the service area are upward; whether the airport is either dependent on tourism or serves as a vital transfer point; whether passenger enplanements and air cargo handled over the previous five years have been growing; whether increased costs of jet fuel would make such other transportation as trains and automobiles more attractive in that particular region; and whether the airport is a major domestic hub for an airline, which could make the airport particularly vulnerable to route changes caused by schedule revisions and changes in airline corporate management.

The second type of airport revenue bond is secured by a lease with one or more airlines for the use of a specific facility such as a terminal or hangar. The lease usually obligates them to make annual payments sufficient to pay the expenses and debt service for the facility. For many of these bonds, the analysis of the airline lease is based on the credit quality of the lessee airline. Whether the lease should extend as long as the bonds are outstanding depends on the specific airport and facility involved. For major hub airports it may be better not to have long-term leases, because without leases, fees and revenues can be increased as the traffic grows, regardless of which airline uses the specific facility. Of course, for regional or startup airports, long-term leases with trunk (i.e., major airline) carriers are preferred.

BONDS BACKED BY REPURCHASE AGREEMENTS OR "REPOS"

Investors should fully investigate with whom the bond or note issuer is temporarily investing its money. A popular way to do this is with repos. Here, we provide the guidelines for evaluating such instruments.

What Is a Repo?

A repo is a contractual agreement between a municipal issuer (or its bank trustee) and a commercial bank, investment banking firm, or other government bond dealer. In the transaction, the repo issuer (such as a government bond dealer) receives cash and, in turn, usually provides interest-bearing U.S. government securities to a municipal issuer as collateral for the cash with the contractual commitment to repurchase the securities at pre-determined dates and prices. Often, long-term bond proceeds, construction loan note proceeds, and even cash flow revenues are invested through repos until the money is needed to pay either debt service or construction expenses associated with the specific projects. Over the years, investment bankers and municipal issuers have found repos to be attractive short-term investment vehicles because they can match the maturity of the repo to their specific cash flow needs.

Evaluating Repo Agreements

If repos are used in financial transactions, the investor or analyst should consider the following factors.

1. Are construction funds, any other bond proceeds, or project enterprise revenues invested through repos? If so, to what extent is the bond or note issuer dependent on the repo monies? Clearly, construction loan note proceeds, debt reserve funds, mortgage loan repayments, and grant receipts invested in repos are of greater concern to the analyst than are idle funds.

2. Are the repos with well-capitalized, established investment banking firms, government bond dealers, or banking institutions? Repos should not be with under-capitalized government securities arbitrage and trading firms. Inclusion on an approved trading list of the Federal Reserve Bank is not sufficient evidence of creditworthiness.

3. Are the repos fully secured with collateral which is in negotiable form and in the possession and control of the municipality or trustee? Title to the collateral should at all times be with the trustee.

4. The collateral should only include *(a)* direct general obligations of, or obligations for which the payment of principal and interest are unconditionally guaranteed by, the United States of America; *(b)* bonds, debentures, or notes issued by any of the following federal agencies: Federal Home Loan Banks, Federal Land Banks, Bank for Cooperatives, Federal Financing Bank, or Federal Home Loan Mortgage Corporation (including participation certificates); and, *(c)* public housing bonds, temporary notes, or preliminary loan notes fully secured by contracts with the United States of America.

5. Because the vagaries of the bond markets impose the risk that the fair market value of the collateral may substantially decline at any time, the collateral should be valued at least monthly. The "fair market value" of the securities, as stated in the repo agreements, should mean the bid prices as they appear in the *Composite Closing Quotations for Government Securities,* published by the Federal Reserve Bank of New York.

6. If the value of the collateral decreases below the levels agreed upon under the repurchase agreements and are not replenished immediately upon notification, then the bond or note trustees should have the right to sell the respective securities. Similarly, if the repo issuer defaults in an interest payment after one business day's notice, the bank trustee should have the option to declare the repo agreement terminated.

7. The repo agreements should state that third parties are not owners of any of the collateral, and that the collateral is free of all liens.

Repos may perform necessary timing functions in many financial transactions. For bond and note issuers their use is widespread and beneficial in keeping financing costs as low as possible. Repos can play an important role in an investment program of a municipality, but the investor or analyst must look carefully at the structure of the repos, using the guidelines detailed above.

CERTIFICATES OF PARTICIPATION (COPs)*

Certificates of participation (COPs) are a form of debt analogous to a lease-rental obligation, customarily used to finance the acquisition of buildings or equipment for a governmental entity. Although certificate financing was first used primarily in California in an attempt to circumvent the Proposition 13 restrictions, it is now being used fairly widely by other state and local governments across the country. Its increasing popularity is due to the fact that it does not require voter approval and that it is "off-balance-sheet" debt, which is not subject to statutory debt limitations. This discussion examines the structure and legal provisions common to most COPs and points out some of the factors analysts and investors should consider before investing in COPs.

Note that COPs may be issued as either taxable or tax-exempt securities.

Security

To the investor, a certificate of participation represents a proportionate interest in annual lease payments made by the lessee to the trustee during the term of the lease agreement. The certificates are secured only by these lease payments. The obligation of the lessee to make these payments constitutes neither a general obligation nor a moral obligation of the issuer. When a state acts as lessee, its obligation to make lease payments generally is subject to annual legislative appropriation; payments by a local issuer acting as a lessee are likewise subject to annual budgetary appropriation.

In the event of nonappropriation of funds, the lease terminates and the lessee is under no obligation to make any further payments. It should also be noted that an event of nonappropriation does not generally constitute an event of default and that none of the common remedies are available to investors under this scenario.

Selective Factors to Consider

Below we describe the factors to consider in evaluating COPs.

---

*This section is co-authored with Christopher Mauro and John Hallacy of Merrill Lynch & Co.

Essential Nature of the Project

Investors should remember that COPs are subject to the risk of nonappropriation. It is important to determine whether the project has or will have a genuinely useful public purpose, such as a jail or city hall, or is for a nonessential governmental use, such as a convention center. The possibility of increasing political pressure under a worst-case scenario is an important consideration. One should question the willingness of a state legislature or city government to appropriate funds for lease payments on a nonessential facility that has become a "white elephant" during periods of budgetary stress.

Useful Life of the Assets

COPs also carry a risk of technological obsolescence. Many COPs are issued to finance the acquisition of telecommunication or other high-tech equipment. A city or state that sells long-term COPs to finance equipment that could become obsolete within five years could be exposing itself to the political pressures that may arise when paying for a white elephant. If the equipment must be replaced, it is unlikely that any legislative body would appropriate funds twice for the same project. As with any lease-rental financing, the lease term should match, in a reasonably accurate manner, the useful life of the project being financed.

Ability to Relet the Project

If the lease agreement is terminated, the trustee takes possession of the assets and attempts to relet or sell these assets. In many cases the trustee may be unable to do this because the project is too specific in nature to its original purpose or may be prohibited from doing so by the indenture. For example, a state office building may have several alternate uses if vacated, but a prison may not.

Beneficial Security Provisions

Most COPs are similarly structured, but certain provisions can add strength to an issue's credit quality. Some of the questions should be asked. Is there any prohibition against substitution of assets in the event of nonappropriation? (Under some agreements, the lessee is prohibited from allocating funds to acquire any functionally similar assets for 30 to 60 days following termination of the lease.) Is there a grace period following the lease payment date that would allow the lessee to make its overdue payment and avoid termination of the lease agreement? Has interest been capitalized beyond the estimated date of completion for project construction? Has a debt service reserve fund been established? Is the lessee required to maintain an adequate level of casualty insurance or self-insurance on the assets? Such insurance should equal the principal amount of the outstanding certificates or the replacement cost of the assets, whichever is greater.

Call Features
In most cases, COPs are subject to extraordinary redemption at par on any lease payment date. Generally, an extraordinary call may result from any of the following events: the receipt of the net proceeds of an insurance claim or condemnation award, prepayment by the lessee, or termination of the lease agreement.

History of Timely Appropriation
A credit consideration in any COP issue is the lessee's demonstrated willingness to make the necessary appropriations to meet debt service. Investors can take some comfort in the COP structure if the issuer has a track record of meeting all lease-rental obligations and any other payments involving off-balance-sheet debt in a timely manner.

Credit Quality of the Underlying Issuer
After examining the structure and security of the COP, it is important for the investor to analyze the credit quality of the lessee to determine the ultimate ability and willingness of this issuer to meet its lease payments. Using traditional indicators of credit quality, the investor must be cognizant of the underlying economic, financial, and political trends specific to the issuer and how these trends could affect the issuer's ability to meet its COP obligations in the future. It is useful to determine the percentage of operating expenditures that will be used to pay debt service on all outstanding certificates and general obligation bonds. The stronger the economy and budgetary operations of the issuer, the stronger should be the credit quality of the COP.

FHA-INSURED HOSPITAL REVENUE BONDS.

Administered by the U.S. Department of Housing and Urban Development and the Department of Health and Human Services, the Federal Housing Administration (FHA) hospital mortgage insurance program began in 1968 under Section 242 of the National Housing Act, as amended. The Wayne General Hospital bonds of the New Jersey Health Care Facilities Financing Authority and the Buffalo General Hospital bonds of the New York State Medical Care Facilities Finance Agency are examples of tax-exempt hospital revenue bonds that are secured in part by FHA-insured mortgages.

This section describes the security features provided by this program and outlines the questions the investor should ask when determining the creditworthiness of hospital bonds with FHA-insured mortgages. We note that these security structures are very complex and this brief discussion identifies only the general areas to be addressed by the investor or analyst.

What Is FHA Hospital Mortgage Insurance?

Under the FHA hospital mortgage insurance program, once a hospital defaults on its mortgage payment, the bonding authority or the trustee files a claim for the FHA mortgage insurance. The claim can be paid in either case or in debentures in an amount equal to 99 percent of the outstanding mortgage balance. The debentures would be due 20 years from the date of the mortgage default, but could be redeemable at par by the U.S. government on any debenture interest rate. The payment dates are January 1 and July 1 of each year. After the trustee files a claim, FHA pays cash or issues a debenture, though the timing of its doing so is at its discretion. It is reasonable to assume that debenture issuance may take no longer than 12 months, but no time period is guaranteed.

What Is the Credit Risk?

Several features of the FHA hospital mortgage insurance program could present impediments to the timely payment of debt service if the particular hospital involved has a mortgage payment default. These potential problems result because of the following provisions.

1. The FHA insurance covers only 99 percent of the outstanding mortgage balance when the mortgage payment default occurs.

2. Depending on the federal government's cost of money and the interest rate on the debentures, the claim could be paid in 20-year, interest-bearing debentures, not cash.

3. The U.S. government is not required to issue the debentures within a specific time period, and debt service on the bonds could become due before the debentures are issued. Note, however, that FHA should be able to process the claim and issue debentures within 12 months.

4. Thirty days' interest on the mortgage is not covered by the FHA insurance. This occurs because insurance claims bear interest from the date of default (nonpayment) and a missed payment would include interest for the month prior to the payment date.

Of course, these credit features are in addition to the traditional security features of a hospital revenue bond. In the first instance, it is expected that debt service will be paid from hospital revenues. Briefly, the factors to consider include determining the range and quality of health care provided, (i.e., primary, secondary, and tertiary), whether the hospital is a start-up or ongoing facility, the historical and projected annual hospital occupancy rates, the degree of dependency of patient-day revenues derived from Medicare and Medicaid, and the hospital's operating ratio among other ratios and financial-health indicators.

Note, however, that a hospital using the FHA insurance program usually is of far lower credit quality than other hospitals, or it would not go to FHA. Even so, the analyst or investor should still determine if the hospital is of at least "bare bones" investment quality; that is, it has the basic financial viability and cash flow to pay debt service.

What Is the "Prudent Man" Evaluation Approach?

Though the FHA hospital mortgage insurance does not, by itself, provide complete backup security to the bondholders, it does (when properly supplemented by special debt and reserve-fund structures) provide a high degree of safety. For any particular hospital revenue bond that has FHA mortgage insurance, the investor or analyst should be concerned about the following.

1. Is there a reserve fund (which is often called a mortgage reserve fund or collateral account) that contains an amount at least equal to the sum of the 30 days of bond interest that is not covered by the FHA insurance, as well as the difference between the principal amount of the bonds outstanding and 99 percent of the mortgage balance? If this reserve is backed by a letter of credit, it must be irrevocable and from a well-capitalized commercial bank.

2. Is there a debt-service reserve fund containing an amount approximate to maximum annual interest? If repurchases (repos) are used, they must be overcollateralized with direct or indirect U.S. government-guaranteed securities; evaluated periodically with prompt makeup provisions and remedies given to the trustees; and provided by well-capitalized credit-worthy financial institutions. If investment agreements are used, are they from highly rated providers?

3. The structure of the bond issue is very important because the debentures that would be issued by the U.S. government mature 20 years after the date of the mortgage default, and because the hospital bonds generally have maturities of much longer periods. If a mortgage default occurs when less than 20 years remain for ultimate bond maturity, or any intermediate maturity, the debenture interest received should be sufficient to provide for all bond principal and interest payments. If a mortgage default occurs when more than 20 years remain for ultimate bond maturity, the semiannual debenture interest and maturing debenture principal (due 20 years after the date of the default) should be able to provide for bond principal and interest requirements. This is usually accomplished if the bonds are amortized at a more rapid rate than is the mortgage—that is, in general the mortgage and debenture interest rates should be fixed at higher rates than the interest rates of the municipal bond. Consequently, over time as the amount of bonds is reduced, the FHA insurance—which covers 99 percent of the outstanding mortgage—covers more and more bonds outstanding. This structure, along with the mortgage reserve fund and the debt-service reserve fund, should provide strong security to the issue.

4. HUD could redeem the debentures in cash prior to their stated 20-year maturities, so the projected cash flows, if available in the official statement, must demonstrate the ability to retire the outstanding bonds in case of early debenture redemptions.

5. Because of the possible need to draw upon them, the investments in the mortgage reserve and debt-service reserve funds must be of high quality and be liquid. Additionally, the investments must be controlled by the trustee.

Also note that because the FHA hospital mortgage insurance is a remedy for a mortgage default, obviously the stronger the hospital is, on its own merits, the more attractive the overall creditworthiness of the bond issue.

Another concern, though not one of credit, is related to the average life assumption used by the bond issuer in the sinking fund. Investors should be aware that the bonds are redeemed pursuant to sinking fund provisions that could result in bonds being redeemed at a rapid rate.

GENERAL OBLIGATION BONDS

For general obligation bonds, one must ask questions and obtain answers in four specific areas: debt burden, budget soundness, tax burden, and the overall economy.

Debt Burden

Concerning the debt burden of the general obligation bond issuer, some of the more important concerns include the determination of the total amount of debt outstanding and to be issued that is supported by the general taxing powers of the issuer as well as by earmarked revenues. Those general obligation bonds that are additionally secured by earmarked revenues outside the issuer's general fund, such as charges on users and aid payments, are known as being double-barreled in security.

For example, general obligation bonds issued by school districts in New York State are general obligations of the issuer and are also secured by state-aid-to-education payments due the issuer. If the issuer defaults, the bondholder can go to the state comptroller and be made whole from the next state aid payment due the local issuer. An example of another double-barreled general obligation bond is the State of Illinois General Obligation Transportation, Series A Bond. Besides being state general obligations, debt service is secured by gasoline taxes in the state's transportation fund as well.

The debt of the general obligation bond issuer includes, in addition to the general obligation bonds outstanding, leases and moral obligation commitments, among others. Additionally, the amount of the unfunded pension liabilities should be determined. Key debt ratios that reveal the burden on local taxpayers include determining the per capita amount of general obligation debt as well as the per capita debt of the overlapping or underlying general obligation bond issuers. Other key measures of debt burden include determining the amounts and percentages of the outstanding general obligation bonds of the overlapping or underlying jurisdictions to real estate valuations. These numbers and percentages can be compared to the history of the issuer to determine whether the debt burden is increasing, declining, or remaining relatively stable.

Budgetary Soundness

The budgetary operations and budgetary soundness of the general obligation bond issuer give rise to some of the more important questions. How well over (at least) the previous five years has the issuer been able to maintain balanced budgets and fund reserves? How dependent is the issuer on short-term debt to finance annual budgetary operations? How have increased demands by residents for costly social services been handled? That is, how frugal is the issuer? How well have the public-employee unions been handled? They usually lobby for higher salaries, liberal pensions, and other costly fringe benefits. Clearly, a pattern of dealing with the constituent demands and public-employee unions by raising taxes and drawing down nonrecurring budget reserves is undesirable. Finally, another general concern in the budgetary area is the reliability of the budget and accounting records of the issuer. Are interfund borrowings reported? And who audits the books?

Tax Burden

Concerning the tax burden, two initial things are important to learn. First, what are the primary sources of revenue in the issuer's general fund? Second, how dependent is the issuer on any one revenue source? If the general obligation bond issuer relies increasingly on either property tax, wage and income taxes, or sales tax to provide the major share of financing for annually increasing budget appropriations, taxes could quickly become so high as to drive businesses and people away. Many larger northern states and cities with relatively high income, sales, and property taxes experience this phenomenon. Still another concern is the degree of dependency of the issuer on intergovernmental revenues, such as federal or state grants-in-aid to finance its annual budget appropriations. Political coalitions on the state and federal levels that support these financial transfer programs are not permanent and could undergo dramatic change very quickly. Therefore, a general obligation bond issuer that currently has a relatively low tax burden but receives substantial amounts of intergovernmental monies should be carefully reviewed by the investor. If the aid monies are reduced, certain issuers may primarily increase their taxes instead of reducing their expenditures to conform to the reduced federal grants-in-aid.

Overall Economy

The fourth and last area of general obligation bond analysis concerns the issuer's overall economy. For local governments—such as counties, cities, towns, and school districts—key items include learning the annual rate of growth of the full value of all taxable real estate for the previous 10 years and identifying the 10 largest taxable properties. What kinds of business or activity occur on the respective properties? What percentage of the total property tax base do the 10 largest properties represent? What is the building permit trend for at least the previous five years? What percentage of all real estate is tax exempt, and what is the distribution of the taxable ones by purpose such as residential, commercial, industrial, railroad, and public utility? Last, who are the five largest employers? Concerning the final item, those communities that have one large employer are more susceptible to rapid adverse economic change than communities that have more diversified employment and real estate bases. Additional information that reveals either economic health or decline includes determining whether the population of the community over the previous 10 years has been increasing or declining by age, income, and ethnicity, and how the monthly and yearly unemployment rates compare with the comparable national averages as well as to the previous history of the community.

For state governments that issue general obligation bonds, the economic analysis should include many of the same questions applied to local governments. In addition, the investor should determine the annual rates of growth on the state level for the previous five years of personal income and retail sales.

HIGHWAY REVENUE BONDS

There are generally two types of highway revenue bonds. The bond proceeds of the first type are used to build specific revenue-producing facilities such as toll roads, bridges, and tunnels. For these pure enterprise revenue bonds, the bondholders have claims to the revenues collected through the tolls. The financial soundness of the bonds depends on the ability of the specific projects to be self-supporting. Proceeds from the second type of highway revenue bond generally are used for public highway improvements, and the bondholders are paid by earmarked revenues such as gasoline taxes, automobile registration payments, and driver's license fees.

Concerning the economic viability of a toll road, bridge, or tunnel revenue bond, the investor should ask a number of questions.

1. What is the traffic history, and how inelastic is the demand? Toll roads, bridges, and tunnels that provide vital transportation links are clearly preferred to those that face competition from interstate highways, toll-free bridges, or mass transit.

2. How well is the facility maintained? Has the issuer established a maintenance reserve fund at a reasonable level to use for such repair work as road resurfacing and bridge painting?

3. Does the issuer have the ability to raise tolls to meet covenant and debt-reserve requirements without seeking approvals from other governmental actors such as state legislatures and governors? In those few cases where such approvals are necessary, one should ask how sympathetic these other power centers have been in the past in approving toll-increase requests.

4. What is the debt-to-equity ratio? Some toll road, bridge, and tunnel authorities have received substantial nonreimbursable federal grants that have helped to subsidize their costs of construction. This, of course, reduces the amount of debt that has to be issued.

5. What is the history of labor–management relations, and can public employee strikes substantially reduce toll collections?

6. When was the facility constructed? Generally, toll roads financed and constructed in the 1950s and 1960s tend now to be in good financial condition. This is because the cost of financing was much less than it is today. Many of these older revenue bond issuers have been retiring their bonds ahead of schedule by buying them at deep discounts to par in the secondary market.

7. If the facility is a bridge that could be damaged by a ship and made inoperable, does the issuer have adequate "use and occupancy" insurance?

Those few toll road and bridge revenue bonds that have defaulted have done so because of either unexpected competition from toll-free highways and bridges, poor traffic projections, or substantially higher than projected construction costs. An example of one of the few defaulted bonds is the West Virginia Turnpike Commission's Turnpike Revenue Bonds issued in 1952 and 1954 to finance the construction of an 88-mile expressway from Charleston to Princeton, West Virginia. The initial traffic-engineering estimates were overly optimistic, and the construction costs came in approximately $37 million higher than the original budgeted amount of $96 million. Because of insufficient traffic and toll collections, between 1956 and 1979 the bonds were in default. By the late 1970s with the completion of various connecting cross-country highways, the turnpike became a major link for interstate traffic. Since 1979 the bonds have become self-supporting in terms of making interest coupon payments. It was not until 1989 that all the still outstanding bonds were finally redeemed.

Concerning the economics of highway revenue bonds that are not pure enterprise type but instead are secured by earmarked revenues such as gasoline taxes, automobile registration payments, and driver's license fees, the investor should ask the following questions.

1. Are the earmarked tax revenues based on either state constitutional mandates, such as the State of Ohio's Highway Improvement Bonds, or are they derived from laws enacted by state legislatures, such as the State of Washington's Chapters 56, 121, and 167 Motor Vehicle Fuel Tax Bonds? A constitutional pledge is usually more permanent and reliable.

2. What has been the coverage trend of the available revenues to debt service over the previous 10 years? Has the coverage been increasing, stable, or declining?

3. If the earmarked revenue is a gasoline tax, is it based either on a specific amount of cents per gallon of gasoline sold, or on a percentage of the price? With greater conservation and more efficient cars, the latter tax structure is sometimes preferred because it is not as susceptible to declining sales of gasoline and in an inflationary environment it benefits directly from any increased gasoline prices.

4. What has the history of statewide gasoline consumption been through recessions and oil shocks?

HOSPITAL REVENUE BONDS

Two unique features of hospitals make the analysis of their debt particularly complex and uncertain. The first concerns their sources of revenue, and the second concerns the basic structure of the institutions themselves.

During the past 25 years, major sources of revenue for most hospitals have been (1) payments from the federal (Medicare) and combined federal–state (Medicaid) hospital reimbursement programs and (2) appropriations made by local governments through their taxing powers. It is not uncommon for hospitals to receive at least half of their annual revenues from these sources. A national health care program, if enacted into law, would likely increase the ratio even more.

From a technical point of view, hospital bonds are structured as revenue bonds; however, their major revenues come from payment formulas established through the annual political-legislative conflicts and compromises on the federal, state, and local levels of government. Therefore, the analysis of hospital revenue bonds should start on the political-legislative levels and then move to the specific hospitals involved. How well the hospital management markets its service to attract more private-pay patients, how aggressive it is in its third-party collections, such as from Blue Cross, and health maintenance organizations (HMOs) and how conservatively it budgets for the governmental reimbursement payments are key elements for distinguishing weak from strong hospital bonds.

Particularly for community-based hospitals (as opposed to teaching hospitals affiliated with medical schools), a unique feature of their financial structure is that their major financial beneficiaries, physicians, have no legal or financial liabilities if the institutions do not remain financially viable over the long term. An example of the problems that can be caused by this lack of liability is found in the story of the Sarpy County, Nebraska, Midlands Community Hospital Revenue Bonds. These bonds were issued to finance the construction of a hospital three miles south of Omaha, Nebraska that would replace an older one located in the downtown area. Physician questionnaires prepared for the feasibility study prior to the construction of the hospital indicated strong support for the replacement facility. Many doctors had used the older hospital in downtown Omaha as a backup facility for a larger nearby hospital. Unfortunately, once the new Sarpy hospital opened in 1976, many physicians found that the new hospital could not serve as a backup because it was 12 miles farther away from the major hospital than the old hospital had been. With these physicians not referring their patients to the new Sarpy hospital, it was soon unable to make bond principal payments and was put under the jurisdiction of a court receiver.

The above factors raise long-term uncertainties about many community-based hospitals, but certain key areas of analysis and trends reveal the relative economic health of hospitals that have revenue bonds outstanding. The first area is the liquidity of the hospital as measured by the ratio of dollars held in current assets to current liabilities. A five-year trend of high values for the ratio is usually desirable because it implies an ability by the hospital to pay short-term obligations and thereby avoid budgetary problems. The second indicator is the ratio of long-term debt to equity, as measured in the unrestricted end-of-year fund balance. In general, a lower long-term debt to equity ratio indicates a stronger hospital, financially. The third indicator is the actual debt-service coverage of the previous five years as well as the projected coverage. The annual bed-occupancy rates for the previous five years is a fourth indicator. The fifth is the percentage of physicians at the hospital who are professionally approved (board certified), their respective ages, and how many of them use the hospital as their primary institution.

For new or expanded hospitals, much of the above data are provided to the investor in the feasibility study. One item in particular that should be covered for a new hospital is whether the physicians who plan to use the hospital actually live in the area to be served by the hospital. Because of its importance in providing answers to these questions, the national reputation and experience of the people who prepare the feasibility study are of critical concern to the investor.

HOUSING REVENUE BONDS

For housing revenue bonds the questions vary according to the type of bond security involved. There are two basic types of housing revenue bonds—each with a different type of security structure. One is the housing revenue bond secured by *single-family* mortgages, and the other is the housing revenue bond secured by mortgages on *multifamily* housing projects.

Concerning single-family housing revenue bonds, the strongly secured bonds usually have four characteristics.

1. The single-family home loans are insured by the Federal Housing Administration (FHA), Federal Veterans Administration (VA), or an acceptable private mortgage insurer. If the individual home loans are not insured, then they should have a loan-to-value ratio of 80 percent or less.

2. If the conventional home loans have less than 100% primary mortgage insurance coverage, an additional 5–10 percent mortgage-pool insurance policy or its equivalent would be required. The private mortgage insurer should be of high quality in terms of company capitalization and in terms of having conservative underwriting standards and limits.

3. In addition to a debt reserve that has an amount of monies equal at least to six-months' interest on the single-family housing revenue bonds, there is a mortgage reserve fund that has an amount equal at least to 1 percent of the mortgage portfolio outstanding.

4. The issuer of the single-family housing revenue bonds is in a region of the country that has either stable or strong economic growth as indicated by increased real estate valuations, personal income, and retail sales, as well as low unemployment rates.

In the 1970s state agency issuers of single-family housing revenue bonds assumed certain prepayment levels in structuring the bond maturities. In recent years most issuers have abandoned this practice, but investors should review the retirement schedule for the single-family mortgage revenue bonds to determine whether or not the issuer has assumed large, lump-sum mortgage prepayments in the early year cash flow projections. If so, how conservative are the prepayment assumptions, and how dependent is the issuer on the prepayments to meet the annual debt-service requirements?

Note that single-family housing revenue bonds issued by local governments, such as towns, cities, and counties, usually have conservative bond-retirement schedules that have not included any home-mortgage prepayment assumptions. Single-family housing revenue bonds issued by state agencies sometimes include prepayment assumptions. This positive feature of local government-issued bonds is balanced somewhat by the facts that the state-issued bonds generally no longer include prepayment assumptions and usually are secured by home mortgages covering wider geographic areas. Additionally, the state issuing agencies usually have professional in-house staffs that closely monitor the home-mortgage portfolios, whereas the local issuers do not. Finally, many state issuing agencies have accumulated substantial surplus funds over the years that can be viewed as an additional source of security for the bonds.

Multifamily housing revenue bonds have four specific, though overlapping, security structures. The first type of multifamily housing revenue bond is one in which the bonds are secured by mortgages that are federally insured. Usually the federal insurance covers all but the difference between the outstanding bond principal and collectible mortgage amount (usually 1 percent), and all but the *nonasset* bonds (i.e., bonds issued to cover issuance costs and capitalized interest). The attractiveness of the federal insurance is that it protects the investor against bond default within the limitations outlined. The insurance protects the bondholders regardless of whether or not the projects are fully occupied and are generating rental payments.

The second type of multifamily housing revenue bond is one in which the federal government subsidizes under the HUD program all annual costs, including debt service, of the project not covered by tenant rental payments. Under Section 8 the eligible low-income and elderly tenants pay only 15 to 30 percent of their incomes for rent. Because the ultimate security comes from the Section 8 subsidies, which escalate annually with the increased cost of living in that particular geographic region, the bondholder's primary risks concern the developer's ability to complete the project, find tenants eligible under the federal guidelines to live in the project, and then maintain high occupancy rates for the life of the bonds. The investor should carefully review the location and construction standards used in building the project, as well as the competency of the project manager in selecting tenants who will take care of the building and pay their rents. In this regard, state agencies that issue Section 8 bonds usually have stronger in-house management experience and resources for dealing with problems than do the local development corporations that have issued Section 8 bonds. Note that the federal government has eliminated new appropriations for the Section 8 program, however, there are substantial amounts of refundings that have occurred.

The third type of multifamily housing revenue bond is one in which the ultimate security for the bondholder is the ability of the project to generate sufficient monthly rental payments from the tenants themselves to meet the operating and debt-service expenses. Some of these projects may receive governmental subsidies (such as interest cost reductions under the federal Section 236 program and property tax abatements from local governments), but the ultimate security is the economic viability of the project. Key information includes the location of the project, its occupancy rate, whether large families or the elderly will primarily live in the project, if the rents necessary to keep the project financially sound are competitive with others in the surrounding community, and whether or not the project manager has a proven record of maintaining good services and establishing careful tenant-selection standards.

A fourth type of multifamily housing revenue bond is one that includes some type of private credit enhancement to the underlying real estate. These credit enhancements can include guarantees or sureties of an insurance company, securitization by the Federal National Mortgage Association (FNMA), or a bank letter of credit.

Other financial features desirable in all multifamily housing bonds include a debt-service reserve fund, which should contain an amount of money equal to the maximum annual debt service on the bonds, a mortgage reserve fund, and a capital repair and maintenance fund.

Another feature of many multifamily housing revenue bond programs, particularly those issued by state housing agencies, is the state moral obligation pledge. Several state agencies have issued housing revenue bonds that carry a potential state liability for making up deficiencies in their one-year debt-service reserve funds, should any occur. In most cases if a drawdown of the debt reserve occurs, the state agency must report the amount used to its governor and state budget director. The state legislature, in turn, may appropriate the requested amount, though there is no legally enforceable obligation to do so.

In 1975, because the New York State Urban Development Corporation's General Purpose Bonds (UDC) were on the brink of default—and in fact UDC was in default on its notes for several months—the state and its local units of government experienced severe difficulties in selling their own general obligation bonds and notes. Responding to these market pressures the state legislature and the governor provided an appropriation of several hundred million dollars to keep UDC's housing bonds solvent. This experience in New York State has been cited by many on Wall Street who argue now that every state legislature would honor the moral obligation pledge to their respective state housing agencies out of fear of losing market access for their own bonds. For the investor, it is far from certain that this would always be the response.

The moral obligation only provides a state legislature with permissive authority—*not mandatory authority*—to make an appropriation to the troubled state housing agency. Therefore the analysis should determine (1) whether the state has the budgetary surpluses for subsidizing the housing agency's revenue bonds and (2) whether or not there is a consensus within the executive and legislative branches of that particular state's government to use state general-fund revenues for subsidizing multifamily housing projects.

INDUSTRIAL DEVELOPMENT REVENUE BONDS

Generally, industrial development revenue bonds are issued by state and local governments on behalf of individual corporations and businesses. The security for the bonds usually depends on the economic soundness of the particular corporation or business involved. If the bond issue is for a subsidiary of a larger corporation, one question to ask is whether or not the parent guarantees the bonds. Is it only obligated through a lease, or does it not have any obligation whatsoever for paying the bondholders? If the answer is that the parent corporation has no responsibility for the bonds, then the investor must look very closely at the operations of the subsidiary in addition to those of the parent corporation.

For companies that have issued common stock that is publicly traded, economic data are readily available either in the annual reports or in the 10-K reports that must be filed annually with the Securities and Exchange Commission. For privately held companies, financial data are more difficult to obtain.

In assessing the economic risk of investing in an industrial revenue bond, another question to ask is whether the bondholder or the trustee holds the mortgage on the property. Although holding the mortgage is not an important economic factor in assessing either hospital or low-income multifamily housing bonds where the properties have very limited commercial value, it can be an important strength for the holder of industrial development revenue bonds. If the bond is secured by a mortgage on a property of either a fast-food retailer, such as McDonalds, or an industrial facility, such as a warehouse, the property location and resale value of the real estate may provide some protection to the bondholder, regardless of what happens to the company that issued the bonds. Of course, the investor should always avoid possible bankruptcy situations regardless of the economic attractiveness of the particular piece of real estate involved.

LEASE-RENTAL BONDS

Lease-rental bonds are usually structured as revenue bonds, and annual rent payments, paid by a state or local government, cover all costs including operations, maintenance, and debt service. It should be noted that Certificate of Participation bonds, or "COPs," are similar in security structure in that they too are dependent on the annual legislative appropriation process. The public purposes financed by these bond issues include public office buildings, firehouses, police stations, university buildings, mental health facilities, and highways, as well as office equipment and computers. In some instances the payments may only come from student tuition, patient fees, and earmarked tax revenues, and the state or local government is not legally obligated to make lease-rental payments beyond the amount of available earmarked revenues. However, for many lease-rental bonds the underlying lessee state, county, or city is to make payment from its general fund subject to annual appropriation. For example, the Albany County, New York, Lease Rental South Mall Bonds were issued to finance the construction of state office buildings. Although the bonds are technically general obligations of Albany County, the real security comes from the annual lease payments made by the State of New York. These payments are annually appropriated. For such bonds, the basic economic and financial analysis should follow the same guidelines as for general obligation bonds of the state.

MORAL OBLIGATION BONDS*

In several states, state agencies have issued revenue-type bonds that carry a potential state liability for making up deficiencies in their one-year reserve funds, should any occur. In most cases if a drawdown of the reserve occurs, the state agency must report the amount used to the governor and state budget director. The state legislature, in turn, may appropriate the requested amount, although there is no legally enforceable obligation to do so. Bonds with this makeup provision are the so-called moral obligation bonds.

The Moral Obligation Pledge

Below is an example of the legal language that explains this procedure and that is usually enacted into law by the particular state legislature involved

> In order to further assure the maintenance of each such debt reserve fund, there shall be annually apportioned and paid to the agency for deposit in each

---

*This discussion was co-authored with Walter D. Carroll of Merrill Lynch and Company.

debt reserve fund such sum, if any, as shall be certified by the chairman of the agency to the governor and director of the budget as necessary to restore such reserve fund to an amount equal to the debt reserve fund requirement. The chairman of the agency shall annually, on or before December first, make and deliver to the governor and director of the budget his certificate stating the sum or sums, if any, required to restore each such debt reserve fund to the amount aforesaid, and the sum so certified, if any, shall be apportioned and paid to the agency during the then current state fiscal year.

Since 1960 over 20 states have issued bonds with this unique revenue-deficiency makeup feature. The first state was New York State with its housing finance agency (HFA) moral obligation bonds. This feature was developed by a well-known bond attorney, John Mitchell, who had extensive experience and knowledge of state constitutions and laws.

In the history of moral obligation financing, most of this debt has been self-supporting. However, in most of the instances where the moral pledge was called upon, the respective state legislatures responded by appropriating the necessary amounts of monies. This occurred in Pennsylvania with the bonds of the Pennsylvania HFA, in New Jersey with the bonds of the South Jersey Port Authority, and in New York State with the bonds of the UDC and with housing bonds of the HFA.

Determining the Value of the Moral Obligation

In terms of bond quality, although the moral obligation is not legally enforceable by the bondholders, it does indicate legislative support. Of course, the general obligation pledge provides the highest degree of legal comfort to the bondholder, but a moral obligation does provide some comfort as well—though certainly not on the same level and not legally enforceable.

The evaluation of the moral obligation pledge varies widely. To those who place a high degree of emphasis on legal protections, the moral obligation pledge is given no weight whatsoever in the evaluation of the bond because it involves no legally binding obligation upon the governmental unit to replenish the reserve fund; that is, the bond is rated solely on the evaluation of the initial source of payment. To those investors who place a high degree of emphasis on ability and willingness to pay, rather than legal protections, the moral obligation pledge is viewed as almost equal to the general obligation pledge.

Despite the nomenclature of the financial mechanism, the bondholder is not relying on the morality of future legislatures but rather on their practicality. The governmental unit may be expected to replenish the debt reserve fund because the cost of doing so is viewed as less severe than the increase costs associated with the bond market penalizing the governmental unit for not replenishing the fund. Increased costs could arise from higher interest rates that the governmental unit making the moral obligation pledge (and even related units of government) would have to pay on future issues of its own debt.

The investor should investigate certain factors when evaluating a particular moral obligation bond.

The Purpose

What is the purpose for which the moral obligation bond is being issued? A future legislature is more likely to make the necessary appropriation to replenish a debt reserve fund if the issue was sold to finance a governmental building or low-income housing than if it was sold to finance a sports stadium. In the latter case, the legislature being asked to make the appropriation to replenish the reserve fund might seriously question the appropriateness of the actions taken by the legislature that made the moral obligation pledge.

Feasibility of Project

Is the project one that has a strong probability of being self-supporting from its planned source of payment? Even if the project should not attain full self-supporting status, the smaller the amount of the shortfall, the less controversy should result over an appropriation to replenish a reserve-fund shortfall. The debate about the appropriation could be much more heated if such support is so sizable and continuous as to raise concern that the project should never have been undertaken.

History of Moral Obligation Support

Clearly, the bondholder can take more comfort in the moral obligation pledge if the particular state has a demonstrated track record of replenishing a debt reserve fund when necessary, as is the case in New York, New Jersey, and Pennsylvania.

Amount of Moral Obligation Debt

Even the moral obligation believer would prefer a general obligation bond in a worst-case economic and financial scenario. Thus, careful consideration should be given to the budgetary resources and debt burden of the governmental body making the moral obligation pledge, including both its direct debt and the amount of moral obligation debt.

PUBLIC POWER REVENUE BONDS

Public power revenue bonds are issued to finance the construction of electrical generating plants. An issuer of the bonds may construct and operate one power plant, buy electrical power from a wholesaler and sell it retail, construct and operate several power plants, or join with other public and private utilities in jointly financing the construction of one or more power plants. This last arrangement is known as a joint-power financing structure. Although there are revenue bonds that can claim the revenues of a federal agency (for example, the Washington Public Power Supply System's Nuclear Project No. 2 Revenue Bonds, which if necessary can claim the revenues of the Bonneville Power Administration) and many others that can require the participating underlying municipal electric systems to pay the bondholders whether or not the plants are completed and operating (for example, the North Carolina Municipal Power Agency Number 1 Catawba Electric Revenue Bonds), the focus here is how the investor determines which power projects will be financially self-supporting without these backup security features.

There are at least five major questions to ask when evaluating the investment soundness of a public power revenue bond.

1. Does the bond issuer have the authority to raise its electric rates in a timely fashion without going to any regulatory agencies? This is particularly important if substantial rate increases are necessary to pay for either new construction or plant improvements.

2. How diversified is the customer base among residential, commercial, and industrial users?

3. Is the service area growing in terms of population, personal income, and commercial/industrial activity so as to warrant the electrical power generated by the existing or new facilities?

4. Are rates competitive with neighboring IOUs? This is a significant credit factor resulting from the competitive provisions contained in the Energy Policy Act of 1992. What are the projected and actual costs of power generated by the system, and how competitive are they with other regions of the country? Power rates are particularly important for determining the long-term economic attractiveness of the region for those industries that are large energy users.

5. How diversified is the fuel mix? Is the issuer dependent on one energy source, such as hydro dams, oil, natural gas, coal, or nuclear fuel? Concerning electrical generating plants fueled by nuclear power, the aftermath of the Three Mile Island nuclear accident in 1979 has resulted in greater construction and maintenance reviews and costly safety requirements prompted by the Federal Nuclear Regulatory Commission (NRC), which oversees this industry. In the past, although nuclear power plants were expected to cost far more to build than other types of power plants, it was also believed that once the generating plants became operational, the relatively low fuel and maintenance costs would more than offset the initial capital outlays. However, with the increased concern about public safety brought about by the Three Mile Island accident, repairs and design modifications are now expected to be made even after plants begin to operate. This of course increases the ongoing costs of generating electricity and has reduced the attractiveness of nuclear power as an alternative to the oil, gas, and coal fuels.

RESOURCE RECOVERY BONDS

A resource recovery facility converts refuse (solid waste) into commercially salable energy, recoverable products, and a residue to be landfilled. The major revenues for a resource recovery bond usually are the "tipping fees" per ton paid monthly by those who deliver the garbage to the facility for disposal; revenues from steam, electricity, or refuse-derived fuel sold to either an electric power company or another energy user; and revenues from the sale of recoverable materials, such as aluminum and steel scrap.

Resource recovery bonds are secured in one of two ways, or a combination thereof. The first security structure is one in which the cost of running the resource recovery plant and paying the bondholders comes from the sale of the energy produced (steam, electricity, or refuse-derived fuel) as well as from fees paid by the haulers, both municipal and private, who bring the garbage to the facility. In this financing structure the resource recovery plant usually has to be operational and self-supporting for the bondholders to be paid. The second security structure involves an agreement with a state or local government, such as a county or municipality, that contractually obligates the government to haul or to have hauled a certain amount of garbage to the facility each year for the life of the facility and to pay a tipping fee (service fee) sufficient to operate the facility. The tipping fee should include amounts sufficient to pay bondholders regardless of whether or not the resource recovery plant has become fully operational.

When deciding to invest in a resource recovery revenue bond, one should ask the following questions.

1. How proven is the system technology to be used in the plant? *Mass burning* is the simplest method, and it has years of proven experience, primarily in Europe. In mass burning the refuse is burned with very little processing. Prepared fuels and shredding, the next most proven method, requires the refuse to be prepared by separation or shredding so as to produce a higher-quality fuel for burning. More innovative and eclectic approaches require the most detailed engineering evaluations by qualified specialists.

2. How experienced and reliable are the construction contractors and facility operators (vendors)?

3. Are there adequate safeguards and financial incentives for the contractor/vendor to complete and then maintain the facility?

4. What are the estimated tipping fees that will have to be charged, and how do they compare with those at any available nearby landfills? One way for a resource recovery revenue bond issuer to deal with the latter is to enact a law requiring that all garbage within a specified geographic region be hauled to its plant. This is also known as "flow control," which the U.S. Supreme Court in May of 1994 held to be unconstitutional.

5. Is the bondholder protected during the construction stage by reserves and by fixed-price construction contracts?

6. Are the prices charged for the generated energy fixed, or instead are they tied to the changing costs of the fuel sources, such as oil and gas, in that particular marketplace?

Because of the uniqueness of the resource recovery technology, additional questions should be asked. First, even if the plant-system technology is a proven one, is the plant either the same size as others already in operation, or is it a larger-scale model that would require careful investor review? Second, if the system technology used is innovative and eclectic, is there sufficient redundancy, or low-utilization assumptions, in the plant design to absorb any unforeseen problems once the plant begins production? Last, in addition to the more routine reserves—such as debt, maintenance, and special capital-improvement reserves there should be covenants that commercial insurance be placed on the facility, that the contractor (or vendor) pledge to maintain the plant for the life of the bonds, that yearly plant reviews by independent consulting engineers be required, and that the vendor be required to make the necessary repairs so that the facility will be operational for the life of the bonds.

For resource-recovery revenue bonds that have a security structure involving an agreement with a local government, additional questions for the investor to ask are the following. Is the contractual obligation at a fixed rate, or is the tipping fee elastic enough to cover all the increasing costs of operations, maintenance, and debt service? Would strikes or other *force majeure* events prevent the contract either from being enforceable or preclude the availability of an adequate supply of garbage? Last, the investor should determine the soundness of the budgetary operations and general-fund reserves of the local government that is to pay the tipping or service fee. For these bonds, the basic economic analysis should follow the same guidelines as for general obligation bonds.

STUDENT LOAN REVENUE BONDS

Student loan revenue bonds are usually issued by statewide agencies and are used for purchasing either new guaranteed student loans for higher education or existing guaranteed student loans from local banks.

Under the 1993 changes in federal law, student loans are guaranteed to varying degrees. They are either guaranteed directly by the federal government—under the Direct Student Loan Program (FDSLP) or indirectly by the Federal Family Education Loan Program (FFELP) for varying percents of principal and interest. This latter program provides federal reimbursement for a state guaranty agency on an annual basis at rates dependent on when the student loan was originated. For those made before October 1, 1993 the reimbursement is at the following rates: for 100 percent of the payment on defaulted loans up to approximately 5 percent of the amount of loans being repaid, 90 percent for claims in excess of 5 percent but less than 9 percent, and 80 percent for claims exceeding 9 percent. Defaulted student loans that were made after October 1, 1993 are reimbursed at the corresponding reduced rates of 98 percent (versus the previous 100 percent), 88 percent (versus 90 percent), and 78 percent (versus 80 percent). The federal commitments are not dependent on future congressional approvals. Loans made under the FDSLP and FFELP programs are contractual obligations of the federal government.

Although most student loans have federal government support, the financial soundness of the bond program that issues the student loan revenue bonds and monitors the loan portfolio is of critical importance to the investor. This is because of the unique financial structure of a student loan portfolio. Although loan repayments from the student or, in the event of student default, repayments from the guaranty agency are contractually assured, it is difficult to project precisely the actual loan-repayment cash flows because the student does not begin repaying the loan until he or she leaves college or graduate school and all other deferments, such as military service, have ended. Before the student begins the loan repayments, the federal government pays the interest on the loans under prescribed formulas. Therefore, the first general concern of the investor should be to determine the strength of the cash flow protection.

The second general concern is the adequacy of the loan guaranty. Under all economic scenarios short of a depression, the FFELP sliding federal reinsurance scale of 98–88–78 should provide adequate cash flow and bond default protection as long as the student loan revenue bond issuer effectively services the student loan repayments, has established and adequately funded loan-guaranty and debt-reserve funds, employs conservative loan-repayment assumptions in the original bond-maturity schedule, and is required to call the bonds at par if the student loan repayments are accelerated. This final factor prevents a reinvestment risk for the bondholder.

There are eight specific questions for the investor to ask.

1. What percentage of the student loans are FDSLP and FFELP backed, respectively?

2. Has a loan-guarantee fund been established and funded? Usually a fund that is required to have an amount at least equal to 2 percent of the loan principal outstanding is desirable.

3. Is the issuer required to maintain a debt reserve fund? Usually, for notes a fund with at least six months' interest, and for bonds a fund with a one-year maximum annual debt-service amount are desirable.

4. If the bond issuer has purchased portfolios of student loans from local banks, are the local lenders required to repurchase any loans if there are either defaults or improperly originated loans?

5. What in-house capability does the issuer have for monitoring and servicing the loan repayments?

6. What is the historic loan-default rate?

7. How are the operating expenses of the agency met? If federal operating subsidies are received under the "Special Allowance Payment Rate" program, what are the rate assumptions used? In this program the issuer receives a supplemental subsidy, which fluctuates with the 91-day U.S. Treasury bill rate.

8. If a state agency is the issuer, is it dependent on appropriations for covering operating expenses and reserve requirements?

9. Under the 1993 federal law changes, reimbursement at the lowest default rates is only 98 percent. Therefore, the investor must determine the specific financial resources or guarantees that the state authority has established.

Also, some student loan bonds have been issued that also are secured by the general obligation pledge of the particular private college or university involved, but without any substantial federal support. An example would be the Dartmouth College–Series 1 Bonds issued by the New Hampshire Higher Educational and Health Facilities Authority. The investor should ask several questions. Are college endowment funds available if necessary, and if so, are they substantial and sufficiently liquid? How prominent is the school in terms of admission standards and enrollment history? What are the general financial resources of the school? And lastly, is there a debt-service reserve fund available with an amount of monies that are at least equal to maximum annual debt service?

TAX, REVENUE, GRANT AND BOND ANTICIPATION NOTES·

Notes are temporary borrowings by states, local governments, and official jurisdictions to finance a variety of activities.[2] Usually, notes are issued for a period of 12 months, though it is not uncommon for them to be issued

---

[2] Information on the note issues discussed in this chapter is derived from the official statements of the various issues. General analytical concepts are from Luther Gulick, "Debt Administration," in *Municipal Finance*, ed. A. E. Buck in collaboration with other staff members of the National Institute of Public Administration and the New York Bureau of Municipal Research (New York: Macmillan, 1926).

for periods of as short as 3 months and for as long as 3 years. Notes are issued for two general purposes: to even out cash flows and to temporarily finance capital improvements. Each is explained below.

Two Major Purposes of Notes

Evening Out Cash Flows

Many states, cities, towns, counties, and school districts, as well as special jurisdictions sometimes borrow temporarily in anticipation of the collection of taxes or other expected revenues. Their need to borrow occurs because payrolls, bills, and other commitments have to be paid starting at the beginning of the fiscal year, but property taxes and other revenues such as intergovernmental grants are not due and payable until after the beginning of the fiscal year. These notes—identified either as tax anticipation notes (TANs), revenue anticipation notes (RANs), or grant anticipation notes (GANs)—are used to even out the cash flows that are necessitated by the irregular flows of income into the treasuries of the states and local units of government, In some instances, combination tax and revenue anticipation notes (TRANs) are issued, which usually are payable from two sources.

Temporarily Financing Capital Improvements

The second general purpose for which notes are issued is in anticipation of the sale of long-term bonds. Such notes are known as bond anticipation notes (BANs). There are three major reasons why capital improvements are initially financed with BANs.

First, because the initial cost estimates for a large construction project can vary from the construction bids actually submitted, and because better terms are sometimes obtained on a major construction project if the state or local government pays the various contractors as soon as the work begins, BANs are often used as the initial financing instrument. Once the capital improvement is completed, the bills paid, and the total costs determined, the BANs can be retired with the proceeds of a final bond sale.

Second, issuers such as states and cities that have large, diverse, and ongoing capital construction programs will initially issue BANs, and later retire them with the proceeds of a single, long-term bond sale. In this instance, the use of BANs allows the issuer to consolidate various, unrelated financing needs into one bond sale.

The third reason why BANs are sometimes issued is related to market conditions. By temporarily financing capital improvements with BANs, the issuer has greater flexibility in determining the timing of its long-term bond sale and possibly avoiding unfavorable market conditions.

Security behind Tax and Revenue Anticipation Notes

Tax anticipation notes are generally secured by the taxes for which they were issued. For counties, cities, towns, and school districts, TANs are usually issued for expected property taxes. Some governmental units go so far as to establish escrow accounts for receiving the taxes and use the escrowed monies to pay noteholders.

Revenue anticipation notes and grant anticipation notes are also usually, but not always, secured by the revenues for which they were issued. These revenues can include intergovernmental grants and aid as well as local taxes other than property taxes. In one extreme case, and as the result of the New York City financial crisis in 1975, RANs issued by New York City for expected educational aid from the state of New York provided for the noteholder to go directly to the state comptroller and get the state aid monies before they were sent to the city's treasury if that is necessary to remedy a default. Most RANs just require the issuer to use the expected monies to pay the noteholders once they are in hand. Additionally, it must be noted that most TANs, RANs, and GANs issued by states, counties, cities, towns, and school districts are also secured by the *general obligation pledge,* which is discussed later in this section.

Information Needed before Buying Tax or Revenue Anticipation Notes

Before purchasing a TAN, RAN, or GAN, the investor should obtain information in five areas in addition to what is required if long-term bonds are being considered for purchase.

1. The reliability of the expected taxes and revenues
2. The dependency of the note issuers on the expected monies
3. The soundness of the issuers' budgetary operations
4. The problems of "rollovers"

5. The historic and projected cash flows by month

We discuss each of these areas.

Determining the Reliability of the Expected Taxes and Revenues

If a TAN is issued in anticipation of property taxes, a question to ask is What were the tax collection rates over the previous five years? Tax collection rates below 90 percent usually indicate serious tax collection problems. Additionally, if the issuer is budgeting 100 percent of the tax levy while collecting substantially less, serious problems can be expected.

If a RAN or GAN is issued in anticipation of state or federal grant monies, the first question to ask is if the grant has been legislatively authorized and committed by the state or federal government. Some RAN issuers, which included New York City prior to its RAN problems in 1975, would issue RANs without having all the anticipated grants committed by the higher levels of government. This practice may still be used by other local governments that are hard-pressed to balance their budgets and want to obtain quick cash through the sale of RANs. A safeguard against this is to see if the issuer has in its possession a fully signed grant agreement prior to the RAN or GAN sale.

Dependency of the Note Issuers on the Expected Monies

One measure of the creditworthiness of the TAN or RAN issuer is the degree of dependency of the issuer on the temporarily borrowed monies. As examples, some jurisdictions limit the amount of TANs that can be issued in anticipation of property taxes to a percentage of the prior year's levy that was actually collected. The State of New Jersey, which has one of the most fiscally conservative local government regulatory codes in the country, limits the annual sale of TANs and RANs by local governments to no more than 30 percent of the property taxes and various other revenues actually collected in the previous year. Many other states are more permissive and allow local governments to issue TANs and RANs as high as 75 to 100 percent of the monies previously collected or even expected to be received in the current fiscal year.

Soundness of the Issuers' Budgetary Operations

Another critical element of the TAN or RAN issuer's creditworthiness concerns determining whether or not the issuer has an overall history of prudent and disciplined financial management. One way to do this is to determine how well the issuer, over the previous five fiscal years, has maintained end-of-year fund balances in the major operating funds.

Problems of Rollovers

Key indications of fiscal problems are revealed when issuers either retire their TANs and RANs with the proceeds of new issues or issue TANs and RANs to be retired in a fiscal year following the one in which they were originally issued. Such practices are known as *rollovers,* and are sometimes used by hard-pressed issuers to disguise chronic operating budget deficits. To leave no doubt as to the soundness of their budgetary operations, many states, local governments, and special jurisdictions have established, either by statute or by administrative policy, that all TANs and RANs issued in one fiscal year must be retired before the end of that fiscal year. Such a policy reduces the flexibility of the issuer to deal with unexpected emergencies that may occur, but it does help provide protection to the noteholders against TANs and RANs ever being used for hidden deficit financing. [3]

We must note that in some circumstances RANs and GANs can be properly issued for periods greater than 12 months. For an example, RANs of the Alabama Federal Aid Highway Finance Authority were issued in 1981 and were due two and a half years later in 1984. These RANs were in anticipation of the authority's receiving the federal share of its costs of certain interstate-highway construction projects. The Federal Highway Administration had established a 36-month reimbursement schedule. Therefore, in this instance the RANs must be outstanding for a period greater than 12 months.

The Historic and Projected Cash Flows by Month

The last area for investigation by the investor or analyst is the TAN or RAN issuer's cash flow history and projections. Initially, what is required

---

[3]Note that this approach toward rollovers is contrary to the position of the late Jackson Phillips, former head of Moody's municipal department, who wrote in August 1975 that "the ability to refinance (rollover or renew) a maturing note has been regarded as a valuable backstop to notes of the revenue-anticipation type. . . . Evaluation of a note must, therefore, consider . . . the availability of refinancing through market rollover. . . ." From "Liquidity of Temporary Loans," *Moody's Municipal Credit Report,* August 1, 1975. However, this policy statement was made before the New York City general obligation note crisis of 1975—which occurred largely because the use of the rollover

here is a monthly accounting, going back over the previous fiscal year, which shows the beginning fund balances, revenues, expenditures, and end-of-month fund balances. In the analysis of this actual cash flow, the investor should determine how well the issuer has met its fiscal goals by maintaining at least a balanced budget and meeting all liabilities, including debt-service payments.

Security behind Bond Anticipation Notes

BANs are secured principally by the ability of the issuers to have future access to the municipal bond market so as to retire the outstanding BANs with the proceeds of long-term bond sales. Additionally, it must be noted that most BANs issued by states, counties, cities, towns, and school districts are also secured by the general obligation pledge, which is discussed later in this section.

Information Needed before Buying Bond Anticipation Notes

Two factors determine the ability of the issuers to gain market access; therefore, the BAN investors should obtain information in these areas.

1. The creditworthiness of the issuers.
2. Expected future market conditions and the flexibility of the issuers.

Creditworthiness of the Issuers
Because the outstanding BANs are to be retired with the proceeds of long-term bond sales, the creditworthiness of the BANs are directly related to the creditworthiness of the underlying bond issuers. Therefore, investors must obtain the same credit information on the BANs that they would if long-term bonds were being issued. In general, the stronger the bond credits, the greater the abilities of the BAN issuers to successfully complete their respective long-term bond sales. Additionally, the investor or analyst should also make a determination as to the probable market access and acceptance of the BAN issuer. That is, in the past how well have the bonds

---

mechanism had allowed the city to avoid retiring its notes and, instead, to increase annually its short-term debt until it had become unmanageable.

of the issuer been received in the marketplace? Has the issuer had to pay interest costs substantially higher than other bond issuers of similar credit-worthiness? Answers to these questions will determine the credit risks involved when purchasing the BANs.

Expected Future Market Conditions and the Flexibility of the Issuers

While it is not possible for the BAN investors to know in advance the condition of the market when their BANs come due, it is safe to conclude that, if the issuer's creditworthiness is at least of investment-grade quality, there should usually be a market for that issuer's bonds. Of course, the weaker the creditworthiness and the larger the amount of BANs to be retired, the higher the rate of interest would have to be.

If the BANs come due at a time when the municipal bond market is experiencing rising interest rates, the BAN issuer should have the flexibility to retire the maturing BANs with a new BAN issue instead of issuing long-term bonds. Most state and local government finance regulations recognize this need for allowing BANs to be retired from new BAN issues. Also, the ability of the issuer to refund, in the municipal market, the maturing BANs with new BANs is directly related to the credit quality of the issuer. Also note that, unlike most TANs and RANs, BANs can be refunded—that is, rolled over—into new BANs. However, prudent issuers usually are limited by local laws to having their BANs outstanding for no longer than five to eight years. If there is no limit as to how long the BANs can be outstanding, the temptation is great for the BAN issuer to avoid funding out the BANs with a bond issue.

Security behind the General Obligation Pledge

Many TANs and RANs issued by states, cities, towns, counties, and school districts are secured by the general obligation pledge. What this means is that the issuers are legally obligated to use, if necessary, their full taxing powers and available revenues to pay the noteholders. Therefore, if a tax anticipation note is issued by a city secured by property taxes as well as by the general obligation pledge, and if the city's property tax collection rate that particular year does not generate sufficient taxes to pay the noteholder, the city must use other resources to make the noteholder whole, including available monies in its general fund. Of course, the importance of the general obligation pledge is directly related to the diversification of the issuer's revenue base and lack of dependence on note sales, as well as on the soundness of its budgetary operations. Many BANs are also secured by the general obligation pledge of the issuer. If the overall credit quality, revenue structure, and market image of the underlying general obligation issuer are stronger than those of the agency or department that has issued the BANs, then the general obligation pledge would be a positive factor because it would strengthen market access either for a rollover of the BANs or for retiring them with the proceeds of a long-term bond sale.

WATER AND SEWER REVENUE BONDS

Water and sewer revenue bonds are issued to provide for a local community's basic needs and as such are not usually subject to general economic changes. Because of the vital utility services performed, their respective financial structures are usually designed to have the lowest possible user changes and still remain financially viable. Generally, rate covenants requiring that user charges cover operations, maintenance, and approximately 1.2 times annual debt-service and reserve requirements are most desirable. On the one hand, a lower rate covenant provides a smaller margin for either unanticipated slow collections or increased operating and plant maintenance costs caused by inflation. On the other hand, rates that generate revenues in excess of 1.2 times could cause unnecessary financial burdens on the users of the water and sewer systems. A useful indication of the soundness of an issuer's operations is to compare the water or sewer utility's average quarterly customer billings to those of other water or sewer systems. Assuming that good customer service is given, the water or sewer system that has a relatively low customer billing charge generally indicates an efficient operation, and therefore strong bond-payment prospects.

Key questions for the investor to ask include the following.

1. Has the bond issuer, through local ordinances, required mandatory water or sewer connections? Local board of health directives against well-water contaminations and septic tank usage can often accomplish the same objective as the mandatory hookups.

2. Does the issuer have to comply with an EPA consent decree and thereby be issuing significant amounts of bonds.

3. What is the physical condition of the facilities in terms of plant, lines, and meters, and what capital improvements are necessary for maintaining the utilities as well as for providing for anticipated community growth?

4. For water systems in particular, it is important to determine whether the system has water supplies in excess of current peak and projected demands. An operating system at less than full utilization is able to serve future customers and bring in revenues without having to issue additional bonds to enlarge its facilities.

5. What is the operating record of the water or sewer utility for the previous five years?

6. If the bond issuer does not have its own distribution system, but instead charges other participating local governments that do, are the charges or fees either based upon the actual water flow drawn (for water revenue bonds) and sewage treated (for sewer revenue bonds), or upon gallonage entitlements?

7. For water revenue bonds issued for agricultural regions, what kind of produce is grown? An acre of oranges or cherries in California will provide the grower with more income than will an acre of corn or wheat in Iowa.

8. For expanding water and sewer systems, does the issuer have a record over the previous two years of achieving net income equal to or exceeding the rate covenants, and will the facilities to be constructed add to the issuer's net revenues?

9. Has the issuer established and funded debt and maintenance reserves to deal with either unexpected cash flow problems or system repairs?

10. Does the bond issuer have the power to place tax liens against the real estate of those who have not paid their water or sewer bills? Although the investor would not want to own a bond for which court actions of this nature would be necessary before the investor could be paid, the legal existence of this power usually provides an economic incentive for water and sewer bills to be paid promptly by the users.

Additional bonds should be issued only if the need, cost, and construction schedule of the facility have been certified by an independent consulting engineer and if the past and projected revenues are sufficient to pay operating expenses and debt service. Of course, for a new system that does not have an operating history, the quality of the consulting engineer's report is of the uppermost importance.

ZERO COUPON BONDS

A zero coupon bond is one in which no interest coupons are paid to the bondholder. Instead, the bond is usually purchased at a very deep discount and matures at par. The difference between the original issue discount price and par represents a specified compounded annual interest rate on the bond. There is no reinvestment risk as with regular coupon bonds because the compound annual interest is virtually assured provided the bondholder keeps the bond to maturity and the issuer is financially able to make the payment at the time of the issue's maturity. Variations of the zero coupon, compound-interest concept are municipal bonds marketed and sold as municipal multipliers, capital accumulators, capital-appreciation bonds, or compound-interest bonds.

The advantage to the investor of purchasing zero coupon bonds is that reinvestment risk is eliminated. Because of this, the investor should be willing to purchase the issue at a somewhat lower yield than comparable issues with regular coupon payments. The lower interest cost should also be attractive to the issuer. Additionally, no semiannual interest payments are paid, so the issuer does not have to pay cash until the bond matures. Also note that, because the zero coupon bonds do not bear interest on a semiannual basis, the administrative costs should be reduced for the issuer as well.

The risk for the issuer is primarily an increased interest cost risk. Unlike full-coupon municipal bonds where the issuer only pays annual interest, the zero coupon bond issuer eventually has to pay the bondholder compounded annual interest. The issuer may enjoy a yield give-up for providing the investor with this compounded annual interest rate; however, if interest rates substantially decline by the time the zero coupon bonds come due, the issuer may have been better off having paid annual (noncompounded) interest.

Credit Analysis of Zero Coupon Bonds

Zero coupon bonds present a unique credit risk for the investor. On the one hand, if interest rates substantially decline during the time horizon when the zero is outstanding and the zero matures in a relatively low interest-rate environment, the buyer of such a bond will have made a good decision—from an interest-rate perspective—to have bought the zero. On the other hand, if interest rates do substantially decline, it may not have been a very prudent decision for the issuer to have sold the compound interest bonds. A lower interest-rate environment could present financial problems—particularly for weaker revenue bond issuers—in generating sufficient monies to pay the zero coupon bondholders as well as annual operating and routine maintenance expenses.

In determining the relative creditworthiness of specific zero coupon bonds, there are at least three areas of concern.

1. If the zero coupon bond is issued as part of a revenue bond issue, the zero coupon portion should not be a balloon maturity. That is, the issuer's financial plan for its funded debt should be characterized by level debt service.

2. If the interest-rate environment does substantially decline after the zero coupon bonds are issued, the indenture should provide the issuer with the flexibility to call the bonds prior to maturity at a price substantially below par; that is, as a percentage of the bond's compound accreted value. Weak protection from an early call is not an attractive feature to the investor, but from the analyst's point of view zero coupon bonds with early call provisions do provide the issuer with greater financial flexibility. Of course, if a 30-year zero coupon bond is callable after 10 years, the investor should review the bond for investment in terms of its compound annual yield to the first call date and not to its maturity date.

3. Because the time horizon for the maturity of some zero coupon bonds ranges up to 30 years, the bond issuers could be expected to undergo various economic cycles that could negatively affect their ability to make the final debt payments. Clearly, the more insulated the issuer is from financial adversity at the time when the zero coupon bond is issued, the stronger it should be—to cushion adverse economic stresses. Therefore, the most attractive zeros are those of the highest creditworthiness when issued, whether they are state general obligation bonds, or well-secured revenue and hybrid bonds.

RED FLAGS FOR THE GENERAL OBLIGATION BOND INVESTOR

In addition to the areas of analysis described above, certain red flags, or negative trends, suggest increased credit risks for general obligation bonds. The signals that indicate a decline in the ability of a state, county, town, city, or school district to function within fiscally sound parameters include the following.

1. Declining property values and increasing delinquent taxpayers.
2. An annually increasing tax burden relative to other regions.
3. An increasing property tax rate in conjunction with a declining population.
4. Declines in the number and value of issued permits for new building construction.
5. Actual general fund revenues consistently falling below budgeted amounts.
6. Increasing end-of-year general fund deficits.
7. Budget expenditures increasing annually in excess of the inflation rate.
8. Increasing unfunded pension liabilities.
9. General obligation debt increasing while property values are stagnant.
10. Declining economy as measured by increased unemployment and declining personal income.

RED FLAGS FOR THE REVENUE BOND INVESTOR

For the revenue bonds discussed above there are general signals that indicate a decline in credit quality. These are the signals.

1. Annually decreasing coverage of debt service by net revenues.
2. Regular use of debt reserve and other reserves by the issuer.
3. Growing financial dependence of the issuer on unpredictable federal and state-aid appropriations for meeting operating budget expenses.
4. Chronic lateness in supplying investors with annual audited financials.
5. Unanticipated cost overruns and schedule delays on capital construction projects.
6. Frequent or significant rate increases.
7. Deferring capital plant maintenance and improvements.
8. Excessive management turnovers.
9. Shrinking customer base.
10. New and unanticipated competition.

SECTION 4

MUNICIPAL BOND PORTFOLIO MANAGEMENT

CHAPTER 14

ACTIVE TOTAL RETURN MANAGEMENT OF MUNICIPAL BOND PORTFOLIOS

In this chapter we discuss various active strategies that have been employed by municipal bond portfolio managers. As yield measures offer little insight into the potential performance of a municipal bond or municipal bond portfolio over some investment horizon, we need a framework that allows us to assess the potential performance. The framework is the total return. We begin this chapter with a discussion of the investment management process.

MUNICIPAL BOND INVESTMENT MANAGEMENT PROCESS

Regardless of the institutional investor, the investment management process involves the following five steps.

1. Setting investment objectives.
2. Establishing investment policy.
3. Selecting the portfolio strategy.
4. Selecting the assets.
5. Measuring and evaluating performance.

Setting Investment Objectives

The first main step in the investment management process is setting the investment objective. The investment objective depends on the institution. For example, the investment objective of a property and casualty company may be to maximize tax-exempt income when the company is in a profitable cycle. A municipal bond mutual fund may seek to out-perform some municipal bond index. A municipal bond fund that is a target term fund (i.e., regulated investment company with a specified termination date) may have as its investment objective to outperform a benchmark but still return a specified dollar amount at the termination date of the fund. A portfolio must be created to meet these dual investment goals.

Establishing Investment Policy

The second step in the investment management process is establishing policy guidelines to satisfy the investment objectives. Setting policy begins with the *asset allocation decision:* The investor must decide how the institution's funds should be distributed among the major classes of assets in which it may invest. The major asset classes typically include stocks, taxable bonds, tax-exempt bonds, real estate, and foreign securities.

Client and regulatory constraints must be considered in establishing an investment policy. Examples of constraints that might be imposed by a client are the amount that may be invested in a bond of an issuer whose credit rating is below some specified level and a restriction that no more than a predetermined percentage of the assets may be invested in a particular state in the case of municipal bonds or industry in the case of corporate bonds. For state-regulated institutions, such as insurance companies, regulators may restrict the amount of funds allocated to certain major asset classes. Even the amount allocated within a major asset class may be restricted, based on the characteristics of a particular asset.

Tax implications must also be considered when adopting investment policies. For example, pension funds are exempt from taxes, so they are not particularly interested in investing in tax-exempt investments. Pension funds buy these investments purely on their pretax yield. There have been times in the market when these institutional investors, or "flippers," have found it advantageous to invest in the municipal market.

Financial reporting requirements affect the ways in which many institutional investors establish investment policies. Unfortunately, financial reporting considerations sometimes cause institutions to establish investment policies that, in the long run, may not be in the best economic interest of the institution.

Selecting a Portfolio Strategy

Selecting a portfolio strategy that is consistent with the objectives and policy guidelines of the client or institution is the third step in the investment management process. Portfolio strategies can be classified as either *active strategies* or *passive strategies*. Essential to all active strategies are expectations about the factors that could influence the performance of an asset class. The factors that affect performance are related to the risks discussed in earlier chapters.

Active municipal bond portfolios may involve forecasts of future interest rates, spread changes (quality and maturity), or the identification of undervalued issues. Passive strategies involve minimal expectational input. A popular type of passive strategy is *indexing,* in which a manager seeks to replicate the performance of some benchmark index. Although this strategy has been pursued by equity portfolio managers and, in recent years, increasingly by taxable fixed-income portfolio managers, it is not commonly followed by municipal bond portfolio managers.

Between these extremes of active and passive strategies new strategies have sprung up that have elements of both. For example, the core of a portfolio may be indexed with the balance managed actively. Or a portfolio may be primarily indexed but employ low-risk strategies to enhance the indexed portfolio's return. This strategy is commonly referred to as ''enhanced indexing'' or ''indexing plus.''

In the fixed-income area, several investment strategies classified as *structured portfolio strategies* have been commonly used. A structured portfolio strategy is one in which a portfolio is designed to achieve the performance of some predetermined benchmark. These strategies are frequently used when trying to match the cash flow from the portfolio of assets to the projected future liabilities that must be paid. Portfolio managers of taxable target term funds have used zero coupon municipal bonds to accomplish the goal of accumulating sufficient funds to meet the objective of returning a specified principal value to stockholders at the termination date.

Given the choice among active, structured, or passive management, which should be selected? The answer depends on (1) the client or money manager's view of how ''price efficient'' the market is and (2) the nature of the liabilities of the client. By price efficient we mean how difficult it would be to earn a greater return than passive management would, after adjusting for the risks and transaction costs associated with implementing a strategy.

Selecting Assets

Once a portfolio strategy is selected, the next step is to select the specific assets to be included in the portfolio. This requires an evaluation of individual securities. In an active strategy, this means trying to identify mispriced securities.

It is in this phase that the investment manager attempts to construct an *efficient* portfolio. An efficient portfolio is one that provides the greatest *expected* return for a given level of risk, or equivalently, the lowest risk for a given *expected* return.

Measuring and Evaluating Performance

The measurement and evaluation of investment performance is the last step in the investment management process. (Actually, it is improper to say that it is the last step because the investment process is an ongoing process.) This step involves measuring the performance of the portfolio then evaluating that performance relative to some benchmark.

In the equity area, several benchmarks by which money managers can be evaluated have been constructed. These include the Standard & Poor's 500, the Russell indexes, and the Wilshire indexes. Similarly, in the taxable fixed-income area there has been a proliferation of bond indexes published by the major investment banking firms.

Historically, clients have evaluated the performance of municipal bond money managers by simply comparing them to the performance of a taxable bond index and requiring that they earn a specified percentage of that index. To correct this deficiency, several dealers and vendors have formulated various municipal bond indexes.

The most popular municipal bond indexes are those of Merrill Lynch and Lehman Brothers. These indexes are comprised of bonds from multiple sectors of the municipal bond market (such as housing and transportation bonds) as well as a mixture of maturity and quality ratings. The weighted average yield and price as well as duration and convexity are calculated on an unadjusted basis as well as an option-adjusted basis. These values as well as total rates of return are generally reported on a daily, weekly, monthly, quarterly, and year-to-date basis. For example, Merrill Lynch's master index—popularly referred to as simply the municipal bond index—consists of 300 individual securities. (Although most indexes are weighted based on market capitalization, Merrill's indexes are weighted by a proprietary matrix methodology.) This index is comprised of over 100 subindexes to allow for analysis relative to particular sectors of the municipal market, quality or maturity groupings. Two examples are the Institutional Municipal Index and the Insured Bond Index. Because of the increased number of mutual funds investing in municipal bonds, dealer firms have constructed specialized indexes to allow for the evaluation of their relative performance. Examples are Merrill Lynch's Mutual Fund Index, New York Mutual Fund Index, and California Mutual Fund Index.

Although the Bond Buyer municipal bond index described in Chapter 16 is used often as an index for bond quotes and the Bond Buyer publishes simple average characteristics for the index, this is not an appropriate index to use for total return analysis because of the various adjustments made to the index before it is reported. However, many of the bonds in the Bond Buyer index are also included in the indexes of the street firms, as the bonds in the index are relatively active traded bonds.

TOTAL RETURN FRAMEWORK

As explained in Chapter 6, an investor who purchases a municipal bond can expect to receive a *dollar* return from one or more of the following sources.

1. The coupon interest payments made by the issuer.
2. Any capital gain (or capital loss—negative dollar return) when the bond matures, is called, is put, is refunded, or is sold.
3. Income from reinvestment of the coupon interest payments (i.e., interest-on-interest).

If yields to maturity, call, and put offer little insight into the relative value of a municipal bond, what measure of return can be used? The proper measure is one that considers all three sources of potential dollar return over the investment horizon. It is the return (interest rate) that makes the proceeds invested (full price) grow to the projected total dollar return at the end of the investment horizon and is referred to as the *total return*.[1]

---

[1] The total return is also referred to as the *horizon return* and *realized compound yield*.

The total return requires that the investor specify

- An investment horizon.
- A reinvestment rate.
- A selling price of the bond at the end of the investment horizon (which depends on the assumed yield to maturity for the bond at the end of the investment horizon).

More formally, the steps for computing a total return over some investment horizon are:

Step 1: Compute the total coupon payments plus the interest on interest based on an assumed reinvestment rate. The reinvestment rate is one-half the annual interest rate that the investor assumes can be earned on the reinvestment of coupon interest payments.[2]

Step 2: Determine the projected sale price at the end of the planned investment horizon. We refer to this as the *horizon price*. The projected sale price depends on the projected yield on comparable bonds at the end of the planned investment horizon. We refer to the yield at the end of the investment horizon as the *horizon yield*.

Step 3: Add the values computed in steps 1 and 2. The sum is the total future dollars that will be received from the investment given the assumed reinvestment rate and projected horizon yield.

Step 4: To obtain the semiannual total return, use the following formula.[3]

$$\left(\frac{\text{Total future dollars}}{\text{Full purchase price of bond}}\right)^{1/\text{Length of horizon}} - 1$$

Step 5: Because coupon interest is assumed to be paid semiannually, double the interest rate found in step 4. The resulting interest rate is the total return expressed on a bond equivalent basis. Instead, the total

---

[2] An investor can choose multiple reinvestment rates for cash flows from the bond over the investment horizon.

[3] Note that this calculation is the same as the yield calculation for a zero coupon bond.

return can be expressed on an effective interest rate basis by using the following formula.

$$(1 + \text{Semiannual total return})^2 - 1$$

To illustrate the computation of the total return, suppose that an investor with a three-year investment horizon is considering purchasing a 20 year, 8 percent coupon municipal bond for $82.84. The next coupon payment is six months from now. The yield to maturity for this bond is 10 percent. The investor expects to reinvest the coupon interest payments at an annual interest rate of 6 percent and that at the end of the planned investment horizon the 17-year bond will be selling to offer a yield to maturity of 7 percent (i.e., the horizon yield is 7%). The total return for this bond is computed in Exhibit 14–1.

An oft-cited objection to the total return is that it requires the portfolio manager to make assumptions about reinvestment rates and horizon yields, as well as to think in terms of an investment horizon. Unfortunately, some portfolio managers are reluctant to do so, finding comfort in meaningless measures such as the yield to maturity because they do not require them to incorporate their expectations into the calculations. Total return, however, enables the portfolio manager to analyze the performance of a municipal bond based on different interest rate scenarios for reinvestment rates and horizon yields. This type of analysis, referred to as *scenario analysis*, allows a portfolio manager to see how sensitive the municipal bond's performance is to each assumption. Therefore, the portfolio manager can get a much better idea of the possible investment attributes of bonds using total return. There is no need to assume that the reinvestment rate will be constant for the entire investment horizon, which is not realistic for longer investment horizons. We argue that portfolio managers should be more comfortable looking at the bonds' total return profile using different interest rate assumptions rather than blindly relying upon the implicit assumptions incorporated into conventional yield measures.

Using Total Return to Compare Municipal and Corporate Bonds

The conventional method for comparing the relative value of a tax-exempt municipal bond and a taxable corporate bond is to compute the *taxable equivalent yield*. The taxable equivalent yield is the yield that must be

EXHIBIT 14–1
Illustration of Calculation of Total Return

Assumptions

Municipal bond: 8%, 20-year bond selling for $82.84 (yield to maturity is 10%)
Reinvestment rate: 6%
Investment horizon: 3 years
Horizon yield: 7%

Calculation

Step 1
Compute the total coupon payments plus the interest-on-interest assuming an annual reinvestment rate of 6 percent, or 3 percent every six months. The coupon payments are $4 per $100 of par value every six months for three years or six periods (the length of the investment horizon). The total coupon interest plus interest-on-interest is $25.874.

Step 2
The projected sale price at the end of three years (i.e., the horizon price) assuming that the required yield to maturity for 17-year bonds is 7 percent is $109.851.

Step 3
Adding the amount in steps 1 and 2 gives total future dollars of $135.725.

Step 4
Compute the following.

$$\left(\frac{\$135.725}{\$82.840}\right)^{1/6} - 1$$
$$= (1.63840)^{0.16667} - 1$$
$$= 1.0858 - 1 = 0.0858 \text{ or } 8.58\%$$

Step 5
Doubling 8.58 percent gives a horizon return of 17.16 percent on a bond equivalent basis. On an effective interest rate basis, the horizon return is

$$(1.0858)^2 - 1$$
$$= 1.1790 - 1 = 0.1790 = 17.90\%$$

---

earned on a taxable bond in order to produce the same return as a tax-exempt municipal bond. The formula is.

$$\text{Taxable equivalent yield} = \frac{\text{Tax-exempt yield}}{1 - \text{Marginal tax rate}}$$

For example, suppose an investor in the 36 percent marginal tax bracket is considering a 10-year municipal bond with a yield to maturity of 6.04 percent. The taxable equivalent yield is

$$\frac{6.04\%}{1 - 0.396} = 10\%$$

If the investor can earn more than 10 percent on a comparable quality corporate bond with 10 years to maturity, those who use this approach would recommend that the corporate bond be purchased. If, instead, less than 10 percent can be earned on a comparable corporate bond, the investor should invest in the municipal bond.

What's wrong with this approach? The tax-exempt yield of the municipal bond and the taxable equivalent yield suffer from the same limitations, discussed earlier, as yield to maturity. Also, the difference in reinvestment opportunities for a corporate and municipal bond should be considered. For the former, coupon payments are taxed; therefore, the amount to be reinvested is not the entire coupon payment but an amount net of taxes. In contrast, because the coupon payments are free from taxes for a municipal bond, the entire coupon can be reinvested. However, taxes might have to be paid on any capital gain realized at the time the security is sold or matures. The total return framework can accommodate this situation by allowing us to compare the reinvestment opportunities.

The total return framework, as compared to the conventional taxable equivalent yield approach, has another advantage. Changes in tax rates (either because the investor expects his or her tax rate to change or the tax structure to change) can be incorporated into the analysis.

Portfolio Total Return

A more appropriate measure for assessing the potential performance of a portfolio is its total return. This is determined by first calculating the total future dollars of each bond in the portfolio under a given scenario considering horizon yields, reinvestment rates, and spreads. The sum of all the total future dollars for each bond in the portfolio is then calculated. The portfolio total return is found as explained earlier for a given bond: It is the interest rate that makes the market value of the portfolio today grow to the sum of all the total future dollars at the horizon date.

By using scenario analysis, a portfolio manager, an investment (or asset/liability) committee, or a board can assess the potential performance of the portfolio. Corrective action can be taken to rebalance a portfolio if a scenario that is expected to occur will be detrimental to the performance of the portfolio. The other portfolio yield measures discussed in Chapter 6 provide no such warning.

ACTIVE STRATEGIES

Selecting a municipal bond portfolio strategy that is consistent with the objectives and policy guidelines of the client or institution is a major step in the investment management process. Municipal bond portfolio strategies can be classified as either active strategies or passive strategies. Essential to all active strategies is specification of expectations about the factors that influence the performance of municipal bonds.

This section describes active municipal bond portfolio strategies within the context of the total return framework.

The starting point in our discussion of active strategies is an investigation of the various sources of return from holding a fixed-income portfolio. As we explain in Chapter 6, the three sources of return are coupon income, any capital gain (or loss), and reinvestment income. Here we explore the factors that affect one or more of these sources. In general, the following factors affect a portfolio's return.

1. Changes in the level of municipal bond interest rates.
2. Changes in the shape of the municipal yield curve.
3. Changes in yield spreads among municipal bond sectors.
4. Changes in the yield spread for a particular municipal issue.

A money manager who pursues an active strategy positions a portfolio, subject to client and regulatory constraints, to capitalize on expectations about the above factors. Other active strategies are based not on the traditional yield spread approach but on the option-adjusted spread approach discussed in Chapter 9.

The total return framework should be employed to analyze the effect of an expected outcome or outcomes on a portfolio's return. Recall from earlier discussions that yield measures are inadequate for assessing the potential performance of an individual bond. For a bond portfolio, the meaning of a "portfolio yield" is questionable and certainly provides no insight into the return for a portfolio over some investment horizon.

What is critical in assessing strategies that are not based on expected changes in the level of interest rates is to compare municipal bond positions that have the same dollar duration. To understand why, consider two municipal bonds, X and Y. Suppose that the price of X is 80 and has a modified duration of 5, while Y has a price of 90 and has a modified duration of 4. Since modified duration is the approximate price change per 100 basis point change in yield, a 100 basis points change in yield for bond X would change its price by about 5 percent. Based on a price of 80, its price will change by about $4 per $80 of market value. Thus, its dollar duration for a 100 basis point change in yield is $4 per $80 of market value. Similarly, for Y, its dollar duration for a 100 basis point change in yield per $90 of market value can be determined. In this case, it is $3.6. So if bonds X and Y are being considered as alternative investments in some strategy other than one based on anticipating interest rate movements, the amount of each bond in the strategy should be such that they will both have the same dollar duration.

To illustrate this, suppose that a portfolio manager owns $10 million of par value of X, which has a market value of $8 million. The dollar duration of X per 100 basis point change in yield for the $8 million market value is $400,000. Suppose further that this portfolio manager is considering exchanging the X that it owns in its portfolio for Y. If the portfolio manager wants to have the same interest rate exposure (i.e., dollar duration) for Y that he or she currently has for X, the manager will buy a market value amount of Y with the same dollar duration. If the portfolio manager purchased $10 million of *par value* of Y, and therefore $9 million of *market value* of Y, the per 100 basis point change in yield would be only $360,000. If, instead, the portfolio manager purchased $10 million of *market value* of Y, the dollar duration per 100 basis point change in yield would be $400,000. Because Y is trading at 90, $11.11 million of par value of Y must be purchased to keep the dollar duration of the position from Y the same as for X.

Mathematically, this problem can be expressed as:

Let

D_X = Dollar duration per 100 basis point change in yield for bond X for the market value of bond X held

MD_Y = Modified duration for bond Y

MV_Y = Market value of bond Y needed to obtain the same dollar duration as bond X

Then, the following equation sets the dollar duration for bond X equal to the dollar duration for bond Y.

$$\$D_X = (MD_Y/100)\, MV_Y$$

Solving for MV_Y,

$$MV_Y = \$D_X/(MD_Y/100)$$

Dividing by the price per $1 of par value of Y gives the par value of Y that has an approximately equivalent dollar duration as bond X.

In our illustration, $\$D_X$ is $400,000 and MD_Y is 4, then

$$MV_Y = \$400,000/(4/100) = \$10,000,000$$

The market value of Y is 90 per $100 of par value, so the price per $1 of par value is 0.9. Dividing $10 million by 0.9 indicates that the par value of Y that should be purchased is $11.11 million.

Interest Rate Expectations Strategies

A money manager who believes that he or she can accurately forecast the future level of interest rates alters the portfolio's sensitivity to interest rate changes. As duration is a measure of interest rate sensitivity, this involves increasing a portfolio's duration if interest rates are expected to fall and reducing it if interest rates are expected to rise. For those money managers whose benchmark is a bond index, this means increasing the portfolio duration relative to the benchmark index if interest rates are expected to fall and reducing it if interest rates are expected to rise. The degree to which the duration of the managed portfolio is permitted to diverge from that of the benchmark index may be limited by the client.

A portfolio's duration may be altered by swapping bonds in the portfolio for new bonds that can achieve the target portfolio duration. Such swaps are commonly referred to as *rate anticipation swaps*.[4]

---

[4]In the taxable fixed-income market, a more efficient means for altering the duration of a bond portfolio is to use interest rate futures contracts. As we explain in Chapter 16, buying futures increases a portfolio's duration, whereas selling futures decreases it. But as explained in Chapter 16, in the municipal bond area the municipal bond futures contract may not be an effective means for altering duration.

The key to this active strategy is, of course, an ability to forecast the direction of future interest rates. The academic literature, however, does not support the view that interest rates can be forecast so that risk-adjusted excess returns can be consistently realized. It is doubtful whether betting on future interest rates will provide a consistently superior return.

Although a money manager may not pursue an active strategy based strictly on future interest rate movements, there can be a tendency to make an interest rate bet to cover inferior performance relative to a benchmark index. For example, suppose a money manager holds himself or herself out to a client as pursuing one of the active strategies discussed later in this chapter. Suppose further that the money manager is evaluated over a one-year investment horizon, and that three months before the end of the investment horizon, the money manager is performing below the client-specified benchmark index. If the money manager believes the account may be lost because of underperformance, there is an incentive to bet on interest rate movements. If the manager is correct, the account can be saved, although an incorrect bet may result in underperforming the benchmark index by a greater amount. In this case, the account might probably be lost regardless of the level of underperformance. A client can prevent this type of gaming by a money manager by imposing constraints on the degree that the portfolio's duration can vary from that of the benchmark index. Also, in the performance evaluation stage of the investment management process, decomposing the portfolio's return into the factors that generated the return highlights the extent to which a portfolio's return is attributable to changes in the level of interest rates.

Other active strategies also rely on forecasts of future interest rate levels. Future interest rates, for instance, affect the value of options embedded in callable municipal bonds. Callable municipal bonds with coupon rates above the expected future interest rate underperform relative to noncallable bonds or low coupon bonds. This is because of the negative convexity feature of callable bonds described in Chapter 7.

Municipal Yield Curve Strategies

As we explain in Chapter 8, the yield curve is the relationship between maturity and yield on issues of the same credit quality. The shape of the municipal yield curve changes over time. Because a portfolio consists of municipal issues with different maturities, changes in the shape of the municipal yield curve have varying price effects on each bond.

Two portfolios with the same duration perform differently if the yield curve does not shift in a parallel fashion. To see this point, consider the three bonds and two portfolios shown in Exhibit 14–2.[5] The first portfolio consists of only bond C, the ten-year bond, and is referred to as the "bullet portfolio." The second portfolio consists of 50.2 percent of bond A and 49.8 percent of bond B, and we call this portfolio the "barbell portfolio." The dollar duration of the bullet portfolio per 100 basis point change in yield is 6.43409. Note in Exhibit 14–2 that the dollar duration of the barbell—which is just the weighted average of the dollar duration of the two bonds—is the same as that of the bullet portfolio. In fact, the barbell portfolio was designed to produce this result. As we explained in Chapter 7, duration is just a first approximation of the change in price resulting from a change in interest rates. Convexity provides a second approximation. The dollar convexities of the two portfolios, shown in Exhibit 14–2, are not equal. The dollar convexity of the bullet portfolio is less than that of the barbell portfolio.

The "yield" for the two portfolios likewise is not the same. The yield (yield to maturity) for the bullet is simply the yield to maturity of bond C, 9.25 percent. The traditional yield calculation for the barbell portfolio, which is found by taking a weighted average of the yield to maturity of the two bonds included in the portfolio, is 8.998 percent. This approach suggests that the "yield" of the bullet portfolio is 25.2 basis points greater than the barbell portfolio. Although both portfolios have the same dollar duration, the yield of the bullet portfolio is greater than the yield of the barbell portfolio. However, the dollar convexity of the barbell portfolio is greater than that of the bullet portfolio. The difference in the two yields is sometimes referred to as the *cost of convexity*. The column labeled "Parallel Shift—Total Return" in Exhibit 14–3 shows the difference in the total return over a six-month investment horizon for the two portfolios assuming that the yield curve shifts in a parallel fashion.[6] By "parallel" it is meant that the yields for the short-term bond (A), the intermediate-term bond (C), and the long-term bond (B) change by the

---

[5]This illustration is adapted from Ravi E. Dattatreya and Frank J. Fabozzi, *Active Total Return Management of Fixed Income Portfolios* (Chicago: Probus Publishing, 1989).

[6]Note that no assumption is needed for the reinvestment rate because the three bonds shown in the exhibit are assumed to be trading right after a coupon payment has been made and therefore there is no accrued interest.

EXHIBIT 14–2
Bullet-Barbell Analysis

		Three bonds used in analysis				
Bond	Coupon	Maturity (Years)	Price Plus Accrued	Yield	Dollar Duration	Dollar Convexity
A	8.50%	5	100	8.50%	4.00544	19.8164
B	9.50	20	100	9.50	8.88151	124.1702
C	9.25	10	100	9.25	6.43409	55.4506

Bullet Portfolio: Bond C

Barbell Portfolio: Bonds A and B
  Composition of barbell: 50.2% of bond A; 49.8% of bond B

  Dollar duration of barbell = $0.502 \times 4.00544 + 0.498 \times 8.88151 = 6.434$
  Average yield of barbell = $0.502 \times 8.50 + 0.498 \times 9.5 = 8.998$

Analysis based on average yield

  Yield pickup = Yield on bullet − Average yield of barbell
      $= 9.25 - 8.998 = 0.252$, or 25.2 basis points

Analysis based on duration, convexity, and average yield

  Dollar convexity of barbell = $0.502 \times 19.81864 + 0.498 \times 124.1702 = 71.7846$
      Yield pickup = Yield on bullet − Average yield of barbell
        $= 9.25 - 8.998 = 0.252$, or 25.2 basis points
      Convexity giveup = Convexity of barbell − Convexity of bullet
        $= 71.7846 - 55.4506 = 16.334$

Analysis based on duration, convexity, and cash flow yield

  Cash flow yield of barbell* =
  $$\frac{(8.5 \times 0.502 \times 4.00544) + (9.5 \times 0.498 \times 8.88151)}{6.434} = 9.187$$
      Yield pickup = Yield on bullet − Cash flow yield
        $= 9.25 - 9.187 = .063$, or 6.3 basis points
      Convexity giveup = Convexity of barbell − Convexity of bullet
        $= 71.7846 - 55.4506 = 16.334$

*The calculation shown is actually a dollar-duration-weighted yield, a very close approximation to cash flow yield.

---

same number of basis points, shown in the "Yield Change" column of the exhibit. The relative performance reported is

  Bullet portfolio's total return − Barbell portfolio's total return

Thus a positive value in the total return column means that the bullet portfolio outperformed the barbell portfolio, whereas a negative sign means that the barbell portfolio outperformed the bullet portfolio.

Which portfolio is the better investment alternative if the yield curve shifts in a parallel fashion and the investment horizon is six months? The answer depends on the amount by which yields change. Notice that when yields change by less than 100 basis points, the bullet portfolio outperforms the barbell portfolio. The reverse is true if yields change by more than 100 basis points.

Now let's look at what happens if the yield curve does not shift in a parallel fashion. The last two columns of Exhibit 14–3 show the relative performance of the two portfolios for a nonparallel shift of the yield curve. Specifically, the first nonparallel shift column assumes that if the yield on bond C (the intermediate-term bond) changes by the amount shown in the first column, bond A (the short-term bond) changes by the same amount plus 25 basis points; whereas bond B (the long-term bond) changes by the same amount shown in the first column less 25 basis points. That is, the nonparallel shift assumed is a flattening of the yield curve. For this yield curve shift, the barbell always outperforms the bullet. In the last column, the nonparallel shift assumes that for a change in bond C's yield, the yield on bond A changes by the same amount less 25 basis points, whereas that on bond B will change by the same amount plus 25 points. That is, it assumes that the yield curve will steepen. In this case, the bullet portfolio outperforms the barbell portfolio so long as the yield on bond C does not rise by more than 250 basis points or fall by more than 325 basis points.

The key point here is that looking at measures such as yield (yield to maturity or some type of portfolio yield measure), duration, or convexity tells us little about performance over some investment horizon because performance depends on the magnitude of the change in yields and how the yield curve shifts.

Yield Spread Strategies

Yield spread strategies involve positioning a portfolio to capitalize on expected changes in yield spreads between sectors of the bond market. Bond swaps or exchanges undertaken when the money manager believes that the prevailing yield spread between two bonds in the market is out of line with their historical yield spread, and that the yield spread will

EXHIBIT 14-3
**Relative Performance of Bullet Portfolio and Barbell Portfolio over a
Six-Month Investment Horizon***

Yield Change	Parallel Shift	Nonparallel Shift**	Nonparallel Shift***
−4.000%	−4.00%	−6.88%	−1.27%
−3.750	−3.38	−6.13	−0.78
−3.500	−2.82	−5.44	−0.35
−3.250	−2.32	−4.82	0.03
−3.000	−1.88	−4.26	0.36
−2.750	−1.49	−3.75	0.65
−2.500	−1.15	−3.30	0.89
−2.250	−0.85	−2.90	1.09
−2.000	−0.59	−2.55	1.25
−1.750	−0.38	−2.24	1.37
−1.500	−0.20	−1.97	1.47
−1.250	−0.05	−1.74	1.53
−1.000	0.06	−1.54	1.57
−0.750	0.15	−1.38	1.58
−0.500	0.21	−1.24	1.57
−0.250	0.24	−1.14	1.53
0.000	0.25	−1.06	1.48
0.250	0.24	−1.01	1.41
0.500	0.21	−0.98	1.32
0.750	0.16	−0.97	1.21
1.000	0.09	−0.98	1.09
1.250	0.01	−1.00	0.96
1.500	−0.08	−1.05	0.81
1.750	−0.19	−1.10	0.66
2.000	−0.31	−1.18	0.49
2.250	−0.44	−1.26	0.32
2.500	−0.58	−1.36	0.14
2.750	−0.73	−1.46	−0.05
3.000	−0.88	−1.58	−0.24
3.250	−1.05	−1.70	−0.44
3.500	−1.21	−1.84	−0.64
3.750	−1.39	−1.98	−0.85
4.000	−1.57	−2.12	−1.06

*Performance is based on the difference in total return over a six-month investment horizon. Specifically

> Bullet portfolio's total return − Barbell portfolio's total return

Therefore a negative value means that the barbell portfolio outperformed the bullet portfolio.

**Change in yield for Bond C. Nonparallel shift as follows (flattening of yield curve):

> Yield change Bond A = Yield change Bond C + 25 basis points
> Yield change Bond B = Yield change Bond C − 25 basis points

***Change in yield for Bond C. Nonparallel shift as follows (steepening of yield curve):

> Yield change Bond A = Yield change Bond C − 25 basis points
> Yield change Bond B = Yield change Bond C + 25 basis points

realign by the end of the investment horizon, are called *intermarket spread swaps*.

The bond market is classified into sectors in several ways: by type of issue (general obligation or revenue bond), quality or credit, coupon (high-coupon/premium bonds, current-coupon/par bonds, and low-coupon/discount bonds), and maturity (short-, intermediate-, or long-term). Yield spreads between maturity sectors involve changes in the yield curve as we have discussed in the previous section.

Credit or quality spreads change because of expected changes in economic prospects. Credit spreads between triple-A municipal issues and lower-rated issues widen in a declining or contracting economy and narrow during economic expansion. The economic rationale is that in a declining or contracting economy state and local governments experience a decline in revenue and reduced cash flow, making it difficult for issuers to service their contractual debt obligations. Investors attempt a flight to quality, increasing the demand for higher credit quality issues. To induce investors to hold securities of lower quality municipal issuers, the yield spread relative to triple-A rated issues must widen. The converse is that during economic expansion and brisk economic activity, revenue and cash flow pick up, increasing the likelihood that municipal issuers have the capacity to service their contractual debt obligations. And investors, as well, have more money to shelter in tax-exempt municipals.

Spreads attributable to differences in callable and noncallable municipal bonds and differences in coupons of callable municipal bonds change as a result of expected changes in (1) the direction of the change in interest rates and (2) interest rate volatility. An expected drop in the level of interest rates widens the yield spread between callable bonds and noncallable municipal bonds as the prospects that the issuer will exercise the call option increase. The reverse is true: the yield spread narrows if interest rates are expected to rise. An increase in interest rate volatility increases the value of the embedded call option, and thereby increases the yield spread between callable bonds and noncallable municipal bonds.

Individual Security Selection Strategies

Managers of municipal bond portfolios pursue several active strategies to identify mispriced issues. The most common strategy identifies an issue as undervalued because either

1. Its yield is higher than that of comparably rated issues.
2. Its yield is expected to decline (and price therefore rise) because credit analysis indicates that its rating will improve.

A swap in which a money manager exchanges one bond for another bond that is similar in terms of coupon, maturity, and credit quality but offers a higher yield is called a *substitution swap*. This swap depends on a capital market imperfection. Such situations sometimes exist in the bond market owing to temporary market imbalances and the fragmented nature of certain sectors within the municipal bond market. The risk the money manager faces in making a substitution swap is that the municipal issue purchased may not be truly identical to the municipal issue for which it is exchanged. Moreover, typically municipal issues have similar but not identical maturities and coupon, which could lead to differences in the convexity of the two bonds; any yield spread may reflect the cost of convexity.

SUMMARY

Active bond portfolio strategies seek to capitalize on expectations about changes in factors that affect the price and therefore the performance of an issue over some investment horizon. The factors that affect a portfolio's return are (1) changes in the level of municipal interest rates; (2) changes in the shape of the municipal yield curve; (3) changes in yield spreads among municipal bond sectors; and (4) changes in the yield spread for a particular bond. The total return framework should be used to assess how changes in these factors affect the performance of a strategy over some investment horizon.

CHAPTER 15

THE ROLE OF MUNICIPAL DERIVATIVE SECURITIES IN PORTFOLIO MANAGEMENT

In Chapter 4 we described the wide range of derivative securities that have been created. The reasons that investment bankers have worked with municipal issuers to create these securities is to provide instruments that provide risk/return characteristics that are either more appealing to investors from an asset/liability perspective or as a more efficient means to place bets. In this chapter we explain how to value inverse floaters, one of the more popular products in the derivative securities market. We focus on this product because there appears to be a good deal of misunderstanding about the investment characteristics of inverse floaters. Then we explain the investment characteristics of several of the other products described in Chapter 4.

VALUATION OF INVERSE FLOATERS

As we stated in Chapter 5, the value of any financial asset is the present value of the expected cash flow. It is difficult to value an inverse floater using this definition because of the uncertainty about future values for the floating rate and thus the residual interest rate. In our discussion of how to value an inverse floater we shall first discuss the value of an inverse floater created via the bond market, referring to the fixed-rate bond from which the inverse floater is created as the *collateral*.

We can express the relationship between the collateral, the floater, and the corresponding inverse floater as follows.

$$\text{Collateral} = \text{Floater} + \text{Inverse floater}$$

For simplicity, we have ignored any fees associated with the auctions.

In terms of value, the following relationship exists.

Value of collateral = Value of floater + Value of inverse floater

That is, the sum of the value of the floater and the value of the inverse floater must be equal to the value of the collateral from which they were created. If this relationship is violated, arbitrage profits are possible. The right of the holder of these two securities to combine them and receive the fixed-rate collateral or detach them and sell them separately assures this relationship.

Alternatively, the relationship can be expressed as follows.

Value of inverse floater = Value of collateral − Value of floater

The above expression states that the value of an inverse floater can be found by valuing the collateral, valuing the floater, and then calculating the difference between these two values. Thus, the value of an inverse floater is not found directly but, instead, is found indirectly from the value of the collateral and the floater.

Let's look at what affects the value of the floater. The floater trades at its par value unless the cap is reached (i.e, unless market interest rates reach the cap). The floater is effectively a capped floater and can be viewed as a package of an uncapped floater (i.e., a floater without a cap) and a cap.

In terms of value, this can be expressed as follows.

Value of capped floater = Value of uncapped floater − Value of cap

The reason for subtracting the value of the cap from the value of an uncapped floater is that the holder of a capped floater has effectively sold a cap.

The uncapped floater should sell at its par value. Thus, the above expression for the value of a capped floater can be expressed as follows.

Value of capped floater = Par value − Value of cap

As can be seen, the divergence of the value of a capped floater from par depends on the value of the cap. If the short-term market rate (the rate determined at the periodic auction) is far below the cap, then the value of the cap is close to zero and the capped floater trades at par value. However, if the short-term market rate is close to the cap or above the cap, the value of the cap is positive and the value of a capped floater is less than its par value.

The question is how to determine the value of the cap. An over-the-counter market exists for caps. A cap is an agreement between two counterparties whereby one party, for an up-front premium, agrees to compensate the other if a designated reference rate or index is above a pre-determined level (called the *strike rate*).[1]

In this market, caps are valued using an option pricing model as a cap is nothing more than an option. Two key factors that affect the value of the cap are (1) the relationship between the current value of the reference rate and the strike rate, and (2) expected volatility of the reference rate. The farther the reference rate is below the strike rate, the lower the value of the cap. As the reference rate approaches the strike rate, the cap increases in value. With respect to expected volatility of the reference rate, a cap has more value the greater the expected volatility.

Given that the floater created from the collateral is a capped floater, then the value of an inverse floater can be expressed as

Value of inverse floater = Value of collateral − Value of capped floater

The factors that affect the value of inverse floaters are the factors that affect the value of the collateral and the value of a capped floater.

For a bond with a 50/50 split of floaters to inverse floaters and a floating rate significantly lower than the cap (thus with a cap value of zero) and selling at par, the value of the inverse floater is equal to the following.

Value of inverse floater = (2 × Value of collateral) − 100

This is because the principal amount of the inverse floater (and the principal on the floater) is half that of the collateral. It should be noted that some adjustments are required for the pay cycle on the bonds. For example, some floating-rate notes pay interest every 28 days, while the interest on the inverse floater accrues and is paid semiannually. These are relatively straightforward adjustments.

The value of an inverse floater created in the swaps market is simply equal to the value of the underlying bond and the value of the swap. The value of the swap used for this valuation is the value of a swap with the same terms from the valuation date to the date that the bond reverts back to a fixed coupon bond.

---

[1] The terms of an interest rate agreement include: (1) the reference rate; (2) the strike rate that sets the ceiling; (3) the length of the agreement; (4) the frequency of settlement; and (5) the notional principal amount.

Price Performance of an Inverse Floater

A common misconception is that the value of an inverse floater should always change in the direction opposite to the change in the short-term market rate. Thus, if this rate falls the value of an inverse floater should rise. This view is incorrect because the value of an inverse floater is not solely dependent on the short-term market rate. This rate affects the value of the inverse floater only through its effect on the value of the cap of the capped floater and its effect on the collateral. The other factors that we have discussed also affect the value of an inverse floater.

To see the importance of these relationships on the value of an inverse floater, consider the following.

- The coupon rate on the collateral is 4.5 percent.
- The short-term market rate is currently 5 percent.
- The collateral is an intermediate term bond that would trade at a quality spread of 120 basis points relative to a triple-A municipal bond with the same maturity. The yield of that triple-A municipal bond is 6 percent so that the collateral's yield is 7.2 percent (6% plus 1.2%).

Next we consider three scenarios six months from now. For each scenario we make an assumption about (1) the short-term market rate six months from now, (2) the expected volatility of the short-term market rate six months from now, and (3) the yield on a triple-A rated municipal bond of the same maturity and the quality spread to that bond. We look at the effect on the value of the collateral and the value of the capped floater. The difference between these two values is the value of the inverse floater.

Scenario 1. In this scenario we assume that six months from now (1) the short-term market rate declines to 3 percent; (2) expected volatility of the short-term market rate declines; and (3) the quality spread widens to 140 basis points, and the yield on a triple-A municipal bond with the same maturity rises to 7 percent. Thus, we assume that short-term rates have declined and intermediate-term rates have increased. This means that the yield curve is assumed to have steepened.

Given this scenario, the value of the floater will increase for two reasons. First, today the coupon rate on the short-term rate is 3 percent but is capped at 4.5 percent. When the short-term market rate falls below the cap six months from now, the floater's value increases. Second, expected volatility for the short-term market rate increases. The value of the collateral declines because both the benchmark triple-A intermediate-term municipal bond yield has increased and the quality spread has widened. Since the value of an inverse floater is the difference between the value of the collateral (which has decreased) and the value of the floater (which has increased), the value of the inverse floater has declined. *Notice that this has occurred in this scenario despite the short-term market rate's decline.*

Scenario 2. In this scenario we assume six months from now that (1) the short-term market rate rises to 5 percent, (2) expected volatility of the short-term market rate increases, and (3) the quality spread narrows to 90 basis points and the yield on a comparable maturity triple-A benchmark municipal bond falls to 5.5 percent. Thus, we assume that short-term rates rise and intermediate term rates fall. This means that the yield curve has flattened. Because the short-term market rate has risen farther above the cap and expected volatility has increased, the value of the capped floater six months from now falls. The value of the collateral rises. Thus, the value of the inverse floater increases *even though the short-term market rate has increased.*

Scenario 3. In this last scenario we assume six months from now that (1) the short-term market rate declines to 3 percent, as it did in scenario 1; (2) expected volatility of the short-term rate decreases as in scenario 1; and (3) the quality spread widens to 140 basis points—as in scenario 1, and the yield on the benchmark triple-A rated municipal bond falls to 5.5 percent as in scenario 2. Under this scenario, the value of the collateral rises. The value of the inverse floater can either rise or fall since the collateral has risen in value and the floater has risen in value. The net effect depends on the relative increase of the collateral and the floater. For example, if the floater is selling close to par (the value of the cap is zero), then the value of the inverse floater rises in this scenario.

These three scenarios illustrate why the change in the shape of the yield curve and a change in the quality spread for the collateral affect the performance of an inverse floater.

Duration of an Inverse Floater

As explained in Chapter 7, the duration of an asset is a measure of the price sensitivity of that asset to a change in interest rates. The duration of an inverse floater can be found by using the following relationship.

Value of inverse floater = Value of collateral − Value of capped floater

The duration of an inverse floater can be found as follows.

$$\text{Duration of inverse floater} =$$
$$\text{Duration of collateral} - \text{Duration of capped floater}$$

The duration of inverse floaters created in the bond market is roughly twice that of the duration on the collateral if the split between inverse floaters and floaters is 50/50. This is because the duration of the floater is close to zero. The inverse floater accepts all the price risk in this instance, so the volatility of the inverse floater is the volatility of the collateral adjusted for the 2:1 leverage. In other words, the full impact of price changes on the collateral accrues to the inverse floater although the par amount outstanding is half that of the collateral.

The duration of an inverse floater created in the swaps market is generally less than that of the bond created in the cash market. The term of the swap, and thus the length of time that the bond is in the inverse floating payment stage of its life, is usually much less than the term on the underlying bond. For example, the underlying may be a 30-year fixed-rate security with an embedded 5-year interest rate swap. The duration of the inverse floater is equal to the sum of the durations on the bond and swap. Thus, the duration of the inverse floater is longer than that of the underlying, but much less than double. Inverse floaters created via the swaps market can be customized by setting the length of the embedded swap to meet the needs of the investor.

Interpretation of an Inverse Floater Position

Because the floater and inverse floater are created from fixed-rate collateral, the following relationship is true.

$$\text{Long a fixed-rate collateral} =$$
$$\text{Long a capped floater} + \text{Long an inverse floater}$$

Recasting this relationship in terms of an inverse floater, we can write

$$\text{Long an inverse floater} =$$
$$\text{Long a fixed-rate collateral } - \text{ Long a capped floater}$$

Or, equivalently,

$$\text{Long an inverse floater} =$$
$$\text{Long a fixed-rate collateral } + \text{ Short a capped floater}$$

Thus, the owner of an inverse floater has effectively purchased fixed-rate collateral and shorted a capped floater. But shorting a capped floater is equivalent to borrowing funds when the interest cost of the funds is a floating rate in which the interest rate is the short-term market rate that is capped.

Consequently, the owner of an inverse floater has effectively purchased a fixed-rate asset with borrowed funds. Thus, the owner of an inverse floater has effectively created a leveraged position. This also explains the long duration on the inverse floater. An inverse floater has a similar payoff to a swap position in which an investor receives a fixed rate and pays a floating rate.

INVESTMENT CHARACTERISTICS OF DERIVATIVE SECURITIES

Purchasers of inverse floaters are generally investors who desire to increase current income in a declining short-term interest rate environment while lengthening the duration of their portfolios. The inverse floater is an effective means of lengthening duration and is an attractive alternative to other means of lengthening duration, such as investing in zero coupon securities or deep discount bonds. Often the inverse floater created via the cash market is the only way to purchase a security with a very long duration. For example, if the underlying bond has a duration of 20 in an equal allocation of the principal to the floater and inverse floater, the duration of the inverse floater can be 40. There are few securities in the municipal bond market that offer this duration.

The bond that is a combination of the floater and the inverse floater we referred to as the collateral, but it is also called the *fixed-option bond*. It generally trades at lower yields than does a comparable fixed-rate bond. This is because the investor owns an option to detach the underlying securities (floater and inverse floater) should it become attractive or necessary to do so. For example, if investors hold the fixed-option bond, in a liquidity crunch they could detach the bonds and sell the floating-rate piece in the market at near par (if the value of the cap is close to zero) and use the proceeds from the sale. Afterward, an investor can repurchase the securities in the market at close to par as long as the interest rate on the floater is not near its cap.

An investor in an inverse floater created in the swaps market wants floating-rate income that moves inversely to short-term rates while locking in the long-term fixed rate on the bond that will begin to pay fixed after the term of the embedded swap. This allows investors who expect short-term rates to decline to take advantage of it with the inverse-floating phase of the issue, while locking in the long-term interest rate on the bond. These securities are often more attractive to the investor because at creation the investor can set the leverage in the security. This is also often attractive to investors who wish to lengthen the duration of their portfolio, but wish to own bonds with durations less than those on inverse floaters created in the cash market. The investor always has an option to link by reversing the embedded swap in the bond. Here, the fixed interest rate on the linked bond is set at the time of the reverse swap at the current cost of this swap in the market.

Putable floaters are purchased by investors who want floating-rate income but do not want the risk associated with a failure in the remarketing of the bonds. Here, the investor accepts a lower rate because of this protection. The corresponding inverse floating investor accepts this risk but requires a higher return from this bond, thus increasing current income. The price of these securities depends on investors' views on the possibility of a failure in the remarketing of the floating-rate bond.

An investor in reversed inverse floating rate bonds wants to receive floating-rate income for a set period of time, such as five years, while locking in long-term interest rates. An investor in this bond might anticipate short-term interest rates increasing during the next few years while falling in the distant future. In addition, they might be attractive to investors who expect interest rates to increase during the next few years but do not want to make a bet on long-term rates, locking in long-term rates today.

Tender option bonds are attractive to investors who wish to receive floating-rate income but want to protect against a significant fall in interest rates. The investor in this bond has purchased the option to own the underlying fixed-rate bond by paying the opt-out fee. The investor tenders the bond when interest rates have fallen, receiving then interest on the underlying fixed rate bond.

Detached calls are generally purchased by investors who want to protect themselves from falling interest rates. The investor exercises the call when interest rates have fallen, receiving a bond at an exercise price that is usually below the market value of the securities. In addition, the investor now receives above-market interest rates. Detached calls can also be purchased to hedge other callable bonds held in a portfolio. This gives an investor the flexibility to purchase bonds that provide the greatest value in the marketplace while protecting the portfolio from declining interest rates. If the investor's bonds are called, the investor has the option of replacing them with bonds with higher-than-market current income by exercising the call.

CHAPTER 16

MUNICIPAL BOND FUTURES CONTRACTS AND THEIR ROLE IN PORTFOLIO MANAGEMENT

Interest rate futures contracts allow portfolio managers to manage the interest rate risk of their portfolio more effectively and, under certain circumstances, to enhance returns. The Treasury bond futures contract has been widely used by managers of taxable bond portfolios in these ways. Because the municipal bond market has unique risks, the Treasury bond futures contract has not been particularly effective in managing the risk of municipal bonds. Proposed and actual changes in tax legislation that affect the value of municipal bonds, and changing economic conditions that might be expected to increase the likelihood of defaults are two examples of factors that affect the municipal market but not the Treasury market. The Chicago Board of Trade's municipal bond futures contract was designed to give participants in the municipal bond market a more effective means of controlling such risks. Also, municipal bond dealers have entered into forward contracts with investors for delivery of *specific* municipal issues. The terms of the forward contract can be customized to meet the needs of the investor.

In this chapter, we discuss the mechanics of futures trading, the pricing of futures contracts, and the various ways futures can be used by portfolio managers. The unique features of the Chicago Board of Trade's municipal bond index futures contract are discussed because of their implications for the pricing of these contracts and implementing strategies using them. We review Treasury bond futures so that we can compare the features of this contract to those of the municipal bond index futures contract; such contracts are also used in connection with the municipal bond index futures contract in some strategies. Because of the illiquidity of the municipal bond forward contract market, we do not discuss it specifically in this chapter but we do compare forward and futures markets. Many of the principles discussed apply to these contracts as well.

MECHANICS OF FUTURES TRADING

A *futures contract* is a firm legal agreement between a buyer (seller) and an established exchange or its clearinghouse in which the buyer (seller) agrees to take (make) delivery of something at a specified price at the end of a designated period of time. The price at which the parties agree to transact in the future is called the *futures price*. The designated date at which the parties must transact is called the *settlement* or *delivery date*. The "something" that a party agrees to buy or sell is called the *underlying*. When the underlying is a fixed-income instrument, the contract is referred to as an interest rate futures contract. Because a futures contract derives its value from the underlying bond or index, it is often referred to as a *derivative instrument*.

Most financial futures contracts traded in the United States have settlement dates in the months of March, June, September, or December. This means that at a predetermined time in the contract settlement month the contract stops trading, and a price is determined by the exchange for settlement of the contract. The contract with the closest settlement date is called the *nearby futures contract*. The next futures contract is the one that settles just after the nearby contract. The contract farthest away in time from settlement is called the *most distant futures contract*.

When an investor takes a position in the market by buying a futures contract, the investor is said to be in a *long position* or to be *long futures*. If, instead, the investor's opening position is the sale of a futures contract, the investor is said to be in a *short position* or *short futures*.

A party to a futures contract has two choices on liquidation of the position. First, the position can be liquidated prior to the settlement date. For this purpose, the party must take an offsetting position in the same contract. For the buyer of a futures contract this means selling the same number of identical futures contracts; for the seller of a futures contract this means buying the same number of identical futures contracts.

The alternative is to wait until the settlement date. At that time the party purchasing a futures contract accepts delivery of the underlying asset at the agreed-upon price; the party who sells a futures contract liquidates the position by delivering the underlying asset at the agreed-upon price. For the municipal bond futures contracts that we shall describe in this chapter, settlement is made in cash only. Such contracts are referred to as *cash settlement contracts*. Typically, parties in the futures market unwind their position prior to the settlement date.

Commissions on futures contracts are fully negotiable. They are usually quoted on the basis of a *round-trip*, meaning a price that includes the cost of opening and closing the futures contract. In most cases, the commission is the same regardless of the maturity date or type of the underlying instrument.

The Role of the Clearinghouse

Associated with every futures exchange is a *clearinghouse*, which performs several functions. One of these functions is guaranteeing that the two parties to the transaction will perform. When an investor takes a position in the futures market, the clearinghouse takes the opposite position and agrees to satisfy the terms set forth in the contract. Because of the clearinghouse, the investor need not worry about the financial strength and integrity of the party taking the opposite side of the contract. After initial execution of an order, the relationship between the two parties ends. The clearinghouse interposes itself as the buyer for every sale and the seller for every purchase. Thus investors are free to liquidate their positions without involving the other party in the original contract and without worrying that the other party may default. This is the reason why we define a futures contract as an agreement between a party and a clearinghouse associated with an exchange.

Besides its guarantee function, the clearinghouse makes it simple for parties to a futures contract to unwind their positions prior to the settlement date.

Margin Requirements

When an opening position is taken in a futures contract, the investor must deposit with its broker a minimum dollar amount per contract as specified by the exchange. This amount is called *initial margin* and is required as deposit for the contract.[1] The initial margin may be in the form of an interest-bearing security such as a Treasury bill. As the price of the futures contract fluctuates, the value of the investor's equity in the position changes. At the end of each trading day, the exchange determines the settlement price for the futures contract. This price is used to mark to market the investor's position so that any gain or loss from the position is reflected in the investor's margin account.

Maintenance margin is the minimum level (specified by the exchange) by which an investor's equity position may fall as a result of an unfavorable price movement before the investor is required to deposit additional margin. The additional margin required is called *variation margin*, and it is an amount necessary to bring the equity in the investor's account back to its initial margin level. Unlike initial margin, variation margin must be satisfied in cash, not in interest-bearing instruments. Any excess margin in the account may be withdrawn by the investor. If a party to a futures contract who is required to deposit variation margin fails to do so within 24 hours, the futures position is closed out by the clearinghouse.

Although there are initial and maintenance margin requirements for buying securities on margin, the concept of margin differs for securities and futures. When securities are acquired on margin, the difference between the price of the security and the initial margin is borrowed from the broker. The security purchased serves as collateral for the loan, and the investor pays interest. For futures contracts, the initial margin, in effect, serves as good faith money, an indication that the investor will satisfy the obligation of the contract. Normally no money is borrowed by the investor.

FUTURES VERSUS FORWARD CONTRACTS

A *forward contract*, just like a futures contract, is an agreement for the future delivery of something at a specified price at the end of a designated period of time. Futures contracts are standardized agreements as to the delivery date (or month) and quality of the deliverable, and are traded on

---

[1] Individual brokerage firms are free to set margin requirements above the minimum established by the exchange.

organized exchanges. A forward contract differs in that it is usually non-standardized (the terms of each contract are negotiated individually between buyer and seller), there is no clearinghouse (the buyer and seller contract directly), and secondary markets are often non-existent or extremely thin. Unlike a futures contract, which is an exchange-traded product, a forward contract is an over-the-counter instrument.

Although both futures and forward contracts set forth terms of delivery, futures contracts are generally not intended to be settled by delivery. In fact, less than 2 percent of outstanding contracts are settled by delivery. Forward contracts, in contrast, are intended for delivery.

Futures contracts are marked to market at the end of each trading day, whereas forward contracts usually are not. Consequently, futures contracts are subject to interim cash flows as additional margin may be required in the case of adverse price movements, or as cash is withdrawn in the case of favorable price movements. There are no interim cash flow effects with a forward contract due to variation margin if the contract is not marked to market.

Finally, the parties in a forward contract are exposed to credit risk because either party may default on the obligation. Credit risk is minimal in the case of futures contracts because the clearinghouse associated with the exchange guarantees the other side of the transaction.

Other than these differences and the nuances of specific contracts, most of what we say about futures contracts applies equally to forward contracts.

RISK AND RETURN CHARACTERISTICS OF FUTURES CONTRACTS

The buyer of a futures contract realizes a profit if the futures price increases; the seller of a futures contract realizes a profit if the futures price decreases.

When a position is taken in a futures contract, the party need not put up the entire amount of the investment. Thus leverage can be achieved. Although the degree of leverage available in the futures market varies from contract to contract, the leverage attainable is considerably greater than in the cash market. At first, the leverage available in the futures market may suggest that the market benefits only those who want to speculate on price movements, but this is not true. Futures markets can be used to reduce price risk. Without the leverage possible in futures transactions, the cost of reducing price risk using futures would be too high for most market participants.

TREASURY BOND FUTURES CONTRACTS

The Treasury bond futures contract is traded on the Chicago Board of Trade (CBT). The underlying instrument for this futures contract is $100,000 par value of a hypothetical 20-year, 8 percent coupon bond. Prices and yields of the Treasury bond futures contract are quoted in terms of this hypothetical Treasury bond, but the seller of the futures contract has the choice of several acceptable Treasury bonds that can be delivered to satisfy the contract. The CBT allows the seller to deliver any Treasury bond that has at least 15 years to maturity from the date of delivery if not callable; in the case of callable bonds, the issue must not be callable for at least 15 years from the first day of the delivery month. To settle the contract, an acceptable bond must be delivered; that is, the contract is not a cash-settlement contract.

The minimum price fluctuation for the Treasury bond futures contract is a 32nd of one percent. The dollar value of a 32nd for a $100,000 par value (the par value for the underlying Treasury bond) is $31.25 ($\frac{1}{32}$ × $1,000). Thus, the minimum price fluctuation is $31.25 for this contract.

The delivery process for the Treasury bond futures contract makes the contract interesting. At the settlement date, the seller of a futures contract (the short) is required to deliver to the buyer (the long) $100,000 par value of an 8 percent, 20-year Treasury bond. Because no such bond exists, the seller must choose from the acceptable deliverable bonds that the exchange has specified. Suppose the seller is entitled to deliver $100,000 of a 6 percent, 20-year Treasury bond to settle the futures contract. The value of this bond of course is less than the value of an 8 percent, 20-year bond; and if the seller delivers the 6 percent, 20-year bond, this would be unfair to the buyer of the futures contract who contracted to receive $100,000 of an 8 percent, 20-year Treasury bond. Alternatively, suppose the seller delivers $100,000 of a 10 percent, 20-year Treasury bond; the value of this Treasury bond is greater than that of an 8 percent, 20-year Treasury bond, so this would be a disadvantage to the seller.

To make delivery equitable to both parties and to tie cash to futures prices, the CBT has introduced *conversion factors* for determining the invoice price of each acceptable deliverable Treasury issue against the Treasury bond futures contract. The conversion factor is determined by the CBT before a contract with a specific settlement date begins trading. The conversion factor is based on the price that a deliverable bond would sell for at the beginning of the delivery month if it were to yield 8 percent. The conversion factor is constant throughout the trading period of the futures contract. The short must notify the CBT of the actual bond that will be delivered one day before the delivery date should the short want to deliver, rather than unwind, his or her position.

The invoice price paid by the buyer of the Treasury bonds delivered by the seller is determined using this formula:

Invoice price = Contract size × Futures contract settlement price × Conversion factor + Accrued interest

Suppose the Treasury bond futures contract settles at 96 (0.96 in decimal form) and that the short elects to deliver a Treasury bond issue with a conversion factor of 1.15. As the contract size is $100,000, the invoice price is

$$\$100,000 \times 0.96 \times 1.15 + \text{Accrued interest}$$
$$= \$110,400 + \text{Accrued interest}$$

In selecting the issue to be delivered, the short selects from all the deliverable issues the one that is cheapest to deliver. This issue is referred to as the *cheapest-to-deliver* or the *most deliverable issue*; it plays a key role in the pricing of this futures contract and in the strategies employing this contract that we discuss later in this chapter. The procedure for determining the cheapest-to-deliver issue is explained later in this chapter. The cheapest-to-deliver issue can change throughout the life of the contract. In interest rate environments in which the Treasury bond yield is around 8 percent, the cheapest-to-deliver is likely to change. In contrast to the Treasury bond futures contract, there is no cheapest-to-deliver issue associated with the municipal bond futures contract, since the contract is settled in cash.

In addition to the option of which acceptable Treasury issue to deliver—sometimes referred to as the *quality* or *swap option*—the short position has two more options granted under CBT delivery guidelines. The short position is permitted to decide when in the delivery month delivery will actually take place. This is called the *timing option*. The other option is the right of the short position to give notice of intent to deliver up to 8:00 PM Chicago time after the closing of the exchange on the date when the futures settlement price has been fixed. This option is referred to as the *wild card option*. The quality option, the timing option, and the wild card option (in sum, referred to as the *delivery options*) mean that the long position can never be sure of which Treasury bond will be delivered or when it will be delivered.

BOND BUYER'S MUNICIPAL BOND INDEX FUTURES CONTRACT

The municipal bond index futures contract is based on the value of the Bond Buyer Index (BBI) which consists of 40 municipal bonds. Unlike the Treasury bond futures contract, where the underlying to be delivered is $100,000 of a hypothetical 8 percent, 20-year Treasury bond, the municipal bond index futures contract does not specify a par amount of the underlying index to be delivered. Instead, the dollar value of a futures contract is equal to the product of the futures price and $1,000. The settlement price on the last day of trading is equal to the product of the Bond Buyer Index value and $1,000. Delivery on all 40 bonds in the index would be difficult, so the contract is a cash settlement contract. This is unlike the Treasury bond futures contract which requires physical delivery of an acceptable Treasury bond issue.

The contract is quoted in 32nds. So a futures price of 102–21 means 102.65625. If the futures price is 102–21, then the dollar value of the futures contract is $102,656.25 ($1,000 × 102.65625). The minimum price change, or tick, is a 32nd, which therefore has a dollar value of $31.25 ($\frac{1}{32}$ × $1,000). As with the Treasury bond futures contract, the settlement months are March, June, September, and December.

The municipal bond index futures contract is nowhere as liquid as the Treasury bond futures contract. For example, on July 22, 1993, the number of municipal bond index futures contracts traded was 5,860 while the estimated number of Treasury bond futures contracts traded was 455,983. *Open interest* is another gauge of the liquidity of the market. It measures the number of contracts still outstanding. On July 22, 1993, open interest for the municipal bond index futures contract and the Treasury bond futures contract was 23,396 and 465,983, respectively.

In order to understand this futures contract, it is necessary to understand the nuances of how the BBI is constructed.

The BBI

The BBI consists of 40 actively traded general obligation and revenue bonds. To be included in the BBI, the following criteria must be satisfied.

1. The rating of the issue must have a Moody's rating of A or higher and/or an S&P rating of A − or higher.
2. The size of the term portion of the issue must be at least $50 million ($75 million for housing issues).

No more than two bonds of the same issuer may be included in the BBI. In addition, for an issue to be considered it must meet the following three conditions.

1. Have at least 19 years remaining to maturity.
2. Have a first call date between 7 and 16 years.
3. Have at least one call at par prior to redemption.

Exhibit 16–1 shows the 40 bonds in the BBI as of July 23, 1993.

The Bond Buyer serves as the index manager for the contract and prices each issue in the index based on prices received daily from at least four of six dealer-to-dealer brokers. In July 1993, these brokers were Cantor, Fitzgerald Municipal Brokers Inc.; Chapdelaine & Co.; J. F. Hartfield & Co.; J. J. Kenny Inc.; Municipal Partners Inc.; and Titus & Donnelly Inc. After dropping the highest price and the lowest price obtained for each issue, the average of the remaining prices is computed. The average price for each of the 40 issues in the BBI as of July 23, 1993 is shown in Exhibit 16–1 in the column labeled "Dollar Price."

This price is then used to calculate the BBI as follows. First, the price for an issue is multiplied by a conversion factor designed to equate the bond to an 8 percent issue, just as in the case of the Treasury bond futures contract. This gives a converted price for each bond in the BBI. That is, for each bond in the BBI the following is calculated.

$$\text{Converted price of an issue} = \frac{\text{Price of issue}}{\text{Conversion factor of issue}}$$

EXHIBIT 16–1

Municipal Bond Index (as of Friday July 23, 1993)

	Friday, July 23, 1993	Due Date	Par Call Date	Dollar Price	Conversion Factor	Converted Price
1	Puerto Rico 6s	7/1/14	7/1/04	101.5313	0.8493	119.5470
2	NY Local Govt Asst 6¹/₄	4/1/18	4/1/04	103.1875	0.8716	118.3886
3	Phoenix Civic Imprv Ariz 6¹/₈	7/1/23	7/1/05	101.2813	0.8551	118.4437
4	No Calif Transmission 5¹/₄	5/1/20	5/1/05	94.2290	0.7904	119.2169
5	Intermountain Power 5¹/₂	7/1/20	7/1/05	95.4063	0.8069	118.2380
6	Jacksonville Elec Auth 5¹/₂	10/1/13	10/1/03	97.3750	0.8246	118.0876
7	Wisconsin Public Power 5¹/₄	7/1/21	7/1/05	92.2500	0.7876	117.1280
8	Michigan Public Power 5¹/₂	1/1/13	1/1/05	97.0625	0.8117	119.5793
9	Adams Co Colo PCR 5⁷/₈	4/1/14	4/1/04	101.2500	0.8485	119.3282
10	NYS Energy Research Dev 6s	3/15/28	3/15/05	100.9375	0.8493	118.8479
11	LA Co Metro Transp Auth 5⁵/₈	7/1/18	7/1/05	98.3438	0.8189	120.0925
12	Oconee Co SC PCR 5.80	4/1/14	4/1/05	99.7188	0.8305	120.0707
13	South Carolina PSA 5¹/₂	7/1/21	7/1/05	95.7813	0.8094	118.3361
14	Chicago telephone GOs 5⁵/₈	1/1/23	1/1/05	96.6875	0.8236	117.3962
15	Kansas Dept Transp 5³/₈	3/1/13	3/1/05	97.4688	0.8050	121.0792
16	Calif Health Facil 5.60	5/1/33	5/1/05	96.7188	0.8211	117.7917
17	Chicago O'Hare 5.60	1/1/18	1/1/05	96.0313	0.8236	116.5994
18	Farmington NM PCR 5⁷/₈	6/1/23	6/1/05	100.3125	0.8399	119.4339
19	Massachusetts g.o. 5¹/₂	11/1/12	11/1/05	97.6875	0.8069	121.0652
20	Washington Pub Power 5.70	7/1/17	7/1/05	97.5625	0.8285	117.7580
21	Boston Mass 5³/₄	2/15/23	8/15/02	97.7813	0.8576	114.0173
22	Calif Comm Development 5¹/₂	10/1/14	10/1/05	97.3087	0.8069	120.5958
23	Illinois Educ Facs 5.70	12/1/25	12/1/05	97.0625	0.8262	117.4806
24	NYC Health & Hosp Corp 5³/₄	2/15/22	2/15/05	100.0625	0.8329	120.1375
25	Omaha Pub Power Dist Neb 5¹/₂	2/1/17	2/1/05	97.0313	0.8143	119.1591
26	Pennsylvania Higher Educ 6.05	1/1/19	7/1/05	100.5000	0.8475	118.5841
27	Orlando-Orange Co Exp 5¹/₂	7/1/18	7/1/05	96.8125	0.8094	119.6102
28	Orlando-Orange Co Exp 5.95	7/1/23	7/1/03	99.5000	0.8641	115.1487
29	Puerto Rico Pub Bldg 5³/₄	7/1/15	7/1/05	99.2500	0.8285	119.7948
30	Puerto Rico Pub Bldg 5¹/₂	7/1/21	7/1/05	95.8750	0.8094	118.4519
31	Calif Comm Development 5¹/₂	7/1/23	7/1/05	96.1563	0.8094	118.7994
32	Los Angeles Cal wastewtr 5.70	6/1/23	6/1/05	98.9888	0.8305	119.1918
33	Los Angeles Cal wastewtr 5.60	6/1/20	6/1/05	98.0938	0.8211	119.4663
34	Mass Bay Transp 5¹/₂	3/1/22	3/1/05	96.1250	0.8143	118.0462
35	Ohio Muni Electric 5³/₈	2/15/24	2/15/05	95.8438	0.8050	119.0606
36	Puerto Rico 5¹/₂	7/1/13	7/1/05	96.9688	0.8094	119.8032
37	Florida Bd of Educ 5¹/₂	6/1/23	6/1/04	96.7500	0.8218	117.7294
38	Florida Bd of Educ 5.40	6/1/18	6/1/04	96.1250	0.8129	118.2495
39	NY Local Govt Asst 5¹/₂	4/1/18	4/1/05	94.9375	0.8143	116.5879
40	NYS Energy Research 5 60	6/1/25	7/14/07	98.8438	0.8039	122.9553

The Bond Buyer 40	Yesterday	Prev. Day	Week Ago
Average Dollar Price	97.77	97.99	99.38
Yield to Par Call	5.91	5.88	5.71
Yield to Maturity	5.81	5.79	5.69

The Municipal Bond Index presented today employs the coefficient derived from the July 15 pricing, when it was set at 0.8536. The average price represents the simple average of the prices of the 40 bonds. The yield to par call is computed from the average price, the average coupon(5.64%) and the average first call date at par (February 24, 2005). The yield to maturity is computed from the average price, the average coupon, and the average maturity date (December 3, 2019).

Additional information concerning the construction and maintenance of the Municipal Bond Index may be obtained from the Economic Analysis and Planning Section of the Chicago Board of Trade, (312) 347-3889. The average price and yield series as revised on March 11, 1986, are available from July 2, 1984, from The Bond Buyer at (212) 943-8543.

For example, on July 23, 1993, the Jacksonville Electric Authority $5\frac{1}{2}$ due 10/1/13 had a price of 97.3750. Since the conversion factor was 0.8246, the converted price for this issue was 97.3750/0.8246, or 118.0876, which is shown in the last column of Exhibit 16–1.

The converted prices for the bonds in the index are then summed and divided by 40, giving an average converted price for the BBI.

$$\text{Avg. converted price for BBI} =$$
$$\frac{(\text{Converted price of issue 1} + \ldots + \text{Converted price of issue 40})}{40}$$

Finally, because the BBI is revised bimonthly when newer issues are added and older issues or issues that no longer meet the criteria for inclusion in the index are dropped, a smoothing coefficient is calculated on the index revision date so that the value of the BBI does not change due merely to the change in its composition. The average converted price for the BBI is multiplied by this coefficient to get the value of the BBI for a particular date.

$$\text{BBI} = \text{Average converted price} \times \text{Coefficient}$$

The coefficient is calculated as follows.

$$\text{Coefficient} = \frac{\text{BBI value before issues are substituted}}{\text{BBI value with new issues before applying coefficient}}$$

For example, if the BBI value is 89 and several issues are substituted that would increase the BBI value to 100 before applying the coefficient adjustment mechanism, then the new coefficient would be

$$\text{Coefficient} = \frac{89}{100} = 0.890$$

As indicated in the text at the bottom of Exhibit 16–1, the coefficient used in calculating the value of the BBI on July 23, 1993 was 0.8536.

Let's look at what happens to the coefficient and the duration of the BBI index when municipal yields change. Consider first the situation when yields decline. Two things occur. First, issues trading at par are substituted for issues trading at a premium. Without the coefficient adjustment mechanism, the value of the BBI falls. To keep the BBI at the same value before the substitution, the coefficient must be greater than one. Second, the new issues to be included in the index have a lower coupon rate than those in the current index. Although the coefficient adjustment mechanism corrects for the price effect, the index now has a lower average coupon rate, and, as a result, the duration of the index increases.

In a rising yield environment, the opposite occurs when new issues are substituted. That is, issues trading at par are substituted for issues trading at a discount, resulting in a coefficient less than one. Higher coupon rate issues are substituted for lower coupon rate issues resulting in a lower duration for the index.

The Bond Buyer calculates the yield to par call and the yield to maturity for the index. The yield to par call is calculated by using the average of the dollar prices for the 40 bonds, the average coupon, and the average par call date. On July 23, 1993, these values were 97.77, 5.64 percent, and February 24, 2005, respectively, resulting in a yield to par call of 5.91 percent. The yield to maturity is calculated using the average price, average coupon, and average maturity. As the average maturity was December 3, 2019 for the BBI on July 23, 1993, the yield to maturity was 5.81 percent.

But what does the average yield to par call or maturity of the BBI mean? Not much. In general, for *any* bond index an average yield calculation does not mean much. This is why there are times when the average price for a bond index is below par while the average coupon is above the calculated average yield. This would not make sense for an individual bond because a bond trading at discount has a coupon rate less than the yield. The problem is further complicated for the BBI because of the coefficient adjustment mechanism. The value of the BBI is not the average price of the 40 bonds, even though the average price is used in the yield calculations. Similarly, it is incorrect to interpret the BBI as the average price of an 8 percent coupon municipal bond. We discuss this further later in this chapter.

PRICING OF THE MUNICIPAL BOND INDEX FUTURES CONTRACTS

One of the primary concerns that most portfolio managers have when taking a position in futures contracts is whether the futures price at which they transact is a "fair" price. Buyers are concerned that the price may be too high, and that they will be picked off by more experienced futures traders waiting to profit from the mistakes of the uninitiated. Sellers worry that the price is artificially low, and that savvy traders may have manipulated the markets so that they can buy at bargain basement prices. Furthermore, prospective participants frequently find no rational explanation for the sometimes violent ups and downs that occur in the futures markets. Theories about efficient markets give little comfort to anyone who knows of or has experienced the sudden losses that can occur in the highly leveraged futures markets.

Fortunately, the futures markets are not as irrational as they may at first seem; if they were, they would not have become so successful. The Treasury bond futures market is not a perfectly efficient market, but it probably comes about as close as any market. In contrast, because of the nuances we have discussed in this chapter for the municipal bond futures contract, the lack of liquidity, and the valuation difficulties we shall discuss, the market is not highly efficient. Fortunately, for both the Treasury and municipal bond futures contracts, there are very clear reasons why futures prices are what they are and methods by which traders, investors, and borrowers may be capable of quickly eliminating any discrepancy between futures prices and their fair levels.

Basic Principles of Valuing Futures

There are several different ways to price futures contracts. Fortunately, all lead to the same fair price for a given contract. Each approach relies on the "Law of One Price." This law states that a given financial asset must have the same price regardless of the means by which it is created. We explain here one way in which futures contracts can be combined with cash market instruments to create cash flows that are identical to other cash securities.[2] The Law of One Price implies that the synthetically created cash securities must have the same price as the actual cash securities. Similarly, cash instruments can be combined to create cash flows that are identical to futures contracts. By the Law of One Price the futures contract must have the same price as the synthetic futures created from cash instruments.

To understand how futures contracts should be priced, consider the following example. Suppose that a 20-year, par value (100) bond with a coupon rate of 8 percent is selling at par. Also suppose that this bond is the deliverable for a futures contract that settles in three months. If the current

---

[2]For the other ways to price futures contracts, see Chapter 5 in Mark Pitts and Frank J. Fabozzi, *Interest Rate Futures and Options* (Chicago: Probus Publishing, 1990).

three-month interest rate at which funds can be loaned or borrowed is 4 percent per year, what should be the price of this futures contract?

Suppose the price of the futures contract is 107. Consider the following strategy.

Sell the futures contract at 107.

Purchase the bond for 100.

Borrow 100 for three months at 4 percent per year.

The borrowed funds are used to purchase the bond, resulting in no initial cash outlay for this strategy. Three months from now the bond must be delivered to settle the futures contract, and the loan must be repaid. These trades produce the following cash flows:

From settlement of the futures contract

Flat price of bond (on settlement date)	107
Accrued interest (8% for 3 months)	2
Total proceeds	109

From the loan

Repayment of principal of loan	100
Interest on loan (4% for 3 months)	1
Total outlay	101
Profit	8

This strategy guarantees a profit of 8. Moreover, the profit is generated with no initial outlay because the funds used to purchase the bond are borrowed. The profit is realized regardless of the futures price at the settlement date. Obviously, in a well-functioning market, arbitragers would buy the bond and sell the futures, forcing the futures price down and bidding up the bond price so as to eliminate this profit.

In contrast, suppose that the futures price is 92 instead of 107. Consider the following strategy.

Buy the futures contract at 92.

Sell (short) the bond for 100.

Invest (lend) 100 for three months at 4% per year.

Once again, there is no initial cash outlay. Three months from now a bond is purchased to settle the long position in the futures contract. That bond is then used to cover the short position (i.e., to cover the short sale in the cash market). The outcome in three months would be as follows.

From settlement of the futures contract

Flat price of bond (at settlement date)	92
Accrued interest (8% for 3 months)	2
Total outlay	94

From the loan

Principal received from maturing loan	100
Interest earned on investment (4% for 3 months)	1
Total proceeds	101
Profit	7

The profit of 7 is a pure arbitrage profit. It requires no initial cash outlay and is realized regardless of the futures price at the settlement date.

There is a futures price that eliminates the arbitrage profit, however. No arbitrage occurs if the futures price is 99. Using the two previous strategies it can be shown that if the futures price is 99, the profit from either strategy results in a profit of zero. This is the expected outcome for an investment with no initial cash outlay.

Theoretical Futures Price Based on Arbitrage Model

Considering the arbitrage arguments just presented, the fair or theoretical futures price can be determined on the basis of the following information.

1. The price of the bond in the cash market.
2. The coupon rate on the bond.
3. The interest rate for borrowing and lending until the settlement date.

The borrowing and lending rate is referred to as the *financing rate*.

To develop the theoretical futures price, we use the following notation.

r = Financing rate (percent)
c = Current yield, or coupon rate divided by the cash market price
P = Cash market price

$F =$ Futures price

$t =$ Time, in years, to the futures delivery date

Now consider the following strategy that is initiated on a coupon date.

Sell the futures contract at F.

Purchase the bond for P.

Borrow P until the settlement date at r.

The outcome at the settlement date is

From settlement of the futures contract

Flat price of bond	F
Accrued interest	ctP
Total proceeds	$F + ctP$

From the loan

Repayment of principal of loan	P
Interest on loan	rtP
Total outlay	$P + rtP$

The profit will equal

$$\text{Profit} = \text{Total proceeds} - \text{Total outlay}$$
$$\text{Profit} = F + ctP - (P + rtP)$$

In equilibrium the theoretical futures price occurs where the profit from this trade is zero. Thus to have equilibrium, the following must hold.

$$0 = F + ctP - (P + rtP)$$

Solving for the theoretical futures price, we have

$$F = P + Pt(r - c)$$

Alternatively, consider the following strategy

Buy the futures contract at F.

Sell (short) the bond for P.

Invest (lend) P at r until the settlement date.

The outcome at the settlement date leads to the same equation for the theoretical futures price given above. If we apply this equation to our earlier example, we have

$$r = 0.04 \quad c = 0.08 \quad P = 100 \quad t = 0.25$$

Then the theoretical futures price is

$$F = 100 + 100 \times 0.25 (0.04 - 0.08) = 100 - 1 = 99$$

This agrees with the equilibrium futures price we stated earlier.

The theoretical futures price may be at a premium to the cash market price (higher than the cash market price) or at a discount from the cash market price (lower than the cash market price), depending on $(r - c)$. The term $r - c$ is called the *net financing cost* because it adjusts the financing rate for the coupon interest earned. The net financing cost is more commonly called *the cost of carry,* or simply *carry,* because it refers to the cost of carrying the position. *Positive carry* means that the current yield earned is greater than the financing cost (thus, $r - c$ is negative); *negative carry* means that the financing cost exceeds the current yield.

In the case of Treasury futures, carry (the relationship between the short-term financing rate and the current yield on the bond) depends on the shape of the yield curve. When the yield curve is upward sloping, the short-term financing rate generally is less than the current yield on the bond, resulting in positive carry. The futures price is then at a discount to the cash price for the bond. The opposite holds true when the yield curve is inverted. In the case of municipal futures, carry is typically negative since the tax-exempt yield is less than the nondeductible financing rate.

A Closer Look at the Theoretical Futures Price

To derive the theoretical futures price using the arbitrage argument, we made several assumptions that have certain implications for the municipal bond futures contract and the Treasury bond futures contract. Later we present a model for the pricing of municipal bond futures contracts that relaxes these assumptions.

Interim Cash Flows

No interim cash flows due to variation margin or coupon interest payments were assumed in the model. However, we know that interim cash flows can occur for both of these reasons. Because we assumed no variation margin, the price derived is technically the theoretical price for a forward contract, which is not subject to daily marking to market. If interest rates rise, the short position in futures receives margin as the futures price decreases; the margin can then be reinvested at a higher interest rate. In contrast, if interest rates fall, there is variation margin that must be financed by the short position; however, because interest rates have declined, financing is possible at a lower cost. When interest rates fall, the long position in futures increases in value. However, excess margin can only be invested at lower rates. When rates rise, the long position in futures loses money, and additional variation margin can only be financed at higher rates. The interim cash flows associated with futures contracts and the fact that they are not required with forward contracts account for the difference between futures and forward prices.

Incorporating interim coupon payments into the pricing model is not difficult. However, the value of the cash flow from the coupon payments at the settlement date depends on the interest rate at which they can be reinvested. The shorter the maturity of the futures contract and the lower the coupon rate, the less important the reinvestment income is in determining the futures price.

The Short-Term Interest Rate (Financing Rate)

In deriving the theoretical futures price we assume that the borrowing and lending rates are equal. Typically, however, the borrowing rate is higher than the lending rate. Because of this, there is not one theoretical futures price but an upper and lower boundary in which the actual futures price may fall without permitting arbitrage profits.

Letting r_B and r_L denote the borrowing rate and lending rate, the upper and lower boundaries are as follows.

$$F(\text{upper boundary}) = P + P\,t\,(r_B - c)$$
$$F(\text{lower boundary}) = P + P\,t\,(r_L - c)$$

For example, assume that the borrowing rate is 6 percent per year, while the lending rate is 5.6 percent per year. Then

$$F\,(\text{upper boundary}) = 100 + 100 \times 0.25 \times (0.060 - 0.08) = 99.50$$
$$F\,(\text{lower boundary}) = 100 + 100 \times 0.25 \times (0.056 - 0.08) = 99.4$$

The appropriate rate for financing (borrowing) and lending is the repo rate.

Transaction Costs

In calculating the theoretical futures price or its boundaries, we assume no transaction costs are involved in taking the necessary position to capture an arbitrage profit due to mispricing. In actuality, the transaction costs of entering into and closing the cash position as well as the round-trip transaction costs for the futures contract must be considered and do affect the boundaries for the futures contract. In the case of the municipal bond index futures contract, there are significant costs (in terms of the bid-ask spread) associated with buying and selling the underlying municipal bonds. In addition, as the BBI is revised additional transaction costs are incurred to rebalance the replicating portfolio.

Deliverable Bond Is Known

In the pricing model based on arbitrage arguments, we assume that only one instrument is deliverable. But the Treasury bond futures contract is designed to allow the short the choice of delivering one of a number of deliverable issues (the quality or swap option). Because more than one may be deliverable, market participants track the price of each deliverable bond and determine which bond is the cheapest to deliver. The futures price then trades in relation to the cheapest-to-deliver bond. There is the risk that while an issue may be the cheapest to deliver at the time a position in the futures contract is taken, it may not be the cheapest to deliver after that time. A change in the cheapest-to-deliver can dramatically alter the futures price.

What are the implications of the quality (swap) option for the futures price? Because the swap option is an option granted by the long to the short, the long wants to pay less for the futures contract. Therefore, the theoretical futures price after adjusting for the quality option granted to the short should be less than the theoretical futures price given above.

Deliverable Is an Individual Bond

The municipal bond index futures contract is a cash settlement contract based on a basket of securities. The difficulty in arbitraging this futures contract is that it is too expensive to buy or sell every issue included in the index. Instead, a portfolio containing a smaller number of bonds may be constructed to "track" the index. The arbitrage, however, is no longer risk-free because there is tracking-error risk.

Delivery Date Is Known

In the pricing model based on arbitrage arguments, we assume a known delivery date. For the Treasury bond futures contract, the short has a timing option, so the long does not know when the securities will be delivered. The effect of the timing option on the theoretical futures price is the same as with the quality option. These delivery options should result in a theoretical futures price that is lower than the one suggested above.

Tax Factors

The model completely ignores tax factors. Tax complications arise in the arbitrage in several ways. First, consider an investor who finds the municipal bond index futures contract is expensive relative to the cash market. To capitalize on this, the investor would sell the futures contract and buy the underlying bonds. The interest earned by carrying the municipal bonds would be interest free. However, the investor must finance the long position in the municipal bonds by borrowing funds. But, under the current tax law, investors are not entitled to deduct the interest paid to carry a position in municipal bonds. Thus, the interest received is not taxed, but the interest paid is not tax deductible. The model must be modified to take this into account.

In addition, for all futures contracts the tax treatment of the capital gain from a futures contract is different from that of the treatment of the capital gain for a cash market security.

The Theoretical Price for the Municipal Bond Index Futures Contract

By relaxing the assumptions above, a better model for determining the theoretical price of the municipal bond index futures contract can be derived that takes into account the day count conventions, tax consequences (for interest income and futures capital gains or losses), and uses as the financing rate the repo rate. The model, which relies on the same arbitrage principles discussed earlier, is

$$F = \text{BBI} + \text{BBI}\left[\frac{\text{Repo}\,(n/360)\,(1 - d\,T_0) - c\,(n/365)}{1 - T_G}\right]$$

where

  BBI = Value of the Bond Buyer Index
  Repo = The repo or short-term financing rate
  n = Number of days from settlement to the last trading day of the contract
  d = Tax deductible portion of borrowings used to carry municipal bonds in the cash market

T_0 = Marginal tax rate on ordinary income
T_G = Capital gains tax rate applicable futures contracts
c = Cash yield on the BBI

As in our simpler model, there are boundaries for the theoretical futures price. The upper and lower boundaries are determined by the financing and lending rates in the repo market and transaction costs. In addition, the boundaries are affected by the tax rates in our pricing formula and the tax deductible portion for borrowing.

Implied Repo Rate

Often a measure other than price is used to assess the relative value of futures contracts. The implied repo rate is used. The *implied repo rate* is the rate assumed to be the financing rate in the futures price equation that causes the cash plus carry to equate to the observed price of the futures contract. This can also be shown to be the implied rate of return on the synthetic short-term investment from purchasing the underlying cash instrument, selling it in the futures market, and financing the position. If the implied repo rate is above the cost of financing the position, then the investor should buy the cash market security and sell the futures contract. This is referred to as a *cash and carry trade*. If however, the implied repo rate is below the financing rate it would be unprofitable to take on this trade. In equilibrium, the return on the short-term synthetic investment should equal the short-term financing rate.

APPLICATIONS TO PORTFOLIO MANAGEMENT

This section describes various ways in which a portfolio manager can utilize the municipal bond index futures contracts.

Speculating on the Movement of Interest Rates

The price of a futures contract moves in the opposite direction from interest rates: when rates rise (fall), the futures price falls (rises). An investor who wants to speculate that interest rates will rise (fall) can sell (buy) interest rate futures. Before municipal bond futures were available, investors who wanted to speculate on interest rates in the municipal bond market did so by taking an appropriate position in municipal bonds: selling municipal bonds if interest rates were expected to rise, and buying them if interest rates were expected to fall.

Using the municipal bond index futures market instead of the cash markets (trading municipal bonds themselves) has four advantages. First, transactions costs are lower for futures compared to cash markets. Second, margin requirements are lower for futures than for municipal securities; using futures thus permits greater leverage. Third, unlike the cash market for municipal bonds, selling short in the futures market is easy. Finally, using municipal bond futures to create a leveraged position avoids the differential tax treatment of interest earned and the cost of financing.

Controlling the Interest Rate Risk of a Portfolio

Making speculation easier for investors is not the function of futures markets. Their key function is to provide an efficient vehicle for controlling risk. In the case of interest rate futures, they can be used to alter the interest rate sensitivity of a portfolio. Portfolio managers with strong expectations about the direction of the future course of interest rates adjust the durations of their portfolios so as to capitalize on their expectations. Specifically, if a manager expects rates to increase, the duration will be shortened; if interest rates are expected to decrease, the duration will be lengthened. Portfolio managers can alter the durations of their portfolios with cash market instruments, but a quick and relatively inexpensive means for doing so (on either a temporary or permanent basis) is to use futures contracts.

Hedging

Hedging is a special case of controlling interest rate risk wherein the portfolio manager seeks to construct a portfolio with a duration of zero. Hedging with futures calls for taking a futures position as a temporary substitute for transactions to be made in the cash market at a later date. If cash and futures prices move together, any loss realized by the hedger from one position (whether cash or futures) is offset by a profit on the other position.

In practice, hedging is not that simple, particularly for municipal bond portfolios. The amount of net profit is not necessarily as anticipated.

The outcome of a hedge depends on the relationship between the cash price and the futures price both when a hedge is placed and when it is lifted. The difference between the cash price and the futures price is called the *basis*. The risk that the basis may change in an unpredictable way is called *basis risk*.

In most hedging applications, the bond to be hedged is not identical to the bond underlying the futures contract. This kind of hedging is referred to as *cross hedging*. There may be substantial basis risk in cross hedging, particularly when hedging a municipal bond portfolio with municipal bond futures contracts. An unhedged position is exposed to *price risk*, the risk that the cash market price will move adversely. A hedged position substitutes basis risk for price risk.

A *short* (or *sell*) *hedge* is used to protect against a decline in the cash price of a bond. To execute a short hedge, futures contracts are sold. By establishing a short hedge, the hedger has fixed the future cash price and transferred the price risk of ownership to the buyer of the futures contract. To understand why a short hedge might be executed, suppose that the manager of a property and casualty insurance company portfolio knows that some municipal bonds must be liquidated in two months to make a $5 million payment. If interest rates rise during the two month period, more municipal bonds must be liquidated to realize $5 million. To guard against this possibility, the manager can sell municipal bonds in the futures market to lock in a selling price.

A *long* (or *buy*) *hedge* is undertaken to protect against an increase in the cash price of a bond. In a long hedge, the hedger buys a futures contract to lock in a purchase price. A manager of a municipal bond fund might use a long hedge when substantial cash inflows are expected and the manager is concerned that municipal interest rates will fall. Also, a money manager who knows that municipal bonds are maturing in the near future and expects that municipal interest rates will fall can employ a long hedge to lock in a rate for the proceeds to be reinvested.

Conceptually, cross hedging with the municipal bond futures contract is somewhat more complicated than hedging deliverable securities because it involves two relationships. First, there is the relationship between the cash market BBI value underlying the contract and the futures contract. Second, there is the relationship between the portfolio of municipal bonds to be hedged and the cash market BBI.

The key to minimizing risk in a cross hedge is to choose the right *hedge ratio*. The hedge ratio depends on volatility weighting, or weighting by relative changes in value. The purpose of a hedge is to use gains or losses from the municipal bond futures position to offset any difference between the target value and the actual value of the municipal bond portfolio. Accordingly, the hedge ratio is chosen with the intention of matching the *dollar* price volatility (that is, the dollar change) of the municipal bond futures contract to the *dollar* price volatility of the municipal bond portfolio. Consequently, the hedge ratio is given by

$$\text{Hedge ratio} = \frac{\text{Volatility of the municipal bond portfolio}}{\text{Volatility of municipal bond futures}}$$

Although it might be fairly clear why volatility is the key variable in determining the hedge ratio, "volatility" has many definitions. For hedging purposes, however, we are concerned with volatility in absolute dollar terms. To calculate the dollar volatility of a municipal bond portfolio, one must know the precise point in time that volatility is to be calculated (because volatility generally declines as bonds season), as well as the price or yield at which to calculate volatility (because higher yields generally reduce dollar volatility for a given yield change). The relevant point in the life of each municipal bond in the portfolio for calculating volatility is the point at which the hedge will be lifted. Volatility at any other point is essentially irrelevant because the goal is to lock in a price or yield only on that particular day. Similarly, the relevant yield at which to calculate volatility initially is the target yield. Consequently, one measure of volatility of the municipal bond portfolio is the dollar duration of all the municipal bonds on the date the hedge is to be lifted, calculated at their current implied forward rate.[3] The dollar duration is the product of the price of the bond and its effective duration.

The relative price volatilities of the municipal bonds to be hedged and the BBI can be obtained from the assumed sale date and target prices. However, in the formula for the hedge ratio we need the volatility not of the BBI but of the municipal bond index futures contract. Fortunately, knowing the volatility of the municipal bond portfolio to be hedged relative to the BBI and the volatility of the BBI relative to the municipal bond futures contract, the relative volatilities that define the hedge ratio can be easily obtained as follows.

---

[3] See Chapter 8 for an explanation of the implied forward rate.

$$\text{Hedge ratio} = \frac{\text{Volatility of the municipal bond portfolio}}{\text{Volatility of municipal bond futures}}$$

$$= \frac{\text{Volatility of the municipal bond portfolio}}{\text{Volatility of BBI}} \times$$

$$\frac{\text{Volatility of BBI}}{\text{Volatility of municipal bond futures}}$$

The volatility of all of the values in the above ratios are found by calculating the dollar price change for a small change in yields (assuming a parallel shift in the yield curve). Because volatility changes as yield levels change, it is necessary to rebalance the hedged portfolio. Rebalancing must also occur because of the biweekly changing of the composition of the BBI. In addition, often the hedge is adjusted by a factor, called *beta*, that measures the relative yields of long-term Treasuries and long-term municipal bonds.

Creating Synthetic Securities for Yield Enhancement

A cash market security can be created synthetically by using a position in the futures contract together with the deliverable instrument. The yield on the synthetic security should be the same as the yield on the cash market security. Any difference between the two yields can be exploited so as to enhance the yield on the portfolio.

To see how, consider an investor who owns a 20-year Treasury bond and sells Treasury futures that call for the delivery of that particular bond three months from now. The maturity of the Treasury bond is 20 years, so the investor has effectively shortened the maturity of the bond to three months.

Consequently, the long position in the 20-year bond and the short futures position are equivalent to a long position in a three-month riskless security. The position is riskless because the investor is locking in the price to be received three months from now—the futures price. By being long the bond and short the futures, the investor has synthetically created a three-month Treasury bill. The return the investor should expect to earn from this synthetic position should be the yield on a three-month Treasury bill. If the yield on the synthetic three-month Treasury bill is greater than the yield on the cash market Treasury bill, the investor can realize an enhanced yield by creating the synthetic short-term security.

The fundamental relationship for creating synthetic securities is

$$RSP = CBP - FBP$$

where

RSP = Riskless short-term security position

CBP = Cash bond position

FBP = Bond futures position

A negative sign before a position means a short position. In terms of our previous example, CBP is the long cash bond position; the negative sign before FBP refers to the short futures position. RSP is the riskless synthetic three-month security or Treasury bill.

The above equation states that an investor who is long the cash market security and short the futures contract should expect to earn the rate of return on a risk-free security with the same maturity as the futures delivery date.

Solving the above equation for the long bond position, we have

$$CBP = RSP + FBP$$

This equation states that a cash bond position equals a short-term riskless security position plus a long bond futures position. Thus, a cash market bond can be created synthetically by buying a futures contract and investing in a Treasury bill.

Solving the above equation for the bond futures position, we get

$$FBP = CBP - RSP$$

This equation tells us that a long position in the futures contract can be created synthetically by taking a long position in the cash market bond and shorting the short-term riskless security. But shorting the short-term riskless security is equivalent to borrowing money. Notice that this equation was what we used in deriving the theoretical futures price when the futures contract was underpriced. Recall that when the futures price was 107, the strategy to realize the arbitrage profit was to sell the futures contract and create a synthetic long futures position by buying the bond with borrowed funds. This is precisely what this equation states. In this case, instead of creating a synthetic cash market instrument as we did with the two previous equations, we have created a synthetic futures contract. The fact that the synthetic long futures position is cheaper than the actual long futures position provides an arbitrage opportunity. If we reverse the sign of both sides of the previous equation, we can see how a short futures position can be created synthetically.

In an efficient market the opportunities for yield enhancement should not exist very long. In the case of the municipal bond index futures contract, the mispricing of the contract because of the factors that go into its pricing does provide the opportunity for yield enhancement. However, care must be exerted by a portfolio manager when implementing strategies seeking to exploit any perceived mispricing because of the complications introduced by the changing composition of the BBI and the coefficient adjustment mechanism.

Trading the MOB Spread

Investors who have expectations about the relative price movement of Treasury securities versus municipal securities over some investment horizon can position themselves in the cash market accordingly. This would involve a position in a basket of Treasury securities and a basket of high-grade municipal bonds.

Instead of using the cash market to capitalize on expectations of price movements in the two market sectors, positions in the Treasury bond futures and municipal bond index futures contracts can be taken. This type of trade is referred to as a *municipals over bond* (MOB) *spread trade*. If an investor expects the price of municipals to outperform that of Treasuries, an investor buys (goes long) the municipal bond index futures contract and simultaneously shorts an appropriate number of Treasury bond futures contracts. If, instead, an investor expects that Treasuries will outperform municipals, an investor sells (goes short) the municipal bond index futures contract and buys an appropriate number of Treasury bond futures contracts. The ratio of Treasury to municipal futures contracts is not one to one; rather, the inverse of the coefficient is used to adjust the number of municipal contracts for each Treasury contract. For example, if the coefficient of the index was 0.90, then 1.11 (1/0.90) municipal contracts should be purchased for each Treasury contract sold in the case of an investor going long the MOB.

The concern in executing a MOB spread trade is that using yields on the two contracts to measure the yield spread is misleading. In the case of the Treasury bond futures contract, the yield on the futures contract, and therefore its price movement, follows the yield on the cheapest-to-deliver Treasury bond. The yield on the municipal bond index futures contract is not meaningful as explained earlier. Moreover, the bias caused by the coefficient adjustment must be factored into the analysis.

When trading the MOB, it is important to keep in mind some particularities of the municipal bond futures contract. The same principles discussed beforehand apply. However, adjustments are required to take into account inherent biases in the contract. First, the contract is not a direct and unbiased reflection of the yields in the municipal market. This is especially important in trading the MOB. Here, although the Treasury futures contract reflects current Treasury yields, the municipal bond futures contract is not a direct reflection of yields in the municipal market. Instead it reflects average yields of municipal markets adjusted by the coefficient of the index. For example, if the coefficient is less than one, then the index will underestimate changes in municipal bond yields. If the coefficient is greater than one, the index will overestimate changes in municipal bond yields. Thus if municipal bond yields move in exact proportion to Treasury bond yields, the MOB spread will increase or decrease depending on the coefficient of the index.

If yields on municipal bonds decrease, the bonds in the index may begin to sell at premiums to their face value. Thus the municipal index coupon rates are greater than current market interest rates in the municipal market during this period. On an index revision date, new bonds selling near par, are used to replace premium bonds in the index; this causes the coefficient to be greater than one. The opposite occurs if yields in the municipal market increase. Because of this, a negative MOB spread does not necessarily imply that the yield on current coupon municipal bonds is less than the yield on comparable Treasuries.

In addition, because most municipal bonds are callable and most Treasuries are not callable, the spread between the municipal index and Treasuries is expected to fall when interest rates fall, even if the yield spread between current coupon municipals and Treasuries is constant.

Yields on municipal bonds are not as volatile as yields on Treasuries, so when yields decline, the price of Treasuries increases greater than the municipal index. Because the index includes less active bonds than the Treasury market, the index underperforms the Treasury market in periods of rapidly declining yields.

It must be kept in mind that there can be movements in the MOB spread that are not related to the current municipal/Treasury relationship. For example, if rates move significantly, the index will contain bonds with coupons that are quite different from current municipal bond yields. In this case, the bid-ask spreads for older bonds in the index may be significantly wider than that for current municipals. In addition, credit shocks in the municipal market can have a profound impact on the index—and therefore the MOB spread—that are unrelated to yield movements.

All of these features show that the MOB does not necessarily imply a direct relationship between current municipal and Treasury yields. Thus the coefficient adjustment for the index prevents the MOB spread from reflecting the actual spread between current coupon municipal and Treasury bonds. Even though revision of the index is performed to keep bonds "fresh" in the index, the coefficient keeps the index to Treasury spread "stale" relative to the current municipal to Treasury spread.[4]

SUMMARY

Municipal bond index futures contracts can be used by a portfolio manager in a variety of ways: to control interest rate risk, to enhance return by creating synthetic short-term instruments, and to capitalize on expectations of the relative price movement in the municipal and Treasury bond markets.

Before implementing any strategy, a portfolio manager must understand the principles for pricing interest rate futures contracts. Both the Treasury bond futures contract and the municipal bond index futures contract have unique features that make the valuation of these contracts complex. In the case of the municipal bond index futures contract, the complexity arises from the changing composition of the 40 municipal bonds comprising the Bond Buyer Index. Not only must the nuances of any contract be considered in pricing these contracts, but the positions created to implement any strategy must be adjusted to reflect them.

Although the municipal bond futures contract is a useful vehicle for hedging municipal bonds, its biases must be noted when constructing a

---

[4]For a further discussion of the biases in the municipal bond futures contract, see Bruce Phelps, *Understanding the MOB Spread* (Chicago: Chicago Board of Trade Publication, July 1986).

hedge. The index may not be the best representative of current municipal to Treasury spreads. Adjustments are required when trading the MOB spread. However these adjustments are fairly simple to make.

Used wisely, the municipal bond index futures contract is an important instrument for effectively implementing certain portfolio strategies. Failure to understand the pricing and unique features of these contracts may lead to unexpected and possibly adverse portfolio consequences.

APPENDIX

INVESTMENT FEATURES OF NOT WIDELY UNDERSTOOD MUNICIPAL SECURITIES

Under our federal system of government, states in the first instance determine the security structures for local municipal bonds. This is accomplished in their respective state constitutions, statutory laws, and court decisions. Because of the diverse nature of states, the security structures for local bonds sometimes differ significantly from state to state. General obligation bonds issued by school districts in one state may have additional bondholder protection that school bonds issued in another state may not have. Yet many investors are unaware of the differences.

The purpose of this appendix is twofold. First, it describes some of the distinguishing differences between the more important local bonds. Second, it highlights those bonds that have special strengths, as well as those that have weaknesses. In selecting bonds to be discussed in this appendix we have primarily focused on those that are of the larger supply in the industry.

State Revolving Fund Revenue Bonds*

During the last 20 years, probably no sector of the municipal market has been more affected by the legislative activity of the federal government than has the water and sewer utility sector because of the adoption of various versions of federal wastewater and drinking water regulations. Additionally, no municipal bond structure has been more directly linked to a single law than is the State Revolving Fund (SRF) bond to the 1987 Clean Water Act. This section provides a historical perspective to the development of the SRF structure and discusses some of the more prevalent structures as well as some of the more significant credit quality features of these new securities.

---

*Co-authored with Christopher Mauro of Merrill Lynch and Co.

Historical Perspective

Federal wastewater legislation in the United States dates from 1948 with the passage of the Water Pollution Control Act of 1948. For state and local governments, however, the relevant and working law was, until the late 1980s, the Clean Water Act of 1972, officially called the Federal Water Pollution Control Act Amendments of 1972. This was the federal law that originated the familiar and predictable construction grants program. With this legislation, the federal government, through the Environmental Protection Agency, took the lead in control of municipal wastewater discharges by making it a national policy to support wastewater development at the federal level. The most significant elements in the statute were the construction grants program and the requirement that all facilities achieve secondary treatment by July 1, 1977. The federal share of construction grants program was set at 75 percent. Congress authorized $18 billion over three years and gave the program contract status, thereby eliminating the need for annual prior appropriation. The tool the federal government used in enforcing the new requirements was the National Pollution Discharge Elimination System permit program. The program requires each wastewater system discharging effluent into a body of water to obtain a permit issued by either an approved state or the EPA. These permits are at the core of compliance with the regulations of the Clean Water Act because they contain strict sampling and reporting requirements.

For a variety of reasons, the 1972 law realized dismal results. Only 30 percent of the municipal systems were able to meet the July 1, 1977 deadline for secondary treatment. Washington's response to this situation came in the form of the 1977 Clean Water Act. Through this new law, the construction grants program received new authorization through fiscal 1982. Additionally, the new law provided for an extension of the secondary treatment requirement to July 1, 1983 and created a waiver, with restrictions, of secondary treatment requirements for coastal communities that discharge into marine waters. The focus of the construction grants program was revised in 1981 with the Construction Grants Amendments of 1981. Under this law, the grants could only fund construction designed to meet the needs of current population rather than anticipated future needs. The range of applicable projects was also narrowed. The federal share of project costs was reduced from 75 percent to 55 percent beginning fiscal 1985. These amendments also provided for the final extension of the secondary treatment requirements to July 1, 1988.

The Clean Water Act of 1987 and the SRF Program

The 1987 version of the Clean Water Act, officially titled the Water Quality Act of 1987, was enacted by Congress on February 4, 1987 by overriding the president's veto. The new law did not change the objectives of federal clean water legislation, but it did represent a fundamental shift in the form of federal funding of wastewater treatment. It was an attempt to get the federal government out of the business of financing wastewater treatment plant construction; instead, it was to provide a self-perpetuating mechanism to support future funding of construction programs. To this end, the law phased out the construction grants program and replaced it with the State Revolving Fund program. In this program, federal dollars are used to capitalize the state revolving funds, from which localities can borrow to finance construction programs. Loan repayments from the localities are then used to make new SRF loans. The act authorized $9.6 billion in direct construction grants through 1990. Thereafter, $8.4 billion in new monies were authorized to capitalize the SRF program through 1994. Under the law, the states must first use the SRF funds to assist localities in meeting the requirements of the Clean Water Act, most notably the secondary treatment requirement.

In order to receive the federal capitalization grant, the state must establish an SRF and must provide a 20 percent match of the federal money. Loans are to be made at or below market rates for a term not to exceed 20 years. In order to meet the federal requirement the state must submit an Intended Use Plan annually to the EPA along with its application for a capitalization grant. The 20 percent state match may appear in the form of a legislative appropriation or a general obligation or revenue bond issue. There are different legal uses of the revolving fund monies, all of which may impact the municipal industry to some degree. The state may provide direct loans from the SRF, or it may use SRF funds to refinance local debt incurred after March 7, 1985. The fund may be used to guarantee the debt of local issuers, or it may be used to purchase bond insurance for the issuers. The SRF may also be used to provide interest rate buy-downs, funding the difference between the market rate and the rate the municipality can reasonably afford. An alternative concept allows for leveraging the assets of the SRF to provide security for bonds issued by the state if the proceeds of those bonds are deposited in the SRF. It is this last option that has generated the majority of new issuance of municipal bonds. Leveraging makes available the greatest amount of funds to the greatest number of local borrowers.

How a state funds its 20 percent share, whether it funds more than its 20 percent share and exactly how these funds will be used to subsidize local wastewater treatment activity depends both on the ability and willingness of a state to finance statewide local needs and on the magnitude of those needs as projected over time. For the most part, the state agencies that have been designated to manage the SRF mechanism have been formed as extensions to existing state departments of environmental protection. The extent to which the state contributes to its SRF program (above 20%) and the method the state chooses to utilize these funds determines the amount of local bond issuance that is generated. Those states with greater needs have been more aggressive with their SRF programs, and those with more modest needs have provided only the minimal required match.

The capitalization grants are set to expire in 1994, but the importance of understanding the state revolving fund program cannot be underestimated as the current administration in 1994 and congressional leaders generally support extension of the program. Additionally, the administration supports the notion of establishing state revolving funds to finance improvements to municipal drinking water utility systems.

The State Revolving Fund Revenue Bond

There may be as many different state revolving fund structures as there are states that have received the federal capitalization grant. Numerous SRF-related bond issues have come to market since the late 1980s, and all have had some different element to their structures. Some bonds were issued to finance the state match requirement; others were issued to overfund the state match or to set up "sister" SRF programs designed to finance those special needs within the state that do not fit within the parameters set forth in the federal SRF legislation. Complete delineation of all of the different SRF bond structures that have come to market is beyond the scope of this section. We instead focus on the generic SRF leverage structure and the significant credit features that may be included in such bonds. We use the leverage structure because it is that structure which has generated the issuance of many of the sizable high-profile bond issues that have come to market since the inception of the SRF program.

In the simplest form of the basic SRF leverage bond structure, the state sells bonds for the benefit of the SRF and uses the federal capitalization grant, and perhaps the state match, to overfund a debt service reserve fund. This large reserve fund provides additional credit support for the bonds. The overcollateralized reserve fund in turn generates interest earnings which are then used to subsidize the loans to the local borrowers. The bonds may be either state revenue or general obligation bonds, but for the most part they are revenue bonds. The underlying loans made to the municipal borrowers may carry a GO obligation, revenue obligation, or mix of the two. Additionally, these bond proceeds may finance loans for pools of borrowers or for the benefit of a single borrower.

This basic structure provides significant amounts of additional credit support to the loan program. Two currently outstanding bonds illustrate this point. The state revolving funds of the State of New York and the Commonwealth of Massachusetts both issued large SRF revenue bonds for the benefit of a single issuer. The New York State Environmental Facilities Corporation sold SRF bonds for the benefit of the New York City Municipal Water Finance Authority. The credit quality of the bonds was enhanced by the overfunded debt service reserve, which was set at roughly 33 percent of outstanding principal. As a result, the bonds were rated Aa by Moody's and A by Standard & Poor's, whereas the Authority's own revenue bonds were rated A by Moody's and A− by Standard & Poor's. Likewise, the Commonwealth of Massachusetts, through the Massachusetts Water Pollution Abatement Trust sold SRF bonds for the benefit of the Massachusetts Water Resources Authority. The credit quality of the bonds were similarly enhanced by the presence of an overfunded reserve which was set at 50 percent of outstanding loan principal. The bonds were rated Aa by Moody's and A by Standard & Poor's. At the time of issuance of the SRF bonds, the Authority's own bonds were rated A by Moody's and A− by Standard & Poor's. The interesting element of this second transaction was that the payment by the Authority to the Trust was subordinate to the Authority's obligation to meet debt service on its own bonds. In the New York City Water case, the SRF loan repayment was a parity obligation to its outstanding revenue bonds.

One can see from the two preceding examples that the structure of the leveraged SRF bond can have a significant impact on the credit quality of that bond, often negating the perceived credit risk of the underlying loan recipient(s). In light of this factor, the investor should be aware of a number of potential credit features.

We have established the fact that the standard SRF leverage structure is based on the establishment of an overfunded or supplemental reserve fund. However, this does not necessarily have to be the case for the SRF to issue revenue bonds. The bonds can be issued in a standard revenue bond format with a one-year debt service reserve fund and some form of rate covenant and additional bonds test. In such cases, the credit quality is driven to a great extent by typical revenue bond credit analysis factors. Alternatively, the state may elect to replace the reserve fund overcollateralization provision with the state's moral obligation. In these structures the state agrees to make-up any shortfall in the reserve fund resulting from the default of a loan repayment. As with other moral obligation bonds, potential timing problems have to be ironed out before the bonds can be viewed as benefiting from this type of enhancement. Assuming a reserve *is* overfunded, the obvious question is what level of overfunding is specified in the indenture? A higher level of reserves not only provides better security for the bondholder but also provides a greater interest rate subsidy to the borrowers, thereby lowering the borrowers' financial burden and financial risk.

Another issue is the composition of the loan recipient pool itself. In the New York and Massachusetts examples we cited earlier, single borrowers accounted for the entire loan proceeds of a single bond issue. Other SRF bonds can be issued to provide loans to larger pools of borrowers. These pools can be either open to statewide borrowers or can be limited to borrowers in certain counties or regions of the state. The broader the eligibility provisions, the more diverse the pool and the lower the risk to bondholders. Unlike joint-action agency revenue bonds in the public power sector, SRF bonds do not contain step-up provisions; that is, no borrower in the pool is responsible for making the payments or any portion of the payments of a defaulted borrower. Therefore, diversification in the composition of the pool is an important credit consideration. Note that this diversification is important not only in the number of borrowers but also in the dollar amount of loans made to each borrower. If a small number of borrowers accounts for a proportionately large percentage of the outstanding loans to each pool, the bond can be expected to bear a credit-quality concentration penalty, especially if these borrowers are of relatively poor credit quality. In fact, it is often the case that the more sizable borrowers in these pools *are* of poorer credit quality because it is cheaper for these local governments to borrow from the SRF than it is to sell their own bonds in the market. One should also be aware that the composition of the loan pools can and will change over time. Therefore, whether or not the pool is open or closed is a significant factor. The concentration of borrowers and distribution of credit quality on the borrowers can change as new loans are made.

The nature of the loan repayment obligation is a significant credit consideration. This obligation may be a revenue obligation or a general obligation of the loan recipient. General obligation is viewed as providing more security, but all of the typical credit quality criteria that are part of general obligation bond credit analysis must be examined when making a judgment of bonds secured by a general obligation pledge of the borrowers. A revenue bond-type obligation can take several forms, each defined by the lien position of the loan repayment obligation. The obligation can be considered an operating expense of the borrower and as such will be on parity with the operating and maintenance payments of the borrower—but this is very rare. The loan repayment obligation is generally on parity with the borrowers' outstanding revenue bonds or subordinate to those bonds. Again, the perceived weaknesses in a revenue bond-type pledge can be more than offset by other strengthening features in the bond structure. An additional loan payment provision included in many SRF bond structures is the state aid intercept mechanism. This provision allows the SRF to direct the state treasurer to divert state aid payments due the municipality to the SRF in the event the municipality defaults on its loan repayment obligation. Like the state moral obligation provision, timing problems may be a consideration in the determination of the credit enhancing qualities of the state aid intercept. For example, the loan repayment schedule has to be related to the state aid disbursement schedule in some fashion. If it is not, the portion of the loan repayment could be due after all the state aid appropriated in that fiscal year has been disbursed. In this case, in the event of a default on that loan repayment, the state aid intercept would not become effective until the following fiscal year, and the amount of state aid available would be subject to the state budget deliberations in that year. Finally, one must be aware that other financial obligations of the borrower may also have a claim on the state aid payments. In such cases, all claims are on a parity basis, and, generally, the state aid intercept is apportioned on a first come, first served basis. Why is this significant? In the worst case, an issuer defaulting on an obligation to the SRF will default on other obligations that are supported by a state aid intercept. In this scenario, the state aid could potentially be exhausted by the default on other obligations, thereby rendering the state aid intercept feature on the SRF bonds useless.

Conclusions

In general, State Revolving Fund bonds are securities of above average to high credit quality. The bonds provide a diversified pool of underlying borrowers, strong security provisions, an indisputable public purpose, and strong federal and state oversight. Each bond is different, and a thorough examination of indenture provisions and the credit quality of the underlying borrowers is necessary. Nevertheless, the SRF bond program by definition must be soundly maintained. The programs must meet the strict guidelines set forth by the U.S. EPA in 1987. Additionally, the programs must be conservatively managed and tightly structured if the loan program is to function as intended. If the programs were not so structured, the credit quality of the bonds would be depressed, and the interest cost on the bonds would increase, potentially rendering the loan program uneconomic. Therefore, provided a reading of the indenture indicates a conservative tone, investors can purchase SRF bonds with confidence that they are investing in a security of sound credit quality.

BRIDGEPORT, CONNECTICUT "RESCO" BONDS

Bond proceeds were used to finance the construction of a 2,250 tons per day solid waste "mass burn" facility built and operated by the Bridgeport Resco Company on property owned by the State of Connecticut Resources Recover Authority and located in the City of Bridgeport. The plant is leased by the Authority to the company, which is a subsidiary of Wheelabrator Technologies. Steam generated by the hot gases created by combustion in the three furnaces drives a 70 MW turbine generator. The plant is a "qualified facility" under the Public Utility Regulatory Policies Act, and the produced electricity is sold to the United Illuminating Company. The plant design and the von Roll technology are proven and are similar to those utilized by other plants constructed and operated by Wheelabrator in Saugus, Massachusetts; Westchester County, New York; and Baltimore, Maryland. Once the plant became fully operational, debt service began to be paid from revenues derived from the following sources.

1. Annual tipping fees paid by 18 municipalities (including the city of Bridgeport) that are contractually obligated to deliver annually certain tonnage to the plant at specified tipping fees.

2. Revenues derived from noncontracted waste from the other communities in the area that are charged spot market disposal rates.
3. Revenues from United Illuminating from the sale of the produced electricity.

Tight Pollution Controls

During compliance tests the plant had the lowest dioxin levels ever measured at that time in a U.S. facility burning municipal garbage. Levels of less than 0.010 monograms per cubic meter were achieved. The plant has acid gas scrubbers and fabric filters.

Greater Plant Capacity Than Originally Expected

In the original feasibility study it was conservatively assumed that the plant would process 657,000 tons of garbage a year. This represented 63 percent of the plant's design capacity. Because of the plant efficiency and very competitive tipping fees, annual tonnage by June 30, 1992 was approximately 700,000 tons.

Diminished Reliance on the City of Bridgeport and Increased Plant Revenues

In the original feasibility study Bridgeport City was expected to provide approximately 17 percent of the garbage to be processed at the plant. With the increased use of the facility, Bridgeport's share is now less. Additionally, because the tipping fees charged on the spot market are substantially higher than those charged to Bridgeport, the city's share of operating revenues is less.

Security

The bonds are secured by municipal disposal fees from 18 participating municipalities. The payment of the disposal fees are binding general obligations of each participating municipality, and each municipality is required to set payments at an amount sufficient to pay debt service and other project costs.

In addition, there is a debt service reserve funded to one year's maximum debt service, and a mortgage lien on the plant. Wheelabrator Technologies is also obligated to make revenue contributions to the plant to the extent of its net realizable tax benefits.

Exhibit A–1 lists the 18 municipalities that have signed municipal disposal agreements with Bridgeport Resco as of June 30, 1992. At the time of the original bond sale there had been only 14 that had signed the agreements.

EXHIBIT A–1
Municipalities Signing Municipal Disposal Agreements with Bridgeport Resco (As of 6/30/92)

Municipality	Minimum Tonnage	
Bridgeport	110,000	(22.02%)
Norwalk	67,000	(13.41%)
Greenwich	60,000	(12.01%)
Fairfield	42,000	(8.41%)
Milford	40,000	(8.01%)
Shelton	30,000	(6.00%)
Westport	26,000	(5.21%)
Stratford	23,000	(4.60%)
Trumbull	23,000	(4.60%)
East Haven	20,000	(4.00%)
Darien	17,000	(3.40%)
Wilton	11,300	(2.26%)
Orange	10,000	(2.00%)
Monroe	9,500	(1.90%)
Weston	4,200	——
Woodbridge	3,000	——
Easton	2,000	——
Bethany	1,500	——
	499,500	(100%)

By June 30, 1992 annual tonnage at the plant was approximately 700,000 tons, which included the tonnage of the above long-term contracting municipalities as well as tonnage that came into the plant under short-term spot market arrangements.

CALIFORNIA'S HEALTH FACILITIES CONSTRUCTION LOAN INSURANCE FUND-BACKED BONDS

The Health Facilities Construction Loan Insurance Fund program is managed by the California Office of Statewide Health Planning & Development. Five days prior to an interest payment date, the Bond Trustee is to notify the office of any monetary deficiencies. The office, under state law, is to make up any shortfall three days prior to the payment date, first by drawing from the Debt Service Reserve Fund, and then, to the extent necessary, from the Construction Loan Insurance Fund. (As of December 31, 1991, the principal amount of outstanding loans insured was $1,841,853,860. The accumulated balance of the Loan Insurance Fund was $95,588,462.)

After an issuer defaults, the office can continue to make debt service payments from the Loan Insurance Fund, or it can request that the state treasurer issue debentures. The debentures are to be issued in an amount equal to the outstanding face value of the outstanding principal and at an interest rate corresponding to that payable on the outstanding bonds.

Note that the monies in the Loan Insurance Fund are not pledged to pay obligations insured by the office and could be reappropriated by the State of California legislature for any other purpose. In February 1987, the California legislature reappropriated $1.2 million for other uses. In the event that amounts in the Loan Insurance Fund are insufficient to make any payments, the state treasurer is to pay principal and interest to the holders of the debentures out of monies in the state treasury not otherwise appropriated.

Because of this commitment by the state treasurer, Standard & Poor's rates these bonds the same as it does the general obligation bonds of the State of California. Moody's does not take this rating position.

It should be noted that with the bankruptcy filing in February 1994 of Triad Healthcare Inc. (a two-hospital system near Los Angeles) this program may face its first real test. The insured bonds are approximately $167 million, while available monies in the insurance program are estimated to be $120 million.

CALIFORNIA'S "MELLO-ROOS" BONDS

Under the California Constitution, cities, counties, and special districts may approve, by a two-thirds vote of "qualified electors," special taxes for financing public facilities in developing areas and areas undergoing rehabilitation. The Mello-Roos Community Facilities Act (originally enacted in 1982) provides the statutory basis for bonds to be issued through a "community facilities district" (CFD) that is formed by the landowners and developers. The territory within a CFD need not be contiguous. Public facilties financed with the bond proceeds may include streets, water, sewer, and drainage facilities, as well as parks, schools, libraries, police stations, and city or county administration facilities. The facilities may even be outside the CFD.

How Are the Bonds Secured?

Under the Act, a CFD is formed and a special tax formula is voted and approved by the landowners. Although the tax cannot be ad valorem, it typically is a set dollar amount determined on the basis of density of development, square footage of construction, or flat acreage charges and can escalate at any rate set by the original voted formula. In addition, there is usually a raw land tax set at a level sufficient to pay debt service on the bonds until the development is completed. The Mello-Roos tax ranks equal with the property tax in terms of lien status.

Questions to Ask Concerning the General Credit Risk

Generally, the credit risk of a Mello-Roos bond is greatest when the bonds are initially issued. This is because the acreage is for the most part largely underdeveloped, resulting in a low ratio of land value to tax lien; and the ownership of the property primarily is developer based. Credit quality should improve as various landowners purchase the developed property. For these reasons, our focus is on the development and start-up phase of the property improvements.

Who Is the Developer (or Developers)?

Because the security for the bondholders, through the voted special tax formula, largely rests upon the ability of the developers to build and market their improved properties in the CFD, the quality of the developer or developers involved is of prime importance. Clearly, developers with strong balance sheets, reasonable cash flow projections, committed bank financing, partnership contribution agreements or other security enhancements, and recognized successful land development experience are preferred. In a worst-case scenario, a developer bankruptcy could delay tax payments and result in a bond default.

What Is the Socioeconomic Target Market?

An important element in the determination of the credit quality of a Mello-Roos bond is the socioeconomics of the population that will be purchasing property and living in the specific CFD. The more economically upscale the target population is, the more insulated the Mello-Roos bonds should be from low tax collection rates that could be caused by a recession. One critical indication of the socioeconomics of the CFD is the median values of the residential units for the single-family detached homes and attached units such as townhouses, condominiums, and apartments that are projected by the developer. Also, surrounding community wealth can be assessed in terms of personal income levels being above, average, or below state and national medians.

Where Is the CFD Located?

Because of the lack of mass transit systems in many suburban areas of California, the actual location of the CFD in relationship to major population centers, medical facilities, churches, commercial activities, interstate highways, and environmental amenities such as recreational facilities are important elements that could affect the successful development of the district.

Who Did the Property Appraisal and What Is the Minimum Value-to-Lien Ratio?

An independent and experienced consultant must review and favorably judge the feasibility of the project. It is important that there be a professional opinion that any new residential or industrial/commercial development will achieve market acceptance. This may be done in a feasibility study or by a special tax engineer who is to be employed by the bond issuer to review the developer's projections. Generally, the projected fair-market value of the unimproved land as a ratio of debt should be, at a minimum, 3-to-1, both as it relates to the bond issue and to the total amount of authorized Mello-Roos bonds for that particular CFD. If priority liens exist, it must be shown that they are current in tax payment, and that together with the Mello-Roos tax lien, meet the minimum 3-to-1 value-to-lien ratio.

Who Devised the Special Tax Formula?
There are very few tax consultants in California who are experienced in developing the special tax formulas. It is critical to bondholder security that taxes collected under the formula be adequate to meet debt service. Therefore, the investor must determine that the formula was devised by someone knowledgeable and well-experienced in such matters.

How Conservative Is the Developer's Construction Program and Schedule?
The investor must determine if the developer's own construction schedule and financing costs are realistic. Has the developer determined the total construction costs and does the developer's financing plan include enough capitalized interest to cover potential construction delays? If the bond proceeds are to be used for constructing public facilities such as schools or fire stations it is desirable that prior to the sale of the bonds construction bids and awards will have occurred.

Is There a Reserve Fund?
In order to provide additional financial flexibility if problems were to occur, there should be established at the outset of the bond issue a reserve fund. It should contain an amount—or be covered by insurance or another form of financial guarantee to an amount—not less than 5 percent, and preferably more, of the principal amount of the issue.

What Is the Credit Quality of the Larger Local Government Jurisdiction?
The CFD functions within a larger local governmental jurisdiction such as a city, county, or school district which may have general obligation bonds outstanding. The financial condition of the larger jurisdiction should be at least investment grade.

How Reliable Is the Legal Opinion?
The legality of the bond issue is of major importance. An experienced municipal bond attorney must opine (1) that the CFD was created in accordance with the California Mello-Roos Community Facilities Act of 1982 and can issue the

bonds; (2) that the issuer properly prepared for the bond sale by having enacted the various required ordinances, resolutions, and trust indentures and without violating any other laws and regulations; and (3) that the security safeguards and remedies provided for the bondholders and pledged are actually supported by federal, state, and local government laws and regulations. In regard specifically to potential tax payment delinquencies, the bond attorney must opine that the local tax collection jurisdiction covenants to institute judicial foreclosure within at least 150 days of a major tax delinquency. If there is an underwriter's counsel involved it must be a nationally recognized bond counsel firm that is experienced and knowledgeable about California assessment bond issues.

Some General Concerns

In addition to the above questions, credit quality is also affected by a number of other factors.

1. The degree of the overall tax burden on the future homeowners, including any existing and future direct and overlapping debt that is supported by property taxes
2. Future local initiatives in the area to control growth that could hamper the ability of the developers to complete the proposed development
3. Future homeowners and lenders at the time of purchase not made aware of the special tax. This could affect their willingness and ability to pay it. The quality and business experience of the developer is of critical importance if this is to be prevented.
4. Without an additional bonds test of at least 1.1 times proposed maximum annual debt service, additional bond issuance could severely burden the taxpayers.

Conclusion

In 1994 over $3 billion in Mello-Roos bonds are outstanding from over 225 Mello-Roos districts. At the time that many of these bonds were issued the residential and commercial real estate markets in California were expanding. More recently, however, these markets have been shrinking in value. The creditworthiness of California Mello-Roos bonds ranges all the way from high risk and speculative to investment grade. Because of the weak real estate market in California, some bonds in the lower end of the credit quality spectrum are likely to experience far more serious financial stress than previously anticipated at the time the bonds had been sold. Additionally, if a few Mello-Roos bonds do default, that could further taint the market perception of all non-rated Mello-Roos bonds, and thereby weaken their market value. Investors should be made aware that the spread between non-rated California bonds and high-grades historically had been relatively narrow. As the financial problems of some of the Mello-Roos bonds issues have become better known this spread has widened for all non-rated Mello-Roos bonds, regardless of the individual credit quality.

The creditworthiness of California Mello-Roos bonds ranges all the way from the high risk and speculative categories to investment grade. Because of the wide diversity, it is not possible to assign the same quality opinion to all Mello-Roos bonds. Each bond issue has to be analyzed individually. By asking and obtaining answers to questions discussed above, the prudent investor should be able to distinguish Mello-Roos bonds that are strong from those that are less creditworthy.

CALIFORNIA'S TAX ALLOCATION BONDS

Under the California Constitution, municipal bonds can be issued by a city or county government to finance redevelopment projects that are secured by the increased value of the taxable property in a project area once the improvements have been made. Such bonds are known as tax allocation bonds (TABs). Bond proceeds are used generally to acquire, clear, and dispose of the land for development by the private sector, and to provide for ancillary public improvements such as new sidewalks, streets, and other environmental amenities.

How Are the Bonds Secured?

The TABs are secured by property tax revenues collected on properties within the district over and above the amounts collected and distributed to overlapping taxing jurisdictions. The overlapping local governments receive tax revenues limited to the "frozen" base year property assessments. That is, the other jurisdictions do not benefit from the increased assessments resulting from the improvements. The taxes collected on the increase in the assessed value of the property above the base year roll are allocated to the TABs. Of course, it should be noted that if, in a worst-case scenario, the assessed valuations were to drop for economic reasons below the base year roll, only the overlapping taxing jurisdictions would receive whatever tax revenues are produced by applying the current tax rate to the existing valuations.

Property taxes within the redevelopment district are usually collected by the county tax collector. Under the California Constitution, as amended by Proposition 13 in 1978, assessed property values are limited, in general, to annual increases of no more than 2 percent. However, after new construction occurs (which is expected to occur in a redevelopment district) and when property changes ownership, market assessments are used on the tax rolls.

Also, under Proposition 13 the combined overlapping taxing jurisdictions are to levy annually the maximum tax rate of 1 percent of assessed value plus whatever additional levy is necessary to retire their outstanding general obligation bonds. The composite tax rate is then applied to the property assessments including the assessments above the base year amount. One potential risk for the investor in TABs is that if the general obligation debt is sizable and has a significantly more rapid amortization schedule there can be a dramatic reduction in the tax rate as the general obligation bonds are retired. This, in turn, could result in less revenues being available to pay the TABs.

Questions to Ask Concerning the General Credit Risk

Below are eight questions that should be asked concerning the general credit risk.

What Is the Size and Location of the Project Area?
Redevelopment projects can vary in size from a small parcel of land to thousands of acres. Generally, the larger and more diverse the area the greater the potential for property improvements and resulting valuation increases.

What Are the Economics of the Project Area?
In general, the investor should avoid TABs issued to finance speculative projects that are dependent on a single developer or on a single project such as a hotel or office building. If projects are in the planning stages, the investor should determine whether construction financing, permitting, and preleasing have successfully occurred. Additionally, the investor in a new issue TAB should determine if there is sufficient capitalized interest to cover the period of construction through the placing of the improved properties on the tax rolls. If one major project dominates the new tax allocation revenue base, the track record and financial strength or weakness of the developer is a significant credit concern. Generally, project areas characterized by increasing personal income growth, low unemployment rates, and steady population growth are strong positive credit features. Of course, a district that is not fully developed but has strong potential for increased growth is most desirable. Lastly, it should be noted that middle-class communities are more insulated from recessionary forces than are more working-class ones.

If the project area is large, such as a business district, it is still important to learn who owns the largest taxable properties and what percentage of the total assessment they represent. Of course, it should be emphasized that not all new taxable properties within the project area may be subject to the increment taxation. This could be the case if either the property improvements did not occur after the base year for property assessments was established, or if a judicial determination excluded certain properties.

Who Did the Feasibility Study?

The ultimate security for the bondholder of a new issue TAB is the likelihood that increased valuations will occur as planned. The feasibility study should be done by experienced independent consultants who are familiar with the local assessment procedures and can critically assess the practicality of the development plans.

What Is the Quality of the Underlying "Frozen" Assessments?

Reviewing the quality of the underlying frozen property assessments can be a very critical credit consideration as well. This is particularly important when one is looking at the smaller redevelopment districts. One should determine what are the larger taxable properties in the frozen base year roll and the percentage of the total assessments they represent. If there is a major shopping center, condominium, or office building assessment on the roll, any reduction of its assessed value because of economic adversity could bring down the assessment to a level below the original base year amount. If the reduction is large enough, it could substantially reduce or even, in a worst-case scenario, eliminate the increased assessments that resulted from the improvements in the project area and which were being taxed and allocated to the TABs.

What Is the Debt Service Coverage?

When looking at a TAB in the secondary market, one should determine if it has a history of steadily increasing property assessments. Generally, the debt service coverage should not be less than $1.25 \times$ for a medium investment grade TAB and preferably closer to $1.5 \times$. Moreover, there should be an additional bonds test restrictive enough to prevent the outstanding TABs from being significantly diluted.

The coverage test should identify revenues that are solely from property taxes as well as those from the State of California's "business subvention" program if any are involved. Also, if there is a "housing set aside" program involved, its effect on future available revenues should be determined. There could also be a cap on total increment property tax revenues that can be collected within the redevelopment district and available for debt service.

Any Potential Litigation or Tax Revolts?

Because the redevelopment district benefits from the higher assessments while the overlapping local governments do not, sometimes conflicts occur between the various jurisdictions. At times, there are side agreements entered into with the overlapping jurisdictions to allocate to them some of the excess tax allocation revenues. Additionally, large taxpayers may legally challenge their assessed valuations. The investor, particularly when looking at TABs in the secondary market, should determine if there is any potential or actual litigation pending. Another area of concern is to review any potential tax initiatives that may negatively impact the tax levy or assessment base.

When Was the Base Year Established?

The year in which the assessed property valuations were "frozen" and used as the base can be a very important credit variable. This is because the prevailing tax rates are applied to the property valuation increases above the base year amount to pay the TABs. In general, the older the base year the greater should be the amount of property assessments that can be taxed to pay the TABs.

How Reliable Is the Legal Opinion?

The legality of the bond issue is of major importance. A nationally recognized and experienced municipal bond attorney must opine (1) that the redevelopment agency was created in accordance with the California Community Redevelopment Law and can issue bonds; (2) that the issuer properly prepared for the bond sale by having enacted the various required ordinances, resolutions, and trust indentures and without violating any other laws and regulations; and (3) that the security safeguards and remedies provided for the bondholders and pledged are actually supported by federal, state, and local government laws and regulations.

Conclusion and Quality Opinion

The creditworthiness of TABs ranges all the way from the high risk and speculative categories to investment grade. For this reason, it is not possible to assign the same quality opinion to all TAB issues. However, by asking and obtaining answers to questions discussed above, the prudent investor should be able to distinguish TABs that are strong from those that are less creditworthy.

CONNECTICUT'S "SPECIAL CAPITAL RESERVE FUND" BONDS

In Connecticut certain bond issues of some state authorities are revenue-type bonds that carry a potential state liability for making up deficiencies in their respective one-year "special capital reserve funds." Typically, the state law states that if the bond trustee were to make a withdrawal from the specific special capital reserve fund then:

> On or before December first, annually, there is deemed to be appropriated from the state general fund such sums, if any, as shall be certified by the chairman of the authority involved to the secretary of the office of policy and management and treasurer of the state, as necessary to restore each such special capital reserve fund to the amount equal to the required minimum capital reserve of such fund, and such amounts shall be allotted and paid to the authority.

In the opinion of bond counsel, such appropriation and payment from the state's general fund does not require further legislative approval. Connecticut law provides that it will be an event of default if the state authority involved fails to comply with these provisions.

Certain bonds of the Connecticut Resources Recovery Authority (i.e., Mid-Connecticut System Bonds Series A); the Connecticut Housing Finance Authority (the General Resolution Bond Issues); the Connecticut Development Authority (the "Umbrella Program" bonds), and the Connecticut Higher Education Supplemental Loan Authority (the 1990 Series A and B and 1991 Series A and B bonds) have this security feature.

In addition to the above bonds, the City of Bridgeport in 1989 issued $35 million of its General Obligation Bonds—1989 Series B. Besides being general obligations of the city, they are further secured by amounts in a special capital reserve fund. This was created by a state law that states that if on December 1 of any year the special capital reserve fund is below its requirement, the city shall cause its finance director to certify to the secretary of the Office of Policy and Management and the state treasurer the amount necessary to restore the fund to its requirement, and that under the act there is deemed to be appropriated from the general fund such sums as so certified. The law further provides that such amounts shall be allotted and paid to the city. Such appropriation and payment does not require further legislative approval. The maximum aggregate principal amount of bonds authorized to be issued by the city and secured by a special capital reserve fund is $35,000,000. Because of this special reserve fund make-up security feature for the above bonds, Standard & Poor's gives the same rating to these bonds as it does to those of the State of Connecticut general obligation bonds.

FLORIDA'S "PRESERVATION 2000" REVENUE BONDS

The "Preservation 2000" revenue bonds are issued by the State of Florida to finance the acquisition of lands in furtherance of outdoor recreation and natural resources conservation throughout the state. By 1993 out of a $3 billion bond authorization, $600 million had been issued.

The bonds are secured by dedicated tax revenues, not by the pledge of the state's own credit. Specifically, they are secured by a portion (71.29%) of the state's documentary stamp taxes. On July 1, 1995 the effective rate will be 62.63 percent. These excise taxes in 1993 were levied at the following rates:

1. 70 cents per $100 consideration paid in connection with the conveyance or other transfer of interests in realty located in Florida.
2. 35 cents per $100 face value on the original issuance of stock upon the organization or reorganization of corporations, joint stock companies, or other associations.

3. 35 cents per $100 face value on bonds, debentures, and certificates issued in Florida.
4. 35 cents per $100 of debt evidenced by notes, mortgages, or other security agreements, as well as assignments of wages or other compensation in payment of debts.

In addition to being secured by these pledged revenues, there is also a debt service reserve which held in 1993 an amount at least equal to maximum annual debt service on the outstanding bonds. Additional bonds can be issued if they meet an historical revenues additional bonds test of 1.5 times on existing and proposed debt. In 1993 available documentary stamp tax revenues (estimated to be $334,164,857) provided maximum annual debt service coverage of over $3.76 \times$.

MASSACHUSETTS HOSPITAL BONDS UNDER CHAPTER 495

On December 31, 1991, the Commonwealth of Massachusetts enacted Chapter 495 of the Acts of 1991. Under Chapter 372 in 1982, Chapter 574 in 1985, and most recently Chapter 23 in 1988, the amounts that hospitals could receive from inpatients other than those covered by Medicare payments were set by various formulas and regulated by the Massachusetts Rate Setting Commission (RSC). Chapter 495 replaces the previous legislation, which was based on actual cost, and deregulates over a period of time both third-party contract provisions and hospital revenues. The new law is quite comprehensive and has provisions that affect many areas of health-care delivery in Massachusetts. Chapter 495 does exempt children's hospitals and specialty hospitals who treat eye, ear, and nose diseases. In our initial review we have identified three major areas of Chapter 495 that will have great financial significance for hospital bonds in Massachusetts. Each is discussed in this section.

The New Revenue Formula: No Regulation after 1993

Chapter 495 applies to all non-Medicare inpatients. For two years (through fiscal 1993) a special transitional formula was used that set hospital rates by specific DRGs (Diagnostic-Related Groups) at approximately 90 percent of the state-wide charges for each DRG in 1991. This cap was trended forward for 1992 and 1993 by adjusting for inflation. Thereafter, the state's role in rate-setting ended. After 1993, hospitals that are high cost providers in competitive service markets are obviously at a disadvantage compared to low-cost providers. This adversely effects volume and market share and hence the financial performance of these entities. Those hospitals that have either valuable medical specialties or geographic location niches should be impacted to a lesser degree.

Deregulating Blue Cross

Under Chapter 495, Blue Cross is free to negotiate terms with each hospital on a hospital-specific basis. Under previous Massachusetts law Blue Cross had a uniform payment contract with all hospitals under which it was given a 7 percent discount for acute-care hospital services. This discount was to be recovered by the hospital in its charges to other private payers.

With Blue Cross free to negotiate with each hospital, the foresight and expertise of the hospital in negotiating a specific contract with Blue Cross will be critical. Additionally, as a result of Blue Cross's new flexibility, the HMO providers may be able to strengthen their negotiating positions with the less efficient and competitive hospitals again having an adverse effect on the hospitals' finances.

Previous Overcharges

Over the years certain hospitals in Massachusetts have overgenerated amounts from their third-party payors. These liabilities show up on the balance sheet of the specific hospital involved as a current liability. Prior to the enactment of Chapter 495 there was not a set timetable for hospitals with such liabilities to pay them off. Under Chapter 495 this has changed. The overgeneration liability under the previous legislation now must be paid into the Massachusetts uncompensated care pool over the ensuing five years. Besides the fact that a hospital in a sizable overgeneration position may not be charging competitive rates and thus will suffer in the new market force-driven revenue environment caused by Chapter 495, it will have a more immediate financial problem of paying back the overgeneration. Under Chapter 495 the RSC has the regulatory authority to determine the payback schedule over the mandated five-year period.

Conclusion

Note that some hospitals may be adversely affected by these three factors and experience serious financial stress that could cause some of them to close. It is anticipated that the Massachusetts health-care industry will become increasingly competitive as a result of this deregulation.

MICHIGAN'S "QUALIFIED" SCHOOL BONDS

Since 1955 the state of Michigan has had a financial aid program for school districts. The school district is allowed to borrow and the state is required to lend to it an amount necessary for the school district to avoid a default on its own general obligation bonds, or to reduce the local property tax levy that is being used to pay debt service. The amounts borrowed are to be paid back with interest. The qualification for participation in this program is done by the state government prior to the original bond sale. If necessary, the state is required to use monies in its own general fund to pay the debt service. The money goes from the state treasurer to the school district's debt-service fund.

Because of this special security backup with the state, school-district bonds in Michigan are of stronger credit quality. There are over 400 school districts in Michigan with "qualified" bonds outstanding. These bonds were usually rated one notch below the state's ratings by Moody's.

NEW JERSEY "QUALIFIED" SCHOOL AND CITY BONDS

In 1976 the governor of New Jersey signed into law two bills (known as "qualified bond" acts) that provide additional security for certain general obligation bonds issued by New Jersey issuers. The chief characteristic of the two laws (one is for municipalities, and the other is for school districts) is that selected state aid monies, normally paid directly to the municipality or school district, will be paid directly by the state treasurer to the bond-paying agent.

Revenue Features

Municipal Qualified Bonds
The selected state aid monies pledged for debt service are the business personal property tax replacement revenues (Public Law 1966, c. 135), state revenue sharing funds (Public Law 1976, c. 73), and state urban aid funds (Public Law 1971, c. 64). The latter state aid program is available to 24 New Jersey urban municipalities. While these state aid programs could be eliminated or changed, the law provides that any future state aid programs that provide funds in substitution of the above would be pledged as security for the qualified bonds.

School Qualified Bonds
Under this law, state aid monies pledged for debt service are those available under the Public School Education Act of 1975 (Public Law 1975, c. 212) and four other state aid programs. As with the municipal qualified bonds, the law specifies that, while the specific state aid programs may be eliminated or changed, any future substitute state aid programs would be pledged as security for such qualified bonds.

Bond Paying Procedures

After the bonds are sold, the issuer certifies to the state treasurer the name and address of the paying agent, the maturity schedule, the interest rate, and debt-service payment dates. The state treasurer is then required to withhold from the amount of state aid due the issuer an amount sufficient to pay the debt service on the qualified bonds, and to make this payment directly to the paying agent. The issuer still must include the debt-service requirements in its annual budget because the diversion of cash does not represent additional state aid to the issuer, but merely a diversion of cash flow to ensure that the principal and interest on the qualified bonds will be paid promptly.

Bond Strengths

The New Jersey qualified bonds have three strengths:

1. Debt-service payments are made directly by the state treasurer to the paying agents.
2. The State Local Finance Board reviews and authorizes all qualified bond sales under the two laws in order to ensure that state aid more than covers the anticipated debt service.
3. The qualified bonds are also general obligations of the issuing municipalities and school boards.

Conclusion

The original purpose of the qualified-bond acts was to assist municipalities and school districts (particularly those in urban centers) that had had problems issuing bonds as a result of New York City's fiscal difficulties in 1975. In the opinion of the attorney general of New Jersey, once the qualified bond issue has been approved by the State Local Finance Board and certified to the state treasurer, the earmarked state aid funds cannot be used for any purpose by or on behalf of the issuer other than to pay the required debt service on the qualified bonds.

It should also be noted that future New Jersey legislatures are not necessarily bound by prior legislation, though several of the state aid programs pledged under the qualified-bond acts have been in existence for several years.

NEW YORK MAC'S "SECOND RESOLUTION" BONDS*

The Municipal Assistance Corporation (MAC) was created by the State of New York in 1975 to provide financing for the City of New York for capital improvements as well as for funding out the city's budget deficit. As of 1992, it has issued over $9 billion in municipal bonds under three separate bond resolutions. Under the First General Resolution approximately $994.7 million in bonds were outstanding; under the Second General Resolution approximately $5.338 billion in

---

*Co-authored with John Hallacy of Merrill Lynch & Co.

bonds were outstanding,[1] and under the 1991 General Resolution $138.4 million in bonds were outstanding. This section focuses on the largest of the three bond security structures; MAC's Second Resolution bonds.

The Security

Pledged revenues are defined as annual appropriations from the state legislature of (1) general revenue-sharing monies (Per Capita Aid) due the City of New York; (2) sales tax revenues collected by the state from a 4 percent sales tax imposed within the city on most retail sales; and (3) stock-transfer tax revenues collected by the state on the transfer of stock and certain other securities.

Annual debt service, operating expenses, and reserve requirements on MAC's First General Resolution bonds have a prior lien on the sales tax and stock-transfer tax revenues. After MAC expenses are met, including debt service on the bonds, the remaining monies flow to the City of New York's general fund.

The Flow of Funds

Sales taxes *plus* stock-transfer taxes collected *less* operating expenses of MAC, *less* maximum annual debt service (DS) payable on the outstanding First Resolution bonds *plus* available Per Capita Aid *pays* debt service on the Second Resolution bonds. Although stock-transfer taxes are still available for debt service payments, if they are not required for debt service payments they are rebated back to stock-transfer taxpayers. Full rebates have been made since October 1, 1981.

The Additional Bonds Test

Second Resolution bonds can be issued only if available revenues cover maximum annual debt service on the old and to-be-issued Second Resolution bonds by two times. Additionally, no more than $10 billion in total MAC bonds can be issued. Available revenues used for the additional bonds test are derived from several sources.

1. The *lesser* of either the sales and stock-transfer taxes collected over the previous 12 months; or, the amounts estimated to be collected over the next 12 months.
2. The amount of Per Capita Aid paid to MAC during the current year.
3. *Less* maximum annual DS on the First Resolution bonds and MAC operating expenses for the current year.

---

[1] These amounts include bonds that could be issued in connection with MAC's commercial paper program.

The Capital Reserve Aid Fund

A debt-service reserve is to be funded at 1.00 times the amount of debt service to be paid in the succeeding calendar year on Second Resolution bonds outstanding and to be issued. This fund is subject to the legislative makeup provision, the so-called moral obligation. (For additional information about the moral obligation, see Chapter 13).

Conclusion

The bulk of MAC revenues is the 4 percent city sales tax collected out of a total of 8¹/₄ percent. For the 12 months ended 12/31/91, the sales tax receipts increased by 1.1 percent to $2.3563 billion. In the last three months of 1990 comparable change in sales tax receipts over the previous year was a decrease of 4.6 percent. In addition to sales tax revenues the stock transfer tax is also pledged. For the 12 months ended 12/31/91, this tax increased 6.3 percent (going from $1.5549 million collected in 1989 to $1.6523 billion in 1990). If coverage is calculated strictly in accordance with the respective resolutions, coverage is over 15× for First Resolution Bonds and over 6× on Second Resolution Bonds. Reserve funds are in excess of annual debt service for both resolutions at $341.2 million for the First Resolution and at $661 million for the Second Resolution. MAC bonds enjoy exceptional coverage and protection with reserves. A total of $6.9 billion of debt is outstanding with $1.28 billion in First Resolution Bonds and $5.7 billion of Second Resolution Bonds.

The 1991 General Bond Resolution bonds ($138,260,000) issued in 1991 constitute liens on the above revenues after debt service is first paid on the First and Second Resolution Bonds. Estimated debt service coverage on the Bonds was 5× in 1992. Coverage by pledged sales taxes alone was approximately 2.6×. The additional bonds test requires a 2× coverage test by the pledged sales tax revenues only. There is also a debt service reserve fund that contains an amount not less than one-half of maximum annual debt service on the bonds.

NEW YORK STATE LOCAL GOVERNMENT ASSISTANCE CORPORATION (LGAC) BONDS*

Since its market debut in February 1991, LGAC has already sold $4.1 billion. In some respects similar to the NYC Municipal Assistance Corp. (MAC), LGAC bonds are paid from 1 percent of the 4 percent statewide sales tax (i.e., 25% of the current levy). Debt service on all bonds planned to be issued would be covered approximately 3.00 times by the $1.3 billion of available sales tax receipts in fiscal

---

*Co-authored with Kurt van Kuller of Merrill Lynch and Co.

1993. LGAC is a key element in New York State's approach to fiscal reform. Proceeds of LGAC bonds are expected to eliminate New York's traditional "Spring Borrowing," the annual massive sale of notes to finance state aid payments to local governments. LGAC bondholders are protected against over-issuance by a requirement for a minimum of 2.00 times coverage as a prerequisite for selling additional bonds. Over the long-term, if the bond authorization is not raised, coverage should rise inexorably, as inflation and population growth spur sales tax revenues. However, the creditworthiness (and ratings) of LGAC bonds is seen as linked to that of New York State due to the necessity for annual legislative appropriations of sales tax revenues before they may be applied for debt service. Therefore, a return to fiscal stability by New York State would greatly enhance the outlook for LGAC bonds.

Security

Receipts from the 1 percent sales tax are deposited as received into a segregated tax fund held by the State Comptroller and the Commissioner of Taxation and Finance. Annually, the state legislature must appropriate a transfer for LGAC debt service. If no such measure is passed, then *all* 1 percent sales tax receipts are *impounded* indefinitely in the tax fund. Thus, a failure to appropriate deprives the state of over 3 percent of its general fund revenues—an amount far more than LGAC debt service. Once appropriated, all sales tax revenues then flow through the tax fund to the state for its general purposes.

If a shortfall occurs, the comptroller is required by law to immediately transfer (without further appropriation) whatever is needed from the state general fund five days prior to an LGAC debt service date. Hypothetically, impoundment of sales taxes would also proceed indefinitely, if necessary. Moreover, a capital reserve fund is required to maintain at all times an amount equal to maximum annual debt service. If a deficiency exists in the capital reserve, impoundment of 1 percent sales tax receipts is also invoked until cured. These measures offer considerable assurances against the risk of non-appropriation. Non-payment of LGAC bonds would also conceivably deprive New York State of vital market access.

The 1 Percent Sales Tax

Until fiscal 1991, sales tax receipts had risen every single year since the present 4 percent rate was adopted in 1971. Annual increases had ranged from 13.65 percent in fiscal 1986 to 3.22 percent in fiscal 1977. Revenues have been augmented by widening of the tax base in each of the last three years. For fiscal 1991 (ended March 31), tax revenues declined 5.65 percent; however, much of this was due to an adjustment in the collection procedures which resulted in only 11 months of remittances from vendors in fiscal year 1991. Factoring in the effect of the adjustment, coverage of *all* expected LGAC debt service (assuming 8% on future issues) by fiscal year 1991 revenues (a no-revenue growth scenario), would be 3.06 times.

Purpose

LGAC was created in 1990 to bond-out the state's traditional seasonal borrowing. This "Spring Borrowing" evolved from the practice of deferring local aid payments due in the current state fiscal year into the next—a form of deficit financing. Because the state's fiscal year ends March 31, while localities in the state mainly have fiscal years ending June 30, localities suffer no impact from this deferral as long as they receive the proceeds from the Spring Borrowing before the start of their fiscal years. The Spring Borrowing totalled $4.1 billion in 1990 and $3.9 billion in 1991. The amount of the Spring Borrowing has ratcheted down with the amount of LGAC bonds outstanding. By the Spring of 1994, as LGAC completed its authorized issuance, the Spring Borrowing was eliminated.

NEW YORK STATE LOCAL SCHOOL DISTRICT BONDS

New York school district general obligation bonds have two special security features. The first is that any uncollected taxes are reimbursed to the school district by the county, thereby assuring 100 percent school tax collections by the end of the fiscal year. The second is that, if necessary, state aid due the school districts must be used to pay the bondholders.

School Districts in New York State

School districts in New York State are units of local government created to operate public schools. They are authorized to levy real estate taxes, and authorized to issue debt including both general obligation bonds and notes. Under the state constitution this debt is payable, if necessary, from the levy of ad valorem taxes on the full value of all taxable property within the boundaries of the respective school districts. For school districts that are in cities with populations under 125,000, there is a debt limit of 5 percent of the issuer's assessed valuation. Within other districts, the debt limit is 10 percent as determined by the state legislature. There is no limit on the taxes that can be levied for payment of the debt.

Why Is the Tax Collection Rate Always 100 Percent for Most School Districts?

Tax collectors of the school districts collect the school tax levies, except that in cities of 125,000 or more the city tax collectors also collect the school levies. In towns of less than 125,000 people, the same arrangement can be made by mutual agreement. Under New York State law the school districts receive delinquent school tax payments from their respective county treasurers. In this way the school districts receive 100 percent of their annual tax levies, and the counties themselves are responsible for collecting the unpaid taxes. It should also be noted that generally there are two exceptions to this procedure: school districts in Westchester County and school districts located within cities.

Additional Bond Security

If a school district does not pay its debt service, the bondholder (under a New York State law enacted in 1959) can file a statement with the state comptroller, who must deduct and withhold from the next succeeding state aid payment any amount sufficient to pay the bondholder. The security feature is Section 99–b of the State Finance Law.

How Important to the School District's Budget Are the State Aid Payments?

New York State first began to provide local school districts with annual aid in 1925 when the state began to assist in paying for physical improvements. In 1962 the state began providing school districts with annual aid for operating expenses as well. The state aid monies are derived from a special formula that is based on weighted average daily attendance in the respective school districts compared to the statewide average daily attendance. Some school districts receive up to 85 percent of their revenues from the State of New York; many depend on state aid programs for at least 50 percent. In many if not all school districts, the total amount of annual state aid is substantially more than the annual debt service.

Section 99–b Drawbacks

There are three aspects of the Section 99–b security structure that the investor should be aware of:

1. The Section 99–b mechanism only becomes operational when a bond default has already occurred. That is, it is a remedy for a default but does not prevent a default from occurring.
2. State aid-to-education payments are made only at certain times of the year. Therefore, a default may occur at a time when the state comptroller does not have any appropriated state funds available for the specific school district.
3. Where a school district has defaulted in the payment of interest or principal due upon school bonds, the comptroller is first required to withhold and pay from state funds appropriated for the support of common schools the employer's contribution to the New York State Teachers' Retirement System, before payments to the holders of the delinquent bonds can be made.

Additional Case Law Support

Security for bonds of all New York State issuers, including school districts, was further strengthened in November 1976 when the New York State Court of Appeals declared the New York State Emergency Moratorium Act invalid. This was the state law that allowed New York City to postpone redeeming its general obligation notes in November 1975.

NEW YORK STATE "SECURED HOSPITAL" REVENUE BONDS*

In the mid-1980's the state established the Secured Hospital Program in order to provide access to the public credit markets for financially "distressed" hospitals. Since inception through the early part of 1994 transactions have been brought to market for four hospitals with the amount outstanding of $580 million. The outstanding bonds have been issued against an authorization of $1.779 billion that leaves $1.209 authorized but unissued bonds.

The bonds issued under this program benefit from several layers of security. One of the most important features of the security is the status of the bond as a service contract of the State of New York. The State of New York has a complex debt profile. The state indicates a total net tax-supported debt of approximately $26.2 billion as of December 31, 1993 that does not include moral obligation bonds. Out of this total only $5.4 billion represents general obligation debt and $20.6 billion represents Lease Purchase and Contractual Obligation Financing. As a result, the state has placed a great reliance on other obligations away from the general obligation pledge. However, these other obligations are given considerable weight in the state's budgeting and appropriating practices. The Contractual Obligation portion of the existing financing on its own is $9.1 billion of the total. Other prominent entities that share this category are the MTA Service Contract Bonds that account for $2.2 billion outstanding and the New York Local Government Assistance Corporation (LGAC) that accounts for $4.1 billion outstanding. In several respects, the Secured Hospital Program bonds share more features in common with the MTA Service Contract bonds; however, all of the bonds in the contractual obligation category are dependent on appropriations from the state's general fund except for LGAC's primary backing from its share of the sales tax that is also dependent on a state appropriation.

Under the terms of the service contract, the state will make annual appropriations acting through its budget director. The obligation to make the payments is absolute and unconditional and is subject only to the executory clause. The latter

---

*Co-authored with John Hallacy.

means the payment must be included in the proposed budget each year by the budget director who covenants to request sufficient funds from the legislature to make the payment. Actual payment is subject to the executory clause from the standpoint that there must be available funds on hand to make payment. Otherwise there are no offsets or counterclaims to the payment. Only legislative approval is required. In addition, the term of the service contract may not exceed 30 years. None of the parties to the service contract possess the right to terminate the contract. In most of the considerations, the MTA service contract bonds and the Secured Hospital Program bonds are much the same. Available remedies are very broad and include the possibility to request a writ of mandamus by the state on behalf of the bondholders.

Where the MTS Service Contract Bonds and these bonds differ is that with the MTA bonds, the bondholder has no security interest or lien on the operating system. In the case of the Secured Hospital Program, the resolution validly pledges a mortgage and a mortgage note on the hospital facilities and the repayments from the hospital. In the event the state is required to make a payment, the agency would repay the state to the extent payments are forthcoming from the appropriate Secured Hospital borrower. In the experience of the program through 1993 for the four hospitals that have borrowed under the program including Bronx-Lebanon, Jamaica, North General, and Wyckoff Heights, the state has never had to make a payment for these bonds from its general fund. The repayments from the hospitals have always been sufficient. However, the state does consider the necessity of whether or not a full payment would reasonably be expected in each year. In the most recent Executive Budget proposal for FY1995, the recommended appropriation level for the state's potential liability for debt service is recommended at $54 million inclusive of upcoming bond sales. However, at this time there is no expectation that an actual payment for debt service would be required.

Due to the "financially distressed" status of the hospitals in the program, there is a great reliance on disproportionate share monies and on Medicaid as sources for the repayments. Payment for capital improvements is an approved reimbursable item from these two sources of third party revenues. The state's appropriation for FY1994 for disproportionate share medical assistance is $650 million with the same recommendation for FY1995 proposed. A large share of these funds flow to hospitals designated "financially distressed" by the State Department of Health under the program. Medicaid is another significant source for these hospitals. The governor recently announced a plan to assume more of New York City's responsibility for its share of the Medicaid expense. This proposed change could lead to significantly enhanced reliability of the flow of funds under the program in the future.

What may be more important to the integrity of the repayments from the hospitals is that the Commissioner of Health and the Medical Care Facilities Finance Agency (the Agency) have considerable oversight over the borrower institutions.

Monitoring includes monthly review of the timeliness of the mortgage repayments, payment of Agency fees, and deposits to the Renewal, Replacement and Depreciation Account. If these protections fail, there is a Special Debt Service Reserve Fund created pursuant to the Secured Hospital Revenue Bond Program. As additional collateral to the Capital Reserve Fund, the Agency may request the State and the State may fund from State monies a Special Debt Service Reserve Fund up to an amount equal to maximum *semiannual* debt service. If funded, these monies are transferred from the State to the Agency for deposit with the bond trustee and, if needed by the Agency, these monies are available to secure the bondholders. Any monies in this Special Debt Service Reserve Fund are available to make principal and interest payments to the bondholders, if necessary, before the Capital Reserve Fund equal to total aggregate annual debt service would ever be called upon to make payment. If monies in the Special Debt Service Reserve Fund are utilized by the Agency the State may appropriate additional monies to restore the Special Debt Reserve Fund to its allowable level. No assurance can be given that the State will initially fund the Special Debt Service Reserve Fund nor restore the Special Debt Service Reserve Fund to its stated value if monies are withdrawn. However, for the outstanding bond issues the Special Debt Service Reserves are fully funded.

The ultimate security if all of these layers of protection are inadequate remains the state's obligation under the service contract. The Secured Hospital Program service contract has never been tested; but, the State of New York so far has had a spotless record on lease appropriation financing and on its service contract bonds.

OLD MAINE BONDS THAT ARE NOW "FUNDING INTERCEPT" BACKED

On July 14, 1991 the Governor of Maine signed into law a bill that implements a new state "funding intercept" mechanism for bonds that have been issued through the Maine Health and Higher Educational Facilities Authority (the Authority). Under this law (Chapter 584 of the Public Laws of 1991) the Authority can cause the State Treasurer to withhold any funds (such as Medicaid) in the Treasurer's custody that would otherwise be paid to a hospital or other Authority borrower which has failed to make, or is reasonably predicted to fail to make, a debt service payment on any bonds that the Authority has issued on behalf of the borrower. Instead, the monies are directed to the bondholders. This funding intercept mechanism is applicable to all hospitals, colleges, and other borrowers of the Authority and is applicable to future as well as currently outstanding bond issues.

The amount of funds that may be made available to bondholders varies from specific borrower to borrower. Colleges that have issued bonds through the Authority receive little, if any, monies from the state, whereas, nursing homes should receive, in general, higher percentages. This is particularly the case for a nursing home with a large Medicaid population. One nursing home issuing bonds receives over 85 percent of its revenues from the state through the Medicaid program. Hospitals issuing bonds through the Authority are financially less dependent on the state though they do receive Medicaid monies. Recent data show that the percentages of Medicaid monies to total hospital revenues for individual Maine hospitals range from approximately 5 percent to almost 16 percent.

How the New Funding Intercept Works

If the bond borrower is in actual default in debt service payments or *if* the Authority has "reasonable grounds to predict" that a default will occur, the Authority now has the ability to notify the state treasurer. According to the law, once so notified, the treasurer is required to withhold the funds due from the state to the borrower. Funds subject to this state funding intercept include federal and state grants, contracts, allocations, or appropriations, including Medicaid payments. (For hospitals and nursing homes, the largest source of state aid takes the form of Medicaid payments.) If, after activating the state funding intercept, the Authority further notifies the treasurer that the timely payment of debt service is still in question, the law requires the treasurer to deposit into the state's general fund and make available to the Authority any funds so withheld from the borrower. The Authority, in turn, is required to use the funds to pay the bondholders.

If the Authority implements the state funding intercept, the law requires the Authority to also notify those state departments that may exercise regulatory control over the borrower. The relevant state department is required under the law to undertake an immediate project review to assure the prudent operation of the borrower. If necessary, the law permits a take-over of the borrower's facilities by the applicable state regulatory body.

Drawbacks

While the funding intercept mechanism provides enhanced security to the bondholders, it does have certain drawbacks.

1. The amount of state funds the borrower receives may not be enough to cover debt service on a timely basis if the funding intercept has to be used.

2. Even if on an annual basis state aid monies would more than cover debt service on the bonds, a problem or default may occur at a time when the state treasurer does not have any appropriated funds available immediately for the bondholders.

3. In regard to potential Medicaid revenues it should be noted that federal regulations require that payments must be paid to the provider of the health-care services and cannot be assigned to another party (e.g., the Authority or the bond trustee). Therefore, in order to use the Medicaid monies, the state treasurer along with the borrower would have to establish a "joint account" into which the inter-cept monies would be deposited. While none of the current borrowers so far have established joint accounts with the state treasurer, the regulatory role that the state plays could give it strong leverage in encouraging a borrower to agree to setting up such an account if need be.

4. The special withholding measures are not a part of any contractual obli-gation with the bondholders and are based on statutory provisions which may be modified or repealed by the legislature at any time.

5. The Authority has permissive, not mandatory, authority to activate the funding intercept.

However, it should be noted that the mechanism *does* provide the bondholder with added protection, and a state-funded source of debt service payments unavail-able for 501(C)(3) hospital, college, and nursing home bonds in other states.

ORANGE COUNTY, FLORIDA'S "TOURISM" BONDS

This bond was issued to finance the construction of tourism-related facilities such as a convention center and is secured by hotel taxes levied on visitors to Orange County, Florida. Orange County is an established national and international tourist destination. It is the home of the Disney World complex of theme parks and hotels, including the Magic Kingdom, Epcot Center, and MGM Studios. Non-Disney attractions include the Sea World and Universal Studios theme parks. In all, there are over 50,000 hotel rooms in the county with occupancy rates in 1992 of over 70 percent. The strength of the issue is the robust economy that is primarily driven by Disney tourism. In 1992 debt service coverage was a respectable 1.64 times. There is also a debt service reserve that is to hold an amount equal to maximum annual debt service. The additional bonds test only requires that pledged revenues received for any 12 consecutive month period over the previous 24 months cover maximum annual debt service on the outstanding and to-be-issued bonds by 1.33 times. The City of Orlando has also pledged certain sales tax receipts. However, if the pledged hotel taxes provide coverage of 1.33 times of maximum debt service for a two-year period, the city's sales tax pledge is released.

SAN FRANCISCO BAY AREA RAPID TRANSIT DISTRICT (BART) BONDS

The purpose of this section is to provide information on the unique features of the San Francisco Bay Area Rapid Transit District (BART) general obligation bonds. BART was established by the State of California to build and operate 71 miles of double-track urban rail transit routes serving San Francisco, the cities of Berkeley, Oakland, and Daly City,[2] and suburban areas within Alameda and Contra Costa counties. These have been financed by issuing debt, including general obligation bonds, which have been authorized by the electorate, and which are secured by unlimited ad valorem taxes on the full value of all taxable property within the BART boundaries.

Who Collects the Property Taxes?   Annually, the Directors of BART are required by state law to determine the amount of property taxes necessary to pay BART G.O. bond debt service and certain operating expenses.[3] They then levy the taxes, and the tax collectors of the counties that BART overlaps include the BART levies in their tax bills.

How Strong Is This Security?   The bond counsel to BART has indicated that there are no mechanical or legal procedures that he is aware of that make the BART unlimited property tax pledge any weaker than the pledge behind individual county general obligation bonds.[4] If some taxpayers, for whatever reason, do not pay their property taxes, foreclosure proceedings are initiated, and in the meantime, the tax levy is raised to make up the difference. If a county tax collector should ever refuse to levy and collect the property taxes for BART, a mandamus can be obtained by the bondholders or by BART, commanding the county officials to collect the taxes and turn them over to BART.

Did the 1978 Jarvis Tax-Reduction Law Weaken the Security?   *No.* The Jarvis tax-reduction law of 1978 limited ad valorem property taxes to 1 percent of full value. However, taxes levied to pay debt service on voter-approved general obligation bonds (which included the BART G.O.s) were specifically excluded from the limitation.

---

[2] Daly City property owners are not subject to the BART levy.

[3] State of California Public Utilities Code, Sections 28500, 29121, 29122, and 29128 (1957, and amended thereafter).

[4] Interview with C. Richard Walker, Orrick, Herrington & Sutcliffe, San Francisco, February 24, 1978.

SCH HEALTH CARE SYSTEM REVENUE BONDS

The Sisters of Charity of the Incarnate Word (SCH) is a 501(c)(3) non-profit corporation, headquartered in Houston, Texas, which either directly owns or through affiliates operates 16 health-care facilities located in Texas, Louisiana, California, Arkansas, and Utah as well as a 152-bed geriatric center in Ireland. Bond proceeds from the 1991 bond sale were used for the funding of or reimbursement for capital improvements in the hospitals in Texas and in California.

The Series 1991A Bonds are unsecured general obligations of SCH. The Restricted SCH affliates are not obligated to make any debt service payments on the Bonds directly to the issuers. SCH, however, has covenanted to cause the Restricted SCH Affiliates to transfer, to SCH, funds or other assets for the purpose of enabling SCH to satisfy the debt service requirements of the Series 1991A Bonds.

Of SCH's staffed beds approximately 3,749 are acute care and 771 are long-term beds. As Exhibit A–5 shows this health-care system maintains a relatively high overall occupancy rate (68.0% through 3/31/91) and year-in year-out profitability which in part results from the geographic diversity of the system and its focused stable management. As examples of the latter, since 1986 two of the

EXHIBIT A–5
SCH Health Care System

Name	Location	Primary Service	Licensed (and staffed) (3/31/91)	% of SCH Gross Patient Revenues (3/31/91)
St. Joseph Hosp.	Houston, TX	Acute Care	840 (608)	15.2%
St. Mary Med. Center	Long Beach, CA	Acute Care	556 (495)	14.7
Schumpert Med. Center	Shreveport, LA	Acute Care	625 (497)	14.3
St. Elizabeth Hosp.	Beaumont, TX	Acute Care	497 (497)	13.1
St. Bernardine Med. Ctr.	San Bernardino, CA	Acute Care	311 (311)	11.0
St. Michael Hosp.	Texarkandy, AR	Acute Care	254 (243)	6.6
St. Mary Hosp.	Port Arthur, TX	Acute Care	278 (205)	5.8
St. Frances Cabrini Hosp.	Alexandria, LA	Acute Care	304 (243)	5.2
St. Patrick Hosp.	Lake Charles, LA	Acute Care	416 (249)	5.2
St. John Hosp.	Nassau Bay, TX	Acute Care	141 (123)	4.6
St. Mary's Hosp.	Galveston, TX	Acute Care	322 (277)	2.6
St. Joseph Villa	Salt Lake City	Nursing Home	175	0.3
St. Elizabeth Nursing Home	Waco, TX	Nursing Home	179	0.2
St. Joseph Nursing Home	Monroe, LA	Nursing Home	132	0.1
Carrigoran House	(Ireland)	Nursing Home	152	0.1
Regis Retirement Center	Waco, TX	Retirement Home	192	0.1
Total Facilities			5,374	99.1
Clinics			——	0.9
TOTAL (SCH Health Care System)			5,374	100.0

EXHIBIT A–6
SCH Health Care System—Selected Operating Highlights (000s)

Financial Operations	FY 1988 (end 6/30/88)	FY 1989 (end 6/30/89)	Fy 1990 (end 6/30/90)	FY 1991 (thru 3/31/91)
Gross Patient Revenues	$1,061,623	$1,214,564	$1,427,294	$1,215,488
Net Patient Revenues	734,005	810,790	897,653	713,157
Net Operating Revenues	747,658	827,394	916,751	730,395
Operating Expenses	722,054	786,590	866,068	709,055
Net Income	$ 26,317	$ 53,983	$ 72,997	$ 36,363

Operating Statistics	FY 1988 (end 6/30/88)	FY 1989 (end 6/30/89)	Fy 1990 (end 6/30/90)	FY 1991 (thru 3/31/91)
Staffed Beds	4,482	4,461	4,492	4,506
Admissions	133,453	130,497	132,628	97,994
ALOS (Days)	9.0	8.6	8.6	8.6
Occupancy	73.4%	68.8%	69.5%	68.0%
Patient Days	1,204,033	1,119,823	1,139,710	839,719

weaker hospitals have been closed or sold and SCH maintains a cushion ratio (the amount of unrestricted cash available times estimated maximum annual debt service) of $7.44\times$. Its liquid cash and investments of over $275 million and high cushion ratio mitigate against the need for a debt service reserve fund. (Moody's cushion ratio median is $5.5\times$.) Additionally, the relatively low debt to capitalization of 37.2 percent and SCH's plan to fund its five-year capital program with proceeds from the 1991 issue and with cash generated from operations without the need for additional borrowings are the strong credit features. Besides the profitability of this hospital system, another strength is that no one hospital dominates the revenue base of the system. As shown in Exhibit A-6 the largest hospital (St. Joseph Hospital in Houston) contributed only a little over 15 percent of fiscal year 1991 gross patient revenues.

The strength of SCH is derived from a number of other factors as well. They include the geographic diversity of the community-based acute-care hospitals located in a variety of competitive markets and economic settings. The system is not dependent on the reimbursement policies of any one region. Although the hospitals in Houston and Long Beach face intense competition the ones in Beaumont, Texas and Shreveport, Louisiana are highly profitable. Through March 31, 1991, Schumpert Medical Center (Shreveport) had a net gain from operations of $11,334,000 and St. Elizabeth Hospital (Beaumont) had for the period a net operating gain of $7,444,000.

The analysis of the credit risk of a large multihospital system such as SCH is somewhat different from the analysis of a standalone hospital. Because of the economies of scale and magnitude of operations, specific local problems such as physician losses or lawsuits affect the overall system less than it would a single health-care provider. Additionally, there is only one small hospital in SCH's system, St. John Hospital in Nassau Bay, Texas, with 123 staffed beds and which represents only 4.6 percent of SCH's gross patient revenues through March 31, 1991.

Another unique strength of a financially strong system such as SCH is that an historical coverage of 4.23x in fiscal year 1990 and a projected one of 3.14x after its 1991 bond sale is a stronger credit indicator than the coverage numbers actually indicate. Because SCH can transfer funds throughout the system to temporarily strengthen a troubled hospital, should that be necessary, it can be said that the whole is greater than the sum of all of its parts.

In the case of the SCH and the Restricted Affiliates the net income in fiscal year 1990 (after paying interest and charging for depreciation) was $72,997,000 and through 3/31/91 it is $36,363,000. These high absolute numbers provide a strong level of credit support and significantly help to place these bonds in the high grade category.

TAMPA CAPITAL IMPROVEMENT SERIES 1988A REVENUE BONDS

Bond proceeds of the Tampa Capital Improvement Series 1988A revenue bonds were deposited into the program fund, and are to be used to provide financing to local governments within the State of Florida through the acquisition of local government loans, namely, bonds, notes, certificates of indebtedness, and other debt securities issued by these units of government. In addition to the delivery of a cashflow certificate, a tax opinion and a legal opinion stating that the securities constitute local government obligations, such securities must also meet the following criteria.

1. They must be rated AA or higher by Standard & Poor's at the time of purchase by the issuer. The ratings may be supported by credit enhancements such as letters of credit or bond insurance.

2. The local government loans shall not be subject to prepayment, or optional or mandatory redemption prior to October 1, 1998 except for redemptions or prepayments resulting from default, project damage, destruction or condemnation, or unexpended proceeds.

3. Should the local government loans be subject to optional redemption or prepayment between October 1,1998 and 2018, such redemption prices must at least equal par plus accrued interest, the optional redemption price for the bonds as provided by the indenture.

Procedure

Prior to making the loans to local governments, the trustee invested $150,000,000 of the bond proceeds under a ten year investment agreement ending on October 1, 1989 with Home Federal Savings and Loan Association ("Home Federal") and $75,000,000 under the same terms with Pacific First Federal Savings Bank ("Pacific First Federal"). Each investment agreement is collateralized with securities held by the collateral agent, which is Chemical Bank, and could include corporate debt, commercial mortgage pass-through certificates, conventional mortgage pass-through certificates, government securities, demand deposits, insured CDs, short-term money market instruments, cash, and "new eligible" collateral in amounts sufficient to achieve and maintain a minimum rating of AA by Standard & Poor's on the investment agreement. The collateral discount factors range from 100 percent for cash and to 220 percent for certain corporate bonds. The collateral is valued at least monthly.

As of October 30, 1991 the collateral agent was holding securities valued at $245,563,340 which secured the $150,000,000 investment agreement with Home Federal. The collateral agent was also holding securities valued at $176,193,749 which secured the $75,000,000 investment agreement with Pacific First Federal.

Security

The bonds are not the obligations of the City of Tampa. The bonds are secured solely by assets in the trust estate, which are composed of monies in the various funds (except the rebate fund) established by the indenture, including all income and proceeds from investment securities. Note that there is no debt service reserve fund securing the bonds. To date, no loans have been made to local governments.

Special Call

Bonds are not subject to optional redemption before October 1, 1998, but may be redeemed, among other reasons, upon an event of default under the Investment Agreement.

In 1991 it was reported in the press that the financial position of Home Federal deteriorated significantly. At that time it was feared that in a worst-case scenario if Home Federal or Pacific First Federal were to fail, under the Financial Institutions Reform, Recovery and Enforcement Act of 1989 (FIRREA), the Resolution Trust Company (RTC) could have been appointed by the Office of Thrift Supervision (OTS) as conservator or as receiver of the thrift institution.

In an April 10, 1990 policy statement the RTC stated that even if it disaffirms a "secured contract," the collateral may be liquidated with the creditor retaining or being paid the principal of the obligation plus interest to the date of disaffirmance to the extent secured by collateral. The Statement also clarified that FIRREA's provisions apply to contracts disaffirmed after August 9, 1989 when FIRREA was enacted, even if the contract was entered into prior to that date. The Investment Agreement was treated by Home Federal and regarded by the City of Tampa as a secured contract under the April 10, 1990 policy statement. If the RTC had chosen to affirm the Investment Agreement as a secured contract it would have continued to make payments under the terms of the Agreement and to satisfy the collateral maintenance requirements. If RTC had chosen to liquidate the Investment Agreement, bonds would have been redeemed.

Because the RTC had not been requested to review the Investment Agreement in terms of its being a secured contract at that time, there was no assurance of the application of the April 10, 1990, policy statement to the Investment Agreement. Formal confirmation by the RTC of the application of the policy statement to the Investment Agreement would have clarified the status of the bonds.

In late October, 1991 the RTC stated in response to a request for written advice that "if appointed as receiver for Home Federal, the RTC would honor any perfected security interests arising out of the Collateral Pledge and Maintenance Agreement."

RTC's response did not address the issue of whether the collateral securing the Investment Agreement would be liquidated and used to call bonds prior to the Investment Agreement's maturity date of October 1, 1998.

It should be noted that shortly thereafter Home Federal was taken over by the RTC. RTC proceeded to liquidate the collateral securing the investment agreement and take out the $150 million of the Tampa Series 1988A bonds secured by the agreement.

TEXAS MUNICIPAL UTILITY DISTRICT (MUD) BONDS

Municipal Utility District (MUD) bonds in Texas are issued by special districts to finance the construction of certain capital improvements in unincorporated areas of the state. Such MUDs are created by the Texas Water Commission and are subject to the continuing supervision of the Texas Department of Water Resources and the Texas Water Commission. The capital projects are usually water or sewer systems located within the specific MUDs that are undergoing residential and commercial development. Some MUDs are purely residential, some are purely commercial (such as for shopping centers), and some are a combination of the two.

How Are the Bonds Secured?

MUD bonds generally are secured by the pledge of unlimited property taxes on all taxable property, if necessary, that is located within the MUD. Additionally, the net revenues of the water and sewer systems, if there are any, are usually pledged to the MUD bondholders. Of course, while a MUD bond is legally secured by unlimited property taxes, how likely it is that the planned development will occur within projections determines the creditworthiness of the specific MUD bond issue.

Credit risk is in two stages. First, there is the initial risk that the specific public improvements—that are financed by the proceeds of the bond sale—neither will be completed on schedule nor at projected, reasonable cost. Such occurrences may throw into doubt the overall economic soundness of the development plan for the MUD.

The second stage of the credit risk is the ability of the MUD developer to properly construct, market, and sell residential homes or commercial properties in the improved MUD. This is necessary in order to create a strong property valuation base that can be taxed at a moderate to low tax rate to pay debt service on the bonds.

Questions to Ask Concerning the General Credit Risk

The following are some of the questions that should be asked by the investor before purchasing a MUD bond.

Who Is the Developer of the MUD?

The investor must evaluate the competitive ability of the developer to build and effectively market the development. The developers must be judged in terms of their ability both to construct the public utilities (streets, water, and sewer systems) and to build and sell homes in the MUD to the public, or in the case of a commercial MUD, to attract quality commercial tenants. A developer with a long history of successful experience with such projects and strong financial resources in the business is clearly preferred. This is particularly the case since the U.S. Bankruptcy Court has the power to stay tax collection procedures against the developer. Clearly, a MUD that is being developed by a wholly owned subsidiary of a major corporation such as the Exxon Corporation is a stronger credit than one in which the developer is less substantial.

How Conservative Is the Developer's Construction Program and Schedule?

The investor must determine if the developer's construction schedule and financing costs are realistic. Has the developer determined the total construction costs, and does the developer's financing plan include enough capitalized interest to cover potential construction delays? If additional bonds had to be issued to complete the installation of the public utilities, the property tax burden on the property owners, of course, would be increased.

What Is the Maximum Impact on MUD Property Tax Rates?
Assuming the successful issuance of the MUD bonds, the investor must determine the maximum and annual projected debt-service requirements and what the projected tax rate would be per $100 of assessed valuation. If the projected tax rates are substantially higher than rates currently levied in competing areas, the rate of development within the MUD could be adversely impacted.

In this regard it should be noted that, in general, commercial MUDs require less public services—such as police and fire facilities—than do the residential MUDs. Therefore, the tax burdens of the commercial MUDs sometimes are lower.

What Is the Socioeconomic Target Market?
An important element in the determination of the credit quality of a residential MUD bond is the socioeconomics of the population that will be purchasing property and living in the specific MUD. The more economically upscale the target population is, the more insulated the MUD should be from low property tax collection rates that would be caused by recessionary forces. A critical indication of the socioeconomics of the MUD is the median home values projected by the developer.

Of course, it also should be noted that during periods of relatively high interest rates, it may be difficult for high-priced homes to be sold in the purely residential MUDs. In this regard, commercial MUDs, such as those for shopping centers, could be stronger credits if the developer and commercial tenants are financially sound.

Where Is the MUD Located?
Because of the lack of mass-transit systems in many suburban areas, the actual location of the MUD in relationship to major population centers, medical facilities, churches, fire stations, interstate highways, and environmental amenities such as recreational facilities is important; it could affect the successful development of the MUD.

How Reliable Is the Legal Opinion?
The MUD bond issue should have two unqualified legal opinions to the effect that the bonds are valid and legally binding obligations of the MUD. The first should be of the attorney general of Texas, and the second of a recognized and experienced municipal bond attorney.

Is the MUD Located within the "Extraterritorial Jurisdiction" of a Major City?

Some MUDs are located within the exclusive extraterritorial jurisdiction of a major city that could annex the MUD. If this were to occur the MUD bonds would become general obligations of the larger, annexing city. One city that has a history of annexing MUDs is the City of Houston. While a MUD that is located within the exclusive extraterritorial jurisdiction of Houston cannot be assumed to be ultimately annexed by Houston, there is the potential that this could happen. Conversely, the City of Dallas does not have a strong history of annexing MUDs that are located within its extraterritorial jurisdiction. Also, it should be noted that even if the MUD is located within the extraterritorial jurisdiction of Houston, it may have other characteristics (as previously discussed) that make the MUD bond a speculative investment.

Conclusion

The creditworthiness of Texas MUD bonds ranges all the way from the speculative category of risk to investment grade. By asking and obtaining answers to the questions discussed above, the prudent investor should be able to distinguish MUD bonds that are strong credits from those that are not.

INDEX